Aesthetic theory and the video game

MANCHESTER
1824

Manchester University Press

For Theodor

Aesthetic theory and the video game

Graeme Kirkpatrick

Manchester University Press
Manchester and New York
distributed in the United States exclusively
by Palgrave Macmillan

GV
1469.3
.K553
2011

Published by Manchester University Press
Oxford Road, Manchester M13 9NR, UK
and Room 400, 175 Fifth Avenue, New York, NY 10010, USA
www.manchesteruniversitypress.co.uk

Distributed in the United States exclusively by
Palgrave Macmillan, 175 Fifth Avenue, New York,
NY 10010, USA

Distributed in Canada exclusively by
UBC Press, University of British Columbia, 2029 West Mall,
Vancouver, BC, Canada V6T 1Z2

British Library Cataloguing-in-Publication Data
A catalogue record for this book is available from the British Library

Library of Congress Cataloging-in-Publication Data applied for

ISBN 978 0 7190 7717 3 *hardback*
ISBN 978 0 7190 7718 0 *paperback*

First published 2011

Edited and typeset
by Frances Hackeson Freelance Publishing Services, Brinscall, Lancs
Printed in Great Britain
by Bell and Bain Ltd, Glasgow

Contents

Preface and acknowledgements

I would like to thank Matthew Frost, Kim Walker and Reena Jugnarain of Manchester University Press for their patience and support. Throughout the time it took to write the book I have been fortunate to work in the School of Social Sciences at the University of Manchester. I am grateful to all my colleagues in the sociology discipline area for their professionalism and commitment to research, which makes Manchester such an extraordinary place in which to develop and explore ideas. My head of school, Fiona Devine gave me encouragement and guidance during the early stages of this project that were important to its eventual success. I must also thank Ann Cronley whose support with administration has been invaluable and without which Matthew would have been waiting even longer for my manuscript.

Olli Leino kindly read the whole manuscript and provided many helpful comments and criticisms which helped me to understand my own argument better and I am grateful to him. Other academic colleagues and friends at different institutions and at different times have provided convivial contexts for discussion in which I have been able to develop the ideas presented here and for this I am grateful to Nick Thoburn, Helen Wood, Piotr Sitarski, Cheryl Martens, Gareth Crabtree, Paul Brown, Bjarke Liboriussen, Hannah Wirman, Simon Niedenthal, Rune Klevjer, Patrick Crogan, Steve Hall, Espen Aarseth, Bo Kampmann Walther, Elia 'Toops' Tupou, Beth Burgess, Aki Jarvinen, Martin Watkins, Andrew Hill, John Wilson, Andrew Feenberg, Helen Kennedy and Jon Dovey. I must also thank the students on my MA course, 'Cultures of Digital Play' (2009) for several helpful discussions.

My greatest thanks are for my partner, Sarah Carling, who always seems to have the right word when I hit blocks and crises – and there have been a few. Theodor Araby-Kirkpatrick was a constant source of inspiration and an able researcher, providing many ideas and fascinating discussions, as well as offering a unique perspective on contemporary gaming culture that greatly enriched my own appreciation.

I am grateful to all these people and they have all helped make the book better. None of them bear any responsibility for its inevitable failings.

Some sections of Chapter 1 were published previously as 'Between art and gameness: critical theory and computer game aesthetics', in *Thesis Eleven* 89, 2007. Parts of Chapter 3 appeared in 'Controller, hand, screen: Aesthetic form in the computer game', in *Games and Culture* 4 (2), 2009. A couple of sections of Chapter 4 were included in 'Feminism and technical capital: The case of the computer game', in *Information Communication & Society* 13 (6), 2010. They are reproduced by kind permission of the journals and their publishers.

Illustrations

Introduction

The main argument of this book is that ideas from classical aesthetic theory should be used to understand video games. I argue that video games are not communications media in any standard sense but objects that furnish us with particular kinds of experience. These experiences are a variety of game, or structured play, but they are also something more than this. What this 'more' is, what it consists in, is the enigma that has triggered the most heated academic debates about the video game and how we should study it and I argue that it is best understood as an historically specific instance of *aesthetic form*. The book sides with ludology in asserting the novelty of the video game as an object of study and the importance of this newness to understanding its distinctive place within contemporary culture.[1] Ludology's emphasis on structured play is endorsed here but reinterpreted as a defensive operation that guards aesthetic form.

Grasping the implications of this means moderating, or even giving up some of the available positions within cultural and media theory, especially those that are associated with the analysis of discourse or with the insistence on interpreting everything as if it were a medium of communication implicated in the circulation of ideology. In place of this, the video game asserts a revived role for the concept of form, which has itself been much neglected in recent aesthetic theory. If we want to understand how the video game has come to occupy the position it has in contemporary experience we need to analyse it in terms of its form; the way it shapes space to create the possibility of meaning only to stop short of actually providing it. Viewed in this way the video game represents a break in the history of entertainment commodities and is almost the inverted reflection of contemporary art. This book is, therefore, as much a contribution to debates in contemporary cultural theory as it is to game studies. Given the important role of video games in reshaping contemporary cultural life, this is surely appropriate.

Stating that aesthetics are important to video games is not in itself an interesting position – any number of books about video games will include a chapter on aesthetics and few if any will neglect the issue altogether. This book is not aimed at helping people to design more attractive, stunning or pleasing games. Rather, its argument is that only by examining what games feel like to players can we really comprehend the video game. It involves making the claim that video games are aesthetic objects before they are anything else, which has consequences for other parts of the discussion we want to have about them. Most people agree, for example, that play or gameplay as it is referred to in connection with video games, is central to what people do with them and should inform our understanding of them in various ways. But there are several ways to define and understand play. One of them comes from classical aesthetic theory and that is the definition I have used here and developed in investigations of popular games like *Resident Evil 4* (Capcom 2005) and *Mirror's Edge* (Electronic Arts 2008). This makes for somewhat different conclusions than if the concept of play were the one from psychology or anthropology. In particular, it raises the question of form in connection with video games and it points towards a different emphasis on questions of rhythm and movement associated with playing them. These are the central questions addressed in this book.

Although I claim that video games are aesthetic objects and that this is an important way to analyse and understand them, I do not say that it is the only way to gain insights on video games or that aesthetics has any unique rights over the study of games. My sense is that if aesthetic analysis in the sense developed here is excluded the result is often a shallow understanding of what is really going on. I have found in the course of developing the aesthetic approach that it conflicts in important ways with established modes of interpretation and that an analysis that uses the aesthetic concepts of play, form and rhythm is nearly always the most convincing. But other approaches generate insights and ideas that are essential to the development of game studies as a discipline and without them aesthetic analysis would often not be possible. Likewise, it is almost certain that the terms of the analysis advanced here will be unsatisfactory to many peeople and so the aesthetic approach will be corrected by others. My hope, though, is that in clarifying the relevance of such concepts as the aesthetic definition of play and form to video game analysis and by asserting the centrality of physical movement to what goes on when people play video games, the book may form part of the ongoing dialogue about what games are, how we can understand them better and what they might become in the future.

Any methodological approach like this tries to situate its object in a particular historical trajectory. It is a conservative implication of ludology, for instance, that video games stand in the tradition of older games like chess or football and that it is only in light of this that we can see their true novelty. Others find in them a source of cinematic innovations, with new viewing practices and new visual possibilities that extend the history of popular entertainments. An aesthetic approach finds itself in the, perhaps unfortunate, position of seeming to claim that video games are art. The book does not claim video games for art, although in some ways it does claim art for video games.

Contemporary art practice has reduced aspirations in relation to what Jacques Ranciere (2009) calls the 'regime of aesthetic art', and this can be seen in its retreat from form. Through play and form the modern artwork of the late nineteenth and early twentieth centuries was a political intervention that worked on the human sensorium to shape and alter our expectations. The 'free play' of the artwork was a reminder of the role of imagination in shaping reality, while the resulting form spoke of a better world to come. Now discussion of play in the work of art has become exclusively conceptual. Formerly art played with its viewers, heightening the activity of the imagination and presenting various kinds of challenge to cognition. Now play is rarely discussed as an important part of the response triggered by the artwork in its human audience. Instead, its playfulness concerns the medium (which can be anything); the exhibition space (is it art just because it's in a gallery?), and the artist in society (is it art because she made it?). Similarly, the concept of form has been denounced and renounced in much of art practice since the early 1960s. This was also the time that the video game was invented; when William Higginbotham created the first tennis-based game (Poole 2000: 29) and Steve Russell made 'Spacewar!' (Levy 1984). No doubt that is a coincidence, but it is also a curious fulfillment of prophecy. Long before the rise of conceptualism, Walter Benjamin (1968) envisaged a time when imagination might run free from the constraints set by art and thought this might be a good thing. Perhaps there is a space in the culture for expressive experimentation that works with some of these neglected elements of the artistic tradition. When imagination is liberated it gives rise to play and form and in so doing calls forth new containers for those things. If the video game is such a container then the questions raised by its success for cultural politics are not the ones we thought we had to ask when we were preoccupied with whether games are violent, or sexist, or whatever. It is this starting point that distinguishes the aesthetic approach to video games within contemporary cultural theory.

In Chapter 1, I begin by defining what is meant by the aesthetic theory of video games and setting out the main themes of the book. The chapter clarifies the idea of aesthetic art and examines recent claims made about the end of that tradition in the self-understanding of art and art criticism. This enables me to position the video game at a particular intersection of art history and popular entertainments, which became possible in the 1960s. Aesthetic theory begins with the eighteenth-century enlightenment and gains its highest expression in works by Kant (1960 [1795]) and Schiller (2008 [1795]). At this point, the status and value of the artwork was clarified by analysis of its place in the human sensorium. If previously a good artwork was one that represented the world well, now it was the impact that representation could have on human sense and taste that would sort good from bad. In the modern period this definition was sharpened in the direction of abstraction. Starting in the late nineteenth century, modern art tested the limits of the aesthetic paradigm by opposing form to semblance and presenting its audience with a different kind of puzzle. With conceptual art, which has been dominant since the 1960s, it became clear that the sensory aspects of the work were no longer central and could not play the criteriological role assigned to them by classical theory, to such an extent that some argued literally anything could now be art. The location of the work in an institution and not the way the work plays with us to generate pleasing sensations of form and pattern, tells us what is art and what is not. This can be viewed as a liberation of art from aesthetics. But if we assume that play and form are things that humans naturally find pleasurable, surely we are justified in asking what has become of them if they are not to be found any longer in art? In the midst of these changes, Theodor Adorno (2002 [1970]) suggestively alluded to popular culture and electronics as possible alternative locations. Drawing on Ranciere's (2007) concept of the art image, the chapter suggests that the video game object mirrors it and that its inner workings exhibit tensions that require the subject of traditional aesthetic theory in order to function. In this way, the video game makes a kind of call to art and aesthetic theory.

Building on this, Chapter 2 examines play and form in connection with video games and clarifies the meaning of those concepts in contemporary discourses. Looking at the emergent discipline of video game studies, the chapter focuses on ludology. The significance of ludology lies in its assertion that to be understood properly games must be viewed as play that is structured by rules of a certain kind. This stance enables a robust defence of the autonomy of the video game as a cultural form that is not susceptible to established modes of analysis that are entrenched in the academic humanities. This position is justified but the problem for ludology is that it does not recognize the true importance of its own activity, which is to guard the

re-emergence of form and to resist incursions of meaning-oriented disciplines onto territory that is, properly understood,
still undecided. An aesthetic perspective provides tools to describe the experiences people have with video games without
imposing alien principles of meaning-making. Here the territory is not guarded so much as its character as a 'virtual space' to
be occupied is denied or withheld. Ludologists have offered an
exaggeratedly spatial concept of the video game that prioritizes
the apparent lack of abstraction in its visual representations
as the defining feature of video games (their newness). This
becomes the opening to a distinctive kind of fiction (Juul 2006)
that cannot be detached from a notion of virtuality prevalent
in contemporary media studies (Bolter and Grusin 2000). In
place of this, Chapter 2 emphasizes the temporal element in
video games. Drawing on the example of *Max Payne* (Rockstar
2001), it highlights the kinds of rhythmic tension that are integral to video games but not adequately comprehended in a
framework dominated by spatial concepts. The aesthetic perspective reveals a vital dimension of video gameplay, virtual
time, without which our understanding remains incomplete.
Virtual time (Badiou 2005a) is predicated upon the absence of
a decision regarding meaning, which is shared by video games
and dance and distinguishes both from art.

The first two chapters introduce the notion of video games
as plastic objects that have to be played with in order to be
experienced. They also define this concept of play as involving
a specific temporal order, or rhythmic structuring of experience that is patterned and pleasurable. And they question the
idea, which tends to be taken for granted in much video game
scholarship, that space in the video game *is* the three-dimensional illusion laid out for us visually on the two-dimensional
screen. Chapter 3 expands on this idea that space in the video
game is a variable and rhythmic experience constituted out
of the interplay of a variety of visual, on-screen devices that
work on players' eyes, with the work they do with their hands
on the game controller. Using the example of *Resident Evil 4*
(Capcom 2005) this chapter examines the role of the controller
in giving players access to experiences of form and deepens

the connection already referred to with the ideas of Walter Benjamin. Benjamin's clarification of the Marxist theory of reification, as a kind of forgetting, and his positive appraisal of childhood and childishness as counters to this are essential to any understanding of the contemporary culture of play with video games. Focusing on the kind of 'short-circuit' that can occur when hand-held controllers appear among visual, on-screen game imagery, I explore the applicability of his idea of dialectical image to video game criticism. This chapter clarifies the video game object in terms of Henri Bergson's (2007 [1940]) theory of the laugh. If the modern artwork managed its tensions by establishing various kinds of balance between feeling response and textual interpretation, the video game allows them to explode in moments of hilarity.

In Chapter 4 the centrality of manual controls to video game aesthetics is explored further through the thesis that video gameplay is a form of dance. Players dance, mainly with their hands, in response to games as choreographic scripts and it is through this dance that they derive the pleasures and frustrations of form. The chapter positions video game studies alongside dance studies, with both disciplines having struggled to secure validation from the academy and for rather similar reasons. They both involve the body in ways that are problematic for power, especially the power associated with gender norms, and they both involve strange paradoxes of intelligibility and illegibility that are unsettling to an academic culture centred on interpretation. The chapter situates video gameplay alongside other popular cultural developments in which we see the human hand taking on increased importance. Drawing on ideas from Nigel Thrift (2008), I argue that the video game is an example of what he calls 'qualculation': in gameplay we physically test and probe a plastic object whose rules are not readily assimilable into those of the simulation or of narrative story. The combination of expressive performance and restraint necessary to play a game well determines an aesthetic experience that is not contained within any kind of sense-meaning; it is more akin to playing a musical instrument. The dance of the hands is central to this process and it is choreographed at a level apart from that of the schemas of meaning interpretation that predominate in cultural studies. Moreover, the fact that this form of popular dance has been associated with young men has implications, as yet unthought through, for feminist video game criticism.

This thesis has a direct bearing on what video games can mean and on the place of meaning, or signification within them. Here I argue that the video game is in some ways an inversion of the modernist artwork. The latter presented itself as a puzzle to the viewer. It remained physically static but presented us with an experience of form. This form we traced out internally by following the order, or script, set out by the work. The whole process was informed by a sense of semblance – the idea that the work resembles or represents something else – that constantly receded. In its abstraction, its refusal of semblance, the modernist work left us dissatisfied but almost teased by the possibilities it opened up. The experience of form turned against semblance in modernist works was a reminder that a better world is possible. In Adorno's (2002) phrase, the work 'points beyond itself'. With video games, the game object is never static. It presents images and sensations that are familiar, that seem to resemble. But it too is a puzzle. The challenge of the video game lies in extruding play and form, which are no longer located internal to the subject, but have to be performed through manipulating the controller. This active play differentiates video games from 'new media art', which is usually appreciated only contemplatively. Through play, we activate the game and deepen our understanding of its true structure. This takes us past the scattered shards of meaning that seemed, when we first started playing, to be part of a coherent image, perhaps of a virtual world. In the depths of this process, we are no longer in touch with the game's fiction, but endeavour to master its routines. Games often leave us with a feeling of guilt, of having wasted too much time on something meaningless and empty. This feeling is integral to video game aesthetics and reflects their profound ambivalence when viewed in the perspective of contemporary cultural politics.

Chapter 5 suggests that the nearest cultural precedent for such paradoxical meaning dynamics lies in the baroque, as understood by Benjamin (1985). Drawing on Angela Ndalianis's (2004) thesis of a contemporary, neo-baroque, it suggests that we find in video games an excess of form that overrides and negates meaning even as it repeatedly invokes it. Games need meanings; fictions and resemblances are integral to them, but the activity of playing games is powerfully corrosive to these fictions and analysis of these processes undermines the idea of mimesis in the video game object. Moreover, it reveals that the process of corrosion, of dispelling meaning, is essential to gameplay. The chapter relates this to a distinctive mechanics of reading in the neo-baroque as well as to structural features of the game medium. I argue that as a formulaic product of the global culture industry the video game cannot support real character development or facilitate the development of profound examinations of the kind associated with modern tragedy. Drawing on Peter Fenves' (2001) study of baroque signification, I argue that in place of poetic mediation of the individual life in connection with eternal themes, the neo-baroque form presents us with a vertiginous excess of meaning on one side (a sense of yawning profundity) and trivial puzzle-solving on the other. Their inter-relation creates the tension that makes us want to play video games but the meaning of this activity is always limited to allegory, which is an inherently degraded form of signification that limits their communications potential.

In the final chapter I turn to the political significance of the cultural salience of this kind of aesthetic. The chapter draws on the ideas of Ian Bogost (2006), whose notion of 'unit operation' seems to me an important complement to Thrift's notion of qualculation. Unit operations are segments of code that define an action structure for the video gameplayer and for users of programmed artefacts more generally. As Bogost points out, such chunks of programmed activity are becoming increasingly salient in the culture, almost to the point of indiscernibility in some contexts. For Bogost, these operations are inherently meaningful, because they are agreed upon by human beings in

a cultural setting. Indeed, he goes so far as to see unit operations in games as constituting 'procedural rhetorics' (Bogost
2007), or arguments that motivate action. This seems to me to
overload the concept with content it does not need to have in
order to play the important role of clarifying the formal pleasures of video gaming and, indeed, to help develop a theoretical
conception of the character of contemporary life and culture.
Engaging ideas from Alain Badiou, whose work Bogost claims
as foundational for his theory, I suggest a different deployment
of the concept is possible. According to Badiou (2007), the permutations of being that Heidegger and many critical theorists
associate with the ontological politics of a re-aestheticised cultural lifeworld (Habermas 1984) are actually better understood
in terms of mathematics. New world-disclosures, he says, do not
arise where poets present them, but in accordance with procedures he grasps using set theory. Badiou's emphasis on formal
truth, as against sense-meaning, enables us to comprehend the
newness of the video game as a kind of 'truth event' within
gaming as a 'condition' for philosophical thought (including
philosophical aesthetics, or what he calls 'inaesthetics').

In conclusion, I argue that video games are profoundly ambivalent for cultural politics. The experience of form they offer
us is not articulated to any future that is different from the
world we are in now. At the same time, their challenge awakens
in us a sense of our own agency and its importance to activities
of 'world-making'. Choosing to play video games still has the
power to annoy and to cause controversy and can be a form of
deviancy or norm-subversion. But this choice remains purely
gestural – quite literally gestural, by the analysis of Chapter
4 – and politically inconsequential. In its many meaningless
repetitions, video gameplay can involve sensations that in previous times were associated with beauty and self-empowerment
but in the current context can seem cynical and nihilistic. This
is why video games must be understood as a call to aesthetic
theory. Although that theory cannot resolve the indecision
within them and so in a sense fails, in failing it at least clarifies
the nature of their undecidability.

Notes

1   Ludology is a branch of game studies centred mainly in Scandinavian universities that emphasizes the gameness of video games and rejects attempts to analyse them as 'narratives' or texts in which meaning plays the dominant, ordering role.

1

The aesthetic approach

> Whether art is still possible today cannot be decided from above, from the perspective of the relations of production. The question depends, rather, on the state of the forces of production.
>
> T.W. Adorno

This chapter sets out the main theoretical terms and definitions that are used in this book to develop the idea that video games are primarily aesthetic objects. This claim means that the best way to understand modern video games is to focus on what they feel like to the people who play them and to reflect on what the significance of that feeling response might be in the contemporary cultural context. Taking an aesthetic approach to video games is made more complicated by the fact that everyone who writes about them already accepts that they have aesthetic properties and there is even some consensus that these properties matter and should inform our assessment of the medium as a whole as well as of individual games. However, my claim concerns the specific applicability of concepts from classical aesthetic theory to the video game as a cultural form. These concepts offer a way to understand video games and to explain what it is about them that makes people want to play them. The aesthetic theory of what video games are also situates them in contemporary culture, in relation to things like the entertainment industry, the world of art and the texture of lived experience in modern societies, in a way that is not prioritized in other accounts. This chapter describes the relevant concepts from aesthetic theory, focusing particularly on some definitions of form, which is the central idea used throughout the book. Subsequent chapters will explore the applicability of these ideas, drawing on accounts of specific games and relevant features of the contemporary cultural landscape to make the case for the aesthetic approach to video games.

First, it is worth sharpenening the definition of 'aesthetic'. In ordinary speech this term is often associated with visual properties of objects and it tends to be used when we want to highlight the fact that something is pleasing to the eye. Video games are often thought of as visual media and it is not uncommon to find theorists and game reviewers alike discussing game graphics and the spectacular visual effects we sometimes find in games as if these were their defining aesthetic properties. Often missing from such analyses is any sense of what actually makes a visual effect pleasing to the human eye. It tends to be taken for granted that we know what is nice to look at and that this requires no further theoretical analysis. Geoff King and Tanya Krzywinska, for example, suggest that much gameplay is motivated simply by the search for 'visual pleasures', writing at one point that players may find aesthetic pleasure simply from 'the quality of graphical resolution alone' (King and Krzywinska 2006: 130). But what makes a visual experience pleasurable? On what basis do we separate the visual aspects of an experience that also includes other sensory components and say that they specifically are the source of our pleasure? These questions concern aesthetic structure and it is in answering them that the resources of classical aesthetic theory are useful. In particular, the concepts of play and form take us beyond a superficial characterization of visual pleasure towards an appreciation of the whole experience of gameplay in terms of how it feels to players. The first section describes this in greater detail, showing how aesthetic concerns cannot be bracketed off as incidental to gameplay but must be understood as central to and organizing the whole activity. Even ludology, which emphasizes the gameness of video games as against other properties has not established a sufficiently central role for the concept of play. The fact that we play video games and in so doing produce experiences of sufficient coherence and attractiveness that it seems natural to refer to 'game worlds' suggests that they have powerful aesthetic properties. At the deepest levels of our experience, play is what enables us to conjure something out of nothing; it separates us from the void, a proposition that is informed by insights from psychology and psychoanalysis as well as classical aesthetic theory. These ideas are discussed in the second section.

The primary concept that enables us to understand and analyse aesthetic experiences like playing video games is the idea of form. What makes it possible for play to produce the semblance of a world is its organization into determinate forms. Form produces a subjective sensibility and an objective delineation of space and time so that experience coheres and makes sense. This book argues that a proper understanding of the appealing nature of video game experiences requires that we revive this idea from the classical aesthetic theories of Immanuel Kant (1960) and Friedrich von Schiller (2008). With some important exceptions like Suzanne Langer (1953) and Theodor Adorno (2002), twentieth-century theory has largely abandoned the idea of form. To some extent this can be attributed to the rise of conceptualism in art practice. It also reflects a degree of suspicion concerning the very idea that some forms – shapes or patterns in the experiential order – are intrinsically appealing to human beings. The objection to form has been that it posits organic unities unfolding in places where modern science has taught us to perceive discontinuity and randomness. The concept has also been written off as idealist, in so far as it suggests a class of experiences that connect human beings to some kind of transcendent force beyond the reach of scientific-materialist explanations. In contemporary sociology of art it is argued that we need to explain the belief in art as harbouring such a special category of experience (Bourdieu 1993) rather than reproduce it in our readers. However, this view has recently been countered, most forcefully by Jacques Ranciere (2009). In the third section I try to show how his work enables us to radicalize the concept of form and make it serviceable in the twenty-first century, when transcendence seems to be unattainable. Formal structure in an experience – what Raymond Williams (1961) called its 'structure of feeling' – remains a vital ingredient when we encounter objects that take us out of ourselves in order to affirm something important that, perhaps, daily life puts us in danger of forgetting. The fact that form persists and now proliferates in the territory beyond art is suggestive of important changes in the culture. It is in this, quite specific sense that I refer to video games as cultural forms.

Discussing form as a property of video games invites the question of the historical and cultural intersection of this relatively new entertainment technology with established fields and practices that have long been recognized as 'art'. This book argues that the relation between games and art is an important key to understanding either of them properly in the current period. Video games inherit certain of their key properties, especially form, from an art world that has to some extent absented itself from important areas of experience. Even Ranciere, who is keen to secure the enduring significance of aesthetic art, acknowledges a certain etiolation of contempo-rary artworks with regard to the capacity of its images to move us. I argue that some of the charge of the traditional artwork has migrated to other parts of the culture. At the same time, this has been a two-way exchange and art has itself become more playful and gamelike (Palmer 2008). This book is about video games and so there is less opportunity to develop the latter side of the argument but in the fourth section of this chapter and elsewhere, developments in art are cited as illus-trative of the consequences of the creative intersection of the two fields.

This book is also concerned with the cultural politics of video gaming. It does not defend the video game as a cultural form – many able advocates are doing this job sufficiently well (Bartle 2008) – nor does it add to the literature that denounces them from a 'critical' perspective. The theoretical tradition that is used and developed here, which develops from Marx through Adorno and Horkheimer's (1997) study of the culture industry, has produced enough of those (Stallabrass 1995; Kline, Dyer-Witheford and de Peuter 2003). I believe that an aesthetic characterization of video games, which should not be neglectful of the social and economic conditions under which they are produced and consumed, draws out the deep ambivalence of the form. This ambivalence, which is matched by other important strains in contemporary culture, is the topic of the fifth section. Play and form in video games are implicated in a specific kind of cultural politics, namely, one in which meaning is a stake. The metaphoric construct, commonly applied to games, of 'world creation' is indicative of their status in a culture that Geert Lovink (2008) accurately characterizes in terms of 'creative nihilism'. The playful activity that surfaces here at the heart of consumer culture spins webs of meaning that offer some psychic protection from the salient threats of economic precarity and the kinds of subjective desolation associated with life in a manipulative 'culture industry' (Adorno 1991). At the same time, the resulting cultural practices (of gameplay) are hollowed out, transparent in their emptiness and increasingly stand as the sign of choices people are not making.[1]

Why an aesthetic approach?

Playing *Katamari Damacy* (Namco 2004), involves steering a multi-coloured ball around in a series of cartoon environments. As the ball rolls it gathers objects, which adhere to its outer surface and create the amusing impression of a tumbling mass of comic randomness. You steer this thing around until it gains such proportions as to have outgrown its environment, at which point the ball passes into larger spaces with different kinds of objects to collect. So, in the early stages it is on a desk collecting things like stationery and erasers, but soon it is on a street and is big enough to pose a threat to the building it was in at the start. There is a backstory to this game. It involves the notion that you are creating a star to replace ones that have been lost in a kind of cosmic accident. However, even if this story makes sense it is irrelevant to the pleasures of playing the game. *Katamari Damacy* is enjoyed by players because of the tumbling about, the challenges of getting particular objects to stick and of keeping them there when you collide with the 'wrong' kind of person or thing in the environment. The game draws out, toys with and occasionally thwarts players' energies in a way that is exciting and comical. One reviewer enthuses, 'what sums up *Katamari Damacy* for me is the unbridled joy bursting from every pore' (Bramwell 2004). The same reviewer confirms that 'deciphering the plot and understanding the motivations of the characters' are probably impossible.[2] Moreover, he says, this obscurity concerning the significance of the events in the game actually allows him to just get on and play it.

Katamari Damacy is an excellent confirmation of a comment by the ludologist, Markku Eskelinen. In an important paper, he points out the profound difference between video games and story telling media like books by saying, 'If I throw a ball at you I don't expect you to drop it and wait until it starts telling stories' (Eskelinen 2004: 36). The act of throwing the ball is initiating a game and the appropriate and obvious response from you is to play with the ball – to play the game. Eskelinen here counters the suggestion that even quite abstract games, like *Tetris* (Nintendo 1989), have the power to signify – that they are meaningful. It seems to me that he is broadly right about this, in that *Tetris* is primarily a plastic object with which we have experiences and, as such, it resembles a ball more than it is like a book or a film. Those objects hold out experiences too, of course, but they are interpretative or imaginative and their core turns on meanings we extract from them. The experiences we have with balls, playing games, are only marginally concerned with meanings and interpretation is mostly limited to working out the rules. Once we know how to play football, for example, interpretation is not relevant. The lack of meaning associated with such activities does not diminish their attractiveness, popularity or importance. Video games do not have to 'mean' anything to be popular and their popularity can be intelligible without reference to interpretation. This does not mean we should ignore the contents of on-screen imagery or what that imagery might represent or signify in some contexts. However, it does suggest we should assess those features of video games in light of their properties as plastic objects that are physically manipulated and from which we derive a particular kind of experience that is precisely *not* dominated by the interpretative and cognitive practices that are normally foregrounded in accounts of daily life or of other media. This is where we should start the aesthetic analysis of video games.[3] They appear here as the locus of what Raymond Williams (1961) calls a 'structure of feeling', which defines the texture and rhythm of life in a determinate social formation.[4]

Having said all of this, video games are extremely complex balls and complexity in behaviour can be a cue to invoke meaning, as a kind of pragmatically necessitated shorthand for physical processes we cannot practically grasp or express as such.[5] A video game presents initially as its apparatus, which is normally a screen, some speakers and a variety of devices such as a joystick or controller, keyboard or mouse, dance mat, or whatever. Beyond this, shaping our experience with the apparatus is the game program. This is a, typically very large, collection of conditional statements or binary switches that control the flow of events in the game object as it responds to our actions. If you do something then something else, usually many other things, will happen as a result. In addition to this, the program contains events that occur independently of our actions and are triggered by the computer's clock. Contemporary game programs are constituted out of combinations of discrete programmed objects, each with its own rules of behaviour and response (Bogost 2006). Governing each object and the relations between them are the algorithms that regulate the game's behaviour (Galloway 2006). We encounter these through the game's interface as changes in the way the game appears and from these changes we work out its rules. Just as with ball games, we learn the rules principally by testing them out. This involves pressing against the game interface to see what gives and what does not. In conventional games such pressing and probing is applied to physical objects as we project balls through space, between goalposts and so on, as well as to different social conventions that mediate the rules of the game.[6] As Jesper Juul (2006) points out, in video games all of this is handled by the computer, which provides the interface, supports the game object(s) and enforces the rules that govern our interactions with it. These are coded into different elements of the physical apparatus, from the images on the screen to the rumbling of the controller.

The scholarly literature on video games has tended to understand their aesthetics primarily in terms of how the games look. This follows the conventional or popular use of the term aesthetic, associating it with visual appearances and with the principles of attractiveness that apply to visual phenomena. Simon Egenfeldt-Nielsen, Jonas Heide Smith and Susanna Pajares Tosca, in one of the best textbook introductions to video game studies, *Understanding Video Games* (2008), illustrate this point. In their chapter on game aesthetics, Egenfeldt-Nielsen *et al.* do not neglect the issue of how the game feels. They associate it with what is known as 'gameplay' and define this feature of games in terms of the dynamic interplay between two elements integral to most games, namely, the game's rules and its graphical content.

> The term 'gameplay' is often used but rarely defined. As commonly employed it refers to the game dynamics, or more simply, 'how it feels to play a game'. Although this feeling is influenced by a game's audio and visual aspects, gameplay is usually considered a consequence of the game's rules rather than its representation. Using this basic definition, we can say that the gameplay of chess is deliberative and [sic] while the gameplay of *Burnout 3* is frantic and easily accessible.
>
> In line with common use of the term we will define gameplay as the game dynamics emerging from the interplay between rules and game geography. (Egenfeldt-Nielsen, Smith and Tosca 2008: 101–2)

The problem with this approach is that it is too ready to dismiss the feeling associated with playing a game as a relatively 'simple' dimension of gameplay and not one that merits further analysis. Instead, two elements of the game program (the rules and the graphics) are sewn together and *their* interplay is said to explain, or account for the feelings associated with gameplay. 'Gameplay' becomes an unanalysed design feature of the game, with the responses of the player assumed to be following a particular course determined by this other play. As if to reinforce the stitching, they go on to make a strong case for *not separating* the visual appearance of a game on screen from its gamic elements, or what it feels like to play. In the design process, they argue, these aspects are closely related:

> a graphical style may *ideally* be chosen for its ability to support the game mechanics but in the real world of graphical style the causal arrow is sometimes reversed as graphics determine the mechanics. For instance if a game designer starts out with a preference for a certain graphical style, this preference is likely to influence the kind of game she will make. (Egenfeldt-Nielsen, Smith and Tosca 2008: 105)

Egenfeldt-Nielsen *et al.* proceed to focus on a range of graphical styles that tend to be associated with particular game genres. Of particular importance to their discussion is the idea of a systematic relation between the kinds of *space* projected by games of different kinds and with different varieties of rule structure. Their argument takes as given an ideal standard of interface design more generally, which aspires to integrate form and content by giving users functionality in vessels that are pleasant to use.[7] This is surely valid at the high end of video game design and there is no doubt that we do find correspondences of this kind in video games. *Katamari Damacy*, for example, is visually similar to cartoons and this comports well with its light-hearted character. When game designers are thinking about new algorithms, or rules that will set the kinds of constraint that determine the feel of a new game, it would be strange if their thoughts were not informed from the outset by some ideas about the game's imagery; the appearance of its environments and characters, and other aspects of its visual design. However, we also know that many new games, perhaps most, are effectively re-skinnings of game engines, many of which have been in circulation for some years. 'New' games commonly involve a few relatively minor twists in terms of the rules that affect gameplay, with segments of action being re-woven in ways that support a different story and a new vision that alters how the game and its characters look on screen. Indeed, as Alexander Galloway (2006: 125) argues, the development of algorithmic complexity is nothing short of a political-aesthetic demand gamers struggle to impose on the video game industry. For him, it is the key to progress in the development of the medium and cannot be taken for granted.[8]

In video game design the distinction between the formal, algorithmic content and appearance remains a fundamental and problematic feature of the medium. Egenfeldt-Nielsen *et al.*'s strategy of construing gameplay as a conjunction of topography and rules precludes further analysis of the structure of feeling that must be present in the human being who plays the game at this intersection. This neglect is by no means peculiar to these authors. The structure of feeling that defines video game aesthetics has been largely overlooked in game studies. Interestingly, recent work in the field of video game design corroborates this observation. Steve Swink (2009), for example, argues that the feel of video games is all important.[9] He writes,

> game feel is the tactile, kinesthetic sense of manipulating a virtual object. It's the sensation of control in a game.
>
> In digital game design, feel is the elephant in the room. Players know it. Designers know of it. Nobody talks about it and everybody takes it for granted. (Swink 2009: xiii)

Emphasizing the importance of aesthetics to video games involves re-opening this question of the feel of gameplay. Far from being a simple matter, or one that can be left to cognitive psychologists to address in terms of investments and pay-offs for players, we need to analyse the experience on its own terms. So what is play and how should we understand it?

Play and form

Play is a central concept for the reflective discourse of philosophical aesthetics and features prominently in the inner life of art as this was defined in the eighteenth century. If we return to the founding authors of modern aesthetic theory, we find that play is central to their thinking about the feel of experience, especially pleasurable experience. This is nowhere more clear than in Kant's (1960 [1790]) *Critique of Judgement*, the starting point for modern thinking about aesthetics, and Friedrich von Schiller's (2008 [1795]) *Letters on the Aesthetic Education of Man*, which builds on Kant's work. Kant repeatedly emphasizes that what is characteristic of aesthetic experience is play in the mental life of the human subject. What Kant means by play in this context refers primarily to imagination and its relationship to cognition. For him, the play of these faculties with each other, stimulated by particular kinds of experience, is the basis of our experience of the beautiful.

Aesthetic objects have the paradoxical form of a purposeless finality; they are supremely well executed, delightful things and yet we cannot see any purpose in the perfection. They present us with a form so precise that it seems to be mathematically ordered, yet we cannot conceive a formula adequate to describe them.[10] We experience form when beautiful things 'play' with our faculties. This is why Kant puts play at the centre of aesthetic experience, noting that, 'play of every kind ... is attended with no further interest than that of making the time pass by unheeded' (Kant 1960: 166). While it is internal to the subject, the kind of play Kant has in mind is not only an intellectual construct far removed from plastic controllers and imaginary swords.[11] On the contrary, he emphasizes that it is the very same play we associate with fun and with physical actions of the body. Moreover, this play has a formal reality that is independent of considerations of meaning:

> Music ... and what provokes laughter are two kinds of play with aesthetic ideas, or even with representation of the understanding, by which, all said and done, nothing is thought. By mere force of change they are yet able to afford lively gratification. This furnishes pretty clear evidence that the quickening effect of both is physical, despite its being excited by ideas of the mind, and that the feeling of health, arising from a movement of the intestines answering to that of play, makes up that entire gratification of an animated gathering upon the spirit and refinement of which we set such store. (Kant 1960 [1795]: 198–9)

What is already clear from this is that play, however fundamental we take it to be, is not only differentiated historically by games but also by other cultural practices that work with play to generate pleasing sensations and experiences. The centrality of play to aesthetic theory is perhaps even more emphatic elsewhere in German idealism. Friedrich von Schiller, for example, writes that in play we embrace what is contingent in order to gain access to an experience of perfection and harmony. This is essential to liberate the mind and expose us to the possibility of change. Consequently, Schiller argues that 'man only plays when in the full meaning of the word he is a man, and he is only completely a man when he plays' (Schiller 2008 [1795]: 34).

Aesthetic experience occurs when we find that something is pleasing to us by virtue of its form. Such an object stimulates us in the sense that it provokes and incites a feeling response, but it does so in a way that goes beyond merely being pleasing to the eye. In aesthetic experience, which for Kant is almost exclusively about natural beauty, we find our imagination is pitched against our understanding – we can discern 'order and finality' in the object but not its purpose. It seems to be deliberate and yet what it is for is withheld from us. While this might sound annoying, it is a fundamentally pleasurable experience because its resonances bring us to a heightened sense of the harmony that exists between ourselves and the divine, super-sensible, order. In its freedom, the play at the heart of aesthetic experience amplifies our sense of ourselves as free, moral agents. There are, therefore, two kinds of experience that can count as beautiful for Kant. In the first there is the experience of order and pattern that pleases us because of its perfection. More important, and in a sense underscoring this for Kant, is his idea of the sublime. Kant's examples of this are those awesome spectacles in nature that seem to shake our hold on reality when we first encounter them. Huge waterfalls or vast mountainous skylines inspire awe and as we struggle to process them – to contain them in a representation – we experience the sublime. The sublime is a kind of inarticulate marveling at our own power to achieve and establish such a synthesis. Here we discover, according to Kant, a facility in ourselves that mirrors God's power to make a world.

Play is perhaps inherently related to ontology, to human attempts to understand the fundamental character of being. More exactly, the human disposition to play is at the heart of the human creative response to being cast adrift in a meaningless universe. If it is not meaningful in itself, play is the activity that makes meaning possible by spinning forms out of the darkness. The pivotal function of play in the historical development of the species was recognized by Johann Huizinga, art historian and a key source for contemporary ludology. Huizinga's (1950) *Homo Ludens* asserts the naturalness of play and its centrality to all significant cultural forms, up to and including parliamentary systems of democracy. Play is found in all cultures and is not associated with any particular level of social development (Huizinga 1950: 3);[12] it is the creative principle that underscores all the created parts of collective life. Importantly, for the argument of the current book, play has intrinsic rhythm and harmony (1950: 10) and it is present as a kind of beating pulse in the sciences as well as the arts. Play, according to Huizinga, can be childish play that is unserious, but it can also be a way to the sacred, as when shamans work themselves into strange mental states. More commonly, play is associated with contests and with representation, sometimes taking the form of role play. Play always goes on within what Huizinga calls a 'magic circle'; a specially delineated zone where the normal conventions of social life are placed on hold and the rules of play (however minimal) are given free reign. Huizinga discusses the etymology of the word 'play' and suggests that it originates in the Old German word, *pflegan*, which apparently meant 'to vouch or stand guarantee for: to expose oneself to danger for someone or something' (1950: 39). This connects with Espen Aarseth's (1997: 113) observation, returned to in the next chapter, that there is an element of risk or danger that seems to distinguish video games from contemporary media and, indeed, Huizinga insists that there is an 'inner hardness' (1950: 51) that is essential to play.

Relevant insights into the nature and significance of play are also provided by scholars in the field of development psychology. Donald Winnicott, for example, locates play in a 'potential space' that is neither internal to the subject nor straightfor-wardly identifiable in the outer world. This space is a function of the relationship between parent and child (1971: 41) and it concerns the experiences of early infancy, when play is the first way a child has of exerting some kind of control over the world. Its actions and reactions exist in a determinate tension with those of the parent, who plays in response to the child.[13] For Winnicott,

> The thing about playing is always the precariousness of the in-terplay of personal psychic reality with the experience of control of actual objects. This is the precariousness of magic itself, magic that arises in intimacy, in a relationship that is found to be reli-able. (Winnicott 1971: 47)

The importance of play here lies in its foundational role for our ontological security and subsequently personal identity, because it is here that we first gain a sense of ourselves as agents who can act on the world and who must, in turn, adapt ourselves to its reality. Equally important is the fact that this growing sense is based in an activity that is inherently precari-ous. Play is always liable to become frightening. For example, the smiling face of the parent that vanishes and reappears may be gone just a little bit too long and upset the child's sense of security. Winnicott suggests that the development of games, with rules, may be a way of forestalling such eventualities (1971: 50). The fundamental play, however, goes on in this space between parent and child and it opens onto creativity in the healthy adult. It is present, Winnicott says, whenever anyone 'Looks in a healthy way at anything or does anything deliberately' (1971: 69).

For the psychologist, play can have a positive, therapeutic role where the goal is to relax the patient and encourage them to establish a more healthy balance between imagination and reality. This applies to all of us because, 'the task of reality ac-ceptance is never completed ... no human being is free from the strain of relating inner and outer reality, and ... relief from this strain is provided by an intermediate area of experience which is not challenged (arts, religion, etc.). This intermediate area is in direct continuity with the play area of the small child who is "lost in play"'(1971: 13).[14] Play therapy, therefore, involves trying to get the patient into a 'non-purposive state ... a sort of ticking over of the unintegrated personality' (1971: 55), which Winnicott calls 'formlessness' (1971: 55). He elaborates on this as follows:

> This gives us our indication for therapeutic procedure – to afford opportunity for formless experience, and for creative impulses, motor and sensory, which are the stuff of playing. And on the basis of playing is built the whole of man's experiential existence. No longer are we either introvert or extrovert. We experience life in the area of transitional phenomena, in the exciting interweave of subjectivity and objective observation, and in an area that is intermediate between the inner reality of the individual and the shared reality of the world that is external to individuals. (1971: 64)

Viewed in these terms, the video game can be seen as a kind of stand-in for the parent, later the friend, with whom the subject constructs this precarious sense of a self grounded in transitional phenomena. Play here is based on a kind of formlessness that precedes both ego development and a secure sense of reality. This pre-ontological domain is one that we have to play our way out of in order to secure a sense of ourselves and to learn about the world.

Winnicott endorses the positive function of play in normal psychological development, but he also considers the problem of pathological disturbance to play and here he is concerned with fantasy, as against healthy imaginative involvement. He argues that, 'creative play is allied to dreaming and to living but essentially does *not* belong to fantasying' (1971: 31). Fantasy is an excess of imagination. Even short of delusion it can impede our ability to process external reality properly and inhibit the development of our inner personality. Winnicott expressly relates this kind of distortion to the playing of 'joyless, obsessive games' (1971: 29) and relates it to the idea of an inner hardness associated with play. Play can be cynical, corrosive to the meanings that connect human beings to one another and which, most of the time, make life bearable. Viewed in this way, play is profoundly ambivalent. Perched over the inner void (meaninglessness, oblivion), it can be a mechanism that enables us to spin threads of meaning that protect and enclose, but it can also be used to shred illusions. This ambivalence is manifest in video gameplay where we find both aspects are present. Playing games, especially with other people, can be productive and meaningful. Equally, a lot of time spent playing very complex games with difficult routines can be repetitious, mechanical and empty. This kind of play tends to undermine the meaning content of the activity, at least in so far as this was set by the game's ostensible fiction, making players feel that they are up against an anonymous rule structure implemented through a machine. As Jesper Juul points out (2006: 135), it is common for gamers to lose all interest in the fiction projected by the game's interface and to switch their focus onto the rules. Video games incorporate this ambivalence into their structure in a way that marks them off from traditional games, good and bad. The ambivalence of play with video games is only intelligible through an examination of the role of form in the experience. Our play with the game object is a shaping of sensation that involves us weaving and unraveling webs of meaning from experiences of space and rhythm. Classical aesthetic theory was concerned with this idea of form structuring experience.

Form, taste and society

According to Kant, form emerges from play and is the defining characteristic of all aesthetic objects. Form is Kant's term for the patterns that make aesthetic representations pleasing in the sense described above. Because aesthetic experience thus rests on profound and objective properties of the human subject, Kant maintains that aesthetic taste itself has a kind of objectivity: we all have the capacity for such a feeling response and can all register its significance. This underscores our ability to make judgements regarding the quality of experience. At the same time, though, Kant acknowledges the ineliminably subjective character of aesthetic judgement; beauty truly is in the eye of the beholder in that these experiences are not of a kind that is susceptible to objective verification. We all feel that judgements exhibit good and bad taste, but there are no laws with which to establish who is right and wrong in cases of disagreement. Kant argues that an intelligent and autonomous exercise of taste is one that fathoms internal movements excited in the subject, especially in connection with the sublime. He contrasts this with judgements that are based merely on superficial responses to objects:

> Taste that requires an added element of *charm* and *emotion* for its delight, not to speak of adopting this as the measure of its approval, has not yet emerged from barbarism ...
>
> A judgement of taste which is uninfluenced by charm or emotion ... and whose determining ground is, therefore, simply finality of form, is a *pure judgement of taste*. (Kant 1960 [1795]: 65, original emphasis)

True aesthetic judgement centres on the form that emerges from the internal play of the faculties described in the previous section. Aesthetic form exerts the hold it does over successive generations of humans primarily because it rests on the playful and the humorous. Giving play shape and refashioning it in the context of changing cultural constellations, aesthetic form has remained centred on play. Moreover, the essentially purposeless character of play carries over into art too. It is not because they are visually pleasing or even because they are stimulating to the senses that video games are aesthetic. It is because they facilitate play and have the kind of form that appeals to long-standing ideas about aesthetic experience as an autonomous sphere of value. The value in question here can be understood in Kantian terms, as a hint at the divine or as others, like Winnicott and Theodor Adorno (2002), express it, as sparking a sense of the magical. In so far as video games are more than just games, they edge into this contiguous domain.

Artworks communicate by stimulating our sense of play and enabling us to discover form in their compositional order. This is why when we approach a cleverly constructed painting the

resemblance it has to a room or landscape that it represents is
not simply a matter of fidelity to the detail of how those things
appear to us visually. Paintings produced under the aesthetic
regime of art (Ranciere 2009) founded by Kant are pleasing
not just because they are faithful reproductions but rather
because their representational work is in fact subordinate to
the way they stimulate a particular response from us. At first
this concerns the senses, as when a painting is constructed so
that our eye is drawn towards a particular point on a canvas
and then guided out, through a particular route as it were, to
take in the rest of the work. There is a representation here of
some thing, but there is also the way that we take to obtain it
and this is the basis of form in play. Viewed in this way, form
is a property of both the composition and the viewer; there is
no recipe for creating form if you are an artist and as a viewer
you may miss it altogether if you do not engage with the work,
allowing it to play with you and letting yourself play with it.
Play and form precede and make possible our enjoyment of the
meaning content of aesthetic art. It is because the human mind
is naturally inclined to engage in these processes and responds
positively to form that aesthetic theory asserts the best artworks are not mere representations but have that added charge
that Kant associated with beauty.

However, in the second half of the twentieth century the
notion of forms with inherent appeal and especially the idea
that a privileged class of objects have more form than others
became suspect. For the French sociologist Pierre Bourdieu, for
instance, the principles of aesthetic art must be viewed as part
of an elaborate set of social rules that people learn as children.
Once internalized, these rules enable people to recognize situations and objects as 'aesthetic' and effectively train them for
participation in the social game that is art appreciation. This
game is closely related to the practices of art creation, since
artworks are only defined as such under circumstances defined
by the game. For Bourdieu, the interesting thing is to grasp the
social processes whereby this game and its rules get produced
and reproduced. Implicit in his approach is the idea that the
artwork has an element of the 'emperor's new clothes' about

it. Its rules are principles of social inclusion and exclusion and ideas like aesthetic form derive their sense from being deeply implicated in the construction of inequalities in the distribution of what he calls 'cultural capital'. Consequently, Bourdieu writes that the formalist tradition is 'rooted in the institutional doxa' (Bourdieu 1993: 177), the very set of practices it claims to authorize. Its analyses are therefore 'untenable', even though they pervade 'all investigation of an essence of the poetic, of symbol, of metaphor, and so on' (1993: 178) because the way those things work does not involve transhistorical essences but must be understood in social context. Bourdieu rejects structuralism on similar grounds because although it posits arbitrariness in the relation between signifier and signified it still 'seeks to extract the specific code(s)' in cultural products and this emphasis on codification is just another evasion of 'the question of the social conditions of the works'. For Bourdieu, 'the formalism that frees works from the most visible historical determination is itself a historical product' (1993: 178) and this should be a primary focus for critical analysis.

Without dismissing Bourdieu's insights into the social underpinnings of art as an institution (indeed, in Chapter 4 his ideas are used to illuminate the relation of video gameplay to gender), his analysis does invite the question whether all and any formal structures would suffice in constructing artworks, or if the institutions that frame art practice and filter its products do not work with something, a kind of raw material in our object-percept relations that antedates this activity. Evolutionary biology gives us reasons for believing that humans are hard-wired to respond positively to symmetries in the environment, for example, since they may signal the presence of predators, prey or possible mates. Humans are natural animals with responses to match. Under conditions of security and a degree of distance from natural threats the pursuit of pleasure has to work with something. Play and form are, in this sense, prior to meaning and culture and they condition those things. Bourdieu's scepticism about form is expressed in the context of a discussion of literary theory and it seems that the problems of essentialism and idealism really only arise if we overstate the relationship of form to meaning. Meaning is, of course, contingent. It slides about and its rules are variable and elusive. Forms are not in themselves meaningful. One of the intriguing things about video games is that they seem to revel in the principle that human beings enjoy form and can appreciate it for long periods of time pretty much for its own sake, without overloading it with investments of significance. For Winnicott this is pathological but from the standpoint of aesthetic theory the more productive observation would be that it positions them awkwardly (that is to say, in a position that is awkward to grasp) with respect to art and older cultural activities more generally.

Bourdieu's position has been criticized by the philosopher Jacques Ranciere (2009),[15] who argues the modern discourse of aesthetics emerged alongside a new kind of artistic practice. It informs and explains a kind of artwork with distinctive tensions and disparities that were novel and therefore incommensurate with previous discourses on creativity and representation. Traditional evaluative criteria appraised the power of representation as part of the symbolic function of a crafted work so that images were tightly pegged to particular textual meanings, which disclosed what the work was 'about'. In the eighteenth century attention switched to concentrate on how images were shaped by the special activity of artists and to provide a closer analysis of audience reception and response. Aesthetic theory emerges in response to a newly perceived problem in the space between doing, or creative performance, on one side and reception, or understanding, on the other. Ranciere grasps this in terms of a 'lost adequation':

> Aesthetics is the discourse that above all announces this break ... Aesthetics is not a domain of thought whose object is 'sensibility'. It is a way of thinking the paradoxical sensorium that henceforth made it possible to define the things of art. This sensorium is that of a lost human nature, which is to say that of a lost adequation between an active faculty and a receptive faculty. (Ranciere 2009: 12)

Working in the tension between these two aspects has been the defining feature of art since the eighteenth century. Aesthetic theory, which reflects on this space, develops criteria that are also justifications in that they say what makes a work 'art' and explain why it is a good thing. It specifies the aesthetic regime of art. The traditional approach to paintings and sculptures had been to assess them in terms of resemblance, of striking likenesses they established to the world as presented in authoritative textual mediations. However, aesthetic theory reflects the loss of this standard of, or for, mimesis; it expresses a recognition that representation cannot feel the same as the real thing and must be understood on its own terms. In the sphere of literature story emerges to fill this gap, which is why we get the development of the modern novel. Outside of literature the poetic has a reduced but still essential role resolving the tensions in aesthetic experience, which always centre on the paradox of a representation that does not straightforwardly represent, but rather works by playing on its audience. I will argue that this paradox appears in a variety of ways in video games and that it can only be understood if we approach them with a focus on the formal structure of the experiences they offer.

In aesthetic analysis the question of what a work 'means' or signifies is inseparable from the question of how it feels, which Ranciere emphasizes is part of a 'texture of communal existence' (Ranciere 2007: 95). The argument of this book is that the video game as a cultural form may be best understood when analysed in these terms. Aesthetic theory is concerned with understanding how it is that human beings find some situations, objects or artefacts attractive, or even beautiful. The paradigm cases of objects subject to such analysis have been scenes of natural beauty and artworks. Video games merit the concern that has been reserved for such items not because they are beautiful or 'art' but rather because they exist in a very specific tension with beauty and art, edging into the field of tensions that define the artwork and position it in relation to other social elements, and this incursion is essential to understanding them. The experience gamers have with video games is aesthetic, even if most of them would not identify it as such, and the fact that it is aesthetic is probably the most important thing about it. Primarily, it is what games feel like to players that matters, both in the sense of explaining why players play and of accounting for the importance of video games in contemporary culture and cultural theory.

A medium that asserts the centrality of play while being more than just a regular game is intrinsically significant from the perspective of aesthetic theory. However, that is not to claim that video games are art. Nor is it to accept that the era of aesthetic art is over, or the postmodernist thesis that all cultural forms are equally meritorious of our consideration. The point is that video games should be understood in relation to developments within art and aesthetic theory over the last three or four decades. As Ranciere points out, aesthetic theory has become relatively unfashionable during this time and as we will see in Chapter 3, to some extent artists have been responsible, with some rejecting the idea that their work should have to meet any philosophically set standards to guarantee its validity. There are a number of reasons for this. First, the development of a sociology of art has revealed class biases concealed by the rhetoric that justifies some cultural practices as 'high culture' while denying the validity of others. Aesthetic properties have been invoked to justify these kinds of distinction but at bottom they just reflect the influence of class on culture (Bourdieu 2010). A second reason for the unpopularity of aesthetic theory has concerned the development of cultural theory since the early 1990s, which has insisted on being able to position artefacts and practices in social context and in terms of their meanings to social groups. Viewed in this way the dimensions of intertextuality and communication, predominantly understood in linguistic terms or on analogy with linguistic processes, tend to obscure analysis of the other ways in which artefacts can affect and involve human audiences.[16] The dimension of form, which is best understood as prior to and conditioning meaning, has largely been lost, while such aesthetic analysis as there has been has tended to concentrate on the idea of emotional affect, rather than the feelings of a more constitutive order that are associated with form and its structuring of our experience of time and space. Finally, art itself seems to have given up any interest in meeting aesthetic standards, in measuring up to goals set for it by philosophy. This reflects broad changes in the meaning of art and artistic practice.

Art and politics

Arthur C. Danto famously argued in the 1980s that art in the sense defined by aesthetic theory had ceased to exist. What he had in mind was not that art had ceased to be produced, indeed there was a veritable flood of art at and after the time when he made his argument. Rather, what constitutes art from around 1960 has lost any intrinsic connection with the aesthetic, understood as a sensibility, structure of feeling, or organization of the human sensorium. In a retrospective reflection on his earlier intervention Danto writes:

> aesthetical considerations, which climaxed in the eighteenth century, have no essential application to what I shall speak of as 'art after the end of art' – ie. Art produced from the late 1960s on. That there was – and is – art before and after the 'era of art' shows that the connection between art and aesthetics is a matter of historical contingency, and not part of the essence of art. (Danto 1995: 25)

Danto's argument is that prior to the pop and conceptual revolutions of the 1960s, art was still concerned with the question of its own status as representation, or mimesis. Art in 'the era of art' was an answer to the question: 'How does this differ from the real thing?' This changed with conceptual art. Perhaps the most famous expression of this turn came when the surrealist artist, Marcel Duchamp, exhibited a urinal in 1927. Duchamp's work was certainly playful, but his play was with the art establishment and its markets and only tangentially with our sensibilities.[17] As Danto points out, the real significance of the urinal sculpture was that it brought this play of form and semblance within art to a dramatic end – here there is no form. The process whereby aesthetic value gets purged from art altogether starts with this move and leads art into conceptualism and to pop. Danto views these developments positively, effectively casting art as liberated from aesthetics.[18]

However, Ranciere reads the situation differently, arguing that 'there is no art without a specific form of visibility and discursivity which identifies it as such' (Ranciere 2009: 44). For him, contemporary 'relational art' is still art because it creates a space that is not that of politics but corresponds to the way that power structures sensibility in the current period. In other words, art remains critical simply by being recognizable as a contemporary space that is not structured by power. This is a reduction in art's ambitions from modernist movements like the ones associated with the Soviet *avant garde*, which thought of itself as projecting experimental spaces directly into the social, creating possibilities for radical transformation (Kiaer 2005; Ranciere 2009: 39). It is not, however, a break with the aesthetic art regime. Ranciere rejects the idea of such a postmodern break, of which Danto's thesis would be a part:

> the notions of modernity and post-modernity misguidedly project, in the form of temporal succession, antagonistic elements whose tension infuses and animates the aesthetic regime of art in its entirety ...
>
> There is no postmodern rupture. But there is a dialectic of the 'apolitically political' work. And there is a limit at which its very project cancels itself out. (Ranciere 2009: 42)

Ranciere gives us a way here to comprehend the video game in the history of aesthetic art. The video game and its culture of play are ambivalent. On one side, this cultural form possesses the autonomy of the aesthetic artwork. It maintains an internal dissonance that ensures it is encountered and experienced as something that is not the same – it is not like the other things we experience in consumer capitalism. The video game does not pacify; it stimulates us into action and, as the next section will suggest, this places it at odds with the culture industry. Steering the bizarre ball in *Katamari Damacy* and watching it tumble this way and that; leaning from side to side with the controller, and encountering unexpected obstacles and movements, all go on within a sense of *ourselves* as providing the

impetus and momentum. Form is the only way to understand
the pleasurable nature of this process. This is true even despite
the fact that video games are bought and sold as mass-produced
entertainment commodities. It means that the video game is
both autonomous in its inner dissonance and heteronomous in
that it is almost emblematic of the logic of contemporary consumerism. According to Ranciere, such paradoxes are definitive
of the modern aesthetic artwork. Traditional arts constituted
islands of autonomous mimesis, circumscribed by forms of
social organization based on naked domination. In contrast,
aesthetic art is a singularity that exists in and against modern
society. Its borders are porous and it has to participate in the
logic of contemporary domination (but not its substance) if it
is to have any effect. Since it is thus determined by its other,
its autonomy is completely contingent on its heteronomy. The
projection of such dissonant objects into social spaces, beyond
galleries and other designated sites is normally associated with
*avant garde*ism – the conscious use of art to make political interventions. Video games are not political art in this sense but
they do seem to inherit and exemplify many of the tensions
and paradoxes of the modern artwork. This raises the question
of the video game's consistency with contemporary sensible
and spatial orderings. Later chapters will suggest that the dynamics of video gameplay can involve surprising discrepancies
with the contemporary regime of power as this is expressed
through distributions of sensible experience.

The primary aesthetic difference between the video game
and the artwork is that in the latter the world and its contents
are all immediately present in an image or object that is essentially static. The work is spatially extended and it falls to the
subject to unlock its rhythms and establish how its elements
work together, to produce something that is both a challenge
and a source of satisfaction, including the lure of semblance.
The drama associated with solving the puzzle of the traditional artwork occurs within the subject and it involves what
Ranciere calls *poiesis* – form is reunited with meaning. With
the video game, this is reversed. The video game as encountered by the player lacks (perceptible) physical extension until

they instantiate it.[19] Individual screen shots are in themselves rarely fascinating; they are at best pictures we can search for clues. They lack substantial compositional order and form. However, they never stay still for long. The video game is an invitation to spend time and its form is elaborated only when the player finds the rhythmic associations necessary to reveal its possibilities. Viewed in this way, it is clear that the central dynamic possessed by games is that of an *extrusion* of the playful response. At first sight, the two are sharply opposed: modern art in particular is abstract and confusing but video games offer images that are readily intelligible because they resemble familiar situations. However, in the way that form is gener-ated, experienced and integrated the two kinds of object *mirror* one another. Examples of form in video games are not to be located simplistically in the patterns that appear on the game screen, although many games, including abstract ones like *Electroplankton* (Nintendo 2006c), do present players with pat-terns and symmetries that are pleasing to the eye. These would be the ornaments and charms that Kant dismisses as relative-ly superficial attractiveness in a design. Often, however, and *Katamari Damacy* is a good example, game designs articulate these symmetries in the visual aspects of the game to player actions and to other sensory stimuli in ways that are fascinat-ing and challenging. It is when order emerges in these complex force-fields, the ebbs and flows of gameplay, that we can find a variant of the experience that is grasped by the concept of aesthetic form. Whereas with the traditional artwork the core dynamics of this are internal to the subject, with video games form is experienced as extruded, in the physical actions and behaviours of the player. This makes it more like a form of dance than, say, traditional painting and it limits the integra-tion of the activity in anything like poetic meaning. What we find in video games is something like the raw material of art surfacing in another dimension of culture.

For Theodor Adorno, artworks offer us the possibility of a genuine encounter with our deepest desire, which is for rec-onciliation with others in a higher social totality,[20] and in so doing they promote reflection on the fate of that desire, on its thwarted status in the present. Their dual structure means that artworks present as puzzles. There is pleasure in solving them but their effect is to point beyond themselves to a potential that we have to be something more than we are, or (what amounts to the same thing) to a better world in which beauty has a place. This is why artworks are critical of the very thing they seem to promise: fulfilment. In contrast, the products of the culture industry pretend to offer this (success on TV talent shows like *The X-Factor* might be a contemporary example) but cannot provide it. As shallow reflections of what already is, they encourage identification with the present as 'normal' and put responsibility for dissatisfaction onto the consumer. This is what Adorno and Horkheimer meant when they wrote that, 'The secret of aesthetic sublimation is its representation of fulfillment as a broken promise. The culture industry does not sublimate, it represses' (1997: 140). Watching a soap opera, you do not come away with a sense that things might be better, but with your idea of what constitutes normal social relations reinforced. Your thirst for something other than mundane, repetitive life in capitalist society (dominated by objective social demands) is either criticized (you and people like you are at fault), or unaddressed and your real desires are thereby repressed. One of the main social consequences of the culture industry is pacification. People work all day and go home to be comforted by an industry that reassures them this situation is normal and right. Their desire for freedom and for the genuinely new (that is, a new principle of social organization) is deferred and displaced into a desire to acquire the latest objects (the pseudo-new), which are generally the same (in their core structures) as the old ones. Bourgeois, capitalist culture has particular offerings for workers in the form of advertising and fetishized goods designed to distract them and secure their interest in consumption (Marx 1977). Capitalist culture is about the life of commodities. While the real-life processes of individuals remain out of view, people are encouraged to spectate on the world of things, which is exciting in proportion as most of life is drudgery. The emergence of shopping arcades and window displays in the bourgeois towns of Europe in the

mid-nineteenth century is a visible manifestation of this tendency (Hetherington 2008; Williams 1991). In the twentieth
century culture became an industry concerned with manipulating people into making the right purchases and it began to
erode those areas of cultural practice where aesthetic criteria
still possessed some autonomous influence.

Modernism in the aesthetic arts was in part a response to these
circumstances (Lunn 1984). In abstract paintings and sculptures
as well as in atonal music, the tensions and instabilities of the
artwork reach fever pitch. The work of art is an expression of
the residual presence of the truly human in a culture that is
hovering on the edge of an abyss of barbarism. For Adorno,
this is a matter of the interplay of form and semblance, of the
reverberations of the artwork as puzzle and the resources we are
called upon to supply in order to unlock the sense of the work.
Art becomes increasingly demanding in order to maintain its
distance from the prevailing social order. Art's seeming disor-
der is its organized response to the deeply administered chaos
of capitalism. Modern art's refusal to offer easily decoded representations of things in the world is a normative premise for
artistic production, captured in Adorno's famous proscription
on semblance ('no poetry after Auschwitz'). For the artwork
to offer a 'semblance of a continuum grounded in the unity of
subjective experience' (Adorno 2002: 155) would be barbaric.
Art's status as resistance means that its puzzles must grow more
complex. Consequently, modernist art becomes jagged and difficult, it can no longer provide affirmation of the divine, or
our connection with anything transcendent, and so cannot be
beautiful. The only response within art to the crisis of art is for
it to be at war with itself. In modern art, aesthetic objects are in
this state. They are meaningful only by a convoluted process in
which they display both the subjective need for meaning and
its objective denial. As art 'abjured semblance' (Adorno 2002:
155) modern art became increasingly abstract and montage
and construction moved to the fore.

Adorno knew that the situation he was describing was not
one that could continue indefinitely. The combustible tensions
of the abstract modernist works he was describing were such

that eventually they had to burn themselves out and, by the mid-1960s, he believed that play and form were imperilled as properties of the artwork. He even envisaged a situation where art might have to give up aesthetic form to preserve itself as an (albeit residual) locus of value in modern culture. Art, he believed, would soon be unable to support the kind of theological 'meaning', or transcendence of ordinary experience that people looked to it to provide. The expulsion of aesthetic form from art in the name of aesthetic value – preservation of the enigma that exceeds literal description – was, in the mid-1960s, an open question. Indeed, he anticipated a time when such a rejection of art would be the best available defence of the aesthetic (2002: 53). If furnishing such experience is no longer a function art is prepared to take on it seems only likely that people will seek it and create it elsewhere. Although he is still often wrongly derided as some kind of art snob (see Poster 1995), Adorno was able to envisage new sources of play and form in the wider culture, from beyond the horizon of aesthetic art. Adorno often stresses that we should not confuse art with its materials.[21] There is no reason in aesthetic theory why paint and marble should be preferred over circuit boards and graphics cards when it comes to creating play and form. The definitive difference that would mark off and define such emergence lies in the concept of 'autonomous technique':

> The antagonism in the concept of technique as something determined inner-aesthetically and as something developed externally to artworks, should not be conceived as absolute. It originated historically and can pass. In electronics it is already possible to produce artistically by manipulating means that originated extra-aesthetically. (Adorno 2002: 33)

What Adorno has in mind here is precisely the migration of aesthetic form to other areas of culture. There is no intrinsic reason why aesthetic form should be limited to 'highbrow' cultural activities. On the contrary, Adorno observed that there was always a 'plebeian element' (2002: 240) in art. For him, as for Kant, all art starts in play and culminates in form and this should be the guiding thought of aesthetic analysis. Adorno writes that the vulgar play element of the circus prefigures and is present in all great art (2002: 81); that animal, foolish, childish play is an 'essential layer' of art (2002: 119), and he likens artistic experience to fireworks enjoyed by the masses (2002: 79–80). Incorporated into objects fashioned by aesthetic form, these elements provide a 'magic spark', essential to the enigmatic nature of aesthetic experience.

Culture industry re-visited

One difficulty for this thesis concerns the role of semblance, as just defined, in video games. Games have been widely understood as projecting coherent, even unusually complete fictional worlds. Would this not make them barbarous in Adorno's terms? The chapters that follow will argue that all is not as it seems here. The semblance projected by video game interfaces is in tension with the activity of play, so that we are not dealing with the post-modern, uncritical embrace of simulation the surface imagery might suggest. The visual images of play serve to orientate the player towards the game, even if the latter is essentially about the purposeless techniques of rapid-fire puzzle-solving and managing the values attached to variables in a dynamic environment. Gameplay involves an attitude that is cynical and humorous, which says: 'Yes, it's a beautiful image, but you'd be wrong to take it seriously'. Here the subversive or cheeky orientation of someone who plays video games even though, or perhaps even because, the activity is viewed with a degree of suspicion by authority figures in the cultural mainstream can be said to inform gameplay itself. Players do not approach games with anything like the 'willing suspension of disbelief' that applies to theatre-goers or even modern film audiences. Their guiding intention is to understand how the game works, perhaps even to take it apart (in both senses of this phrase), and this is informed by their awareness that it will pretend or purport to be one thing (its fiction, if you will) while actually holding out affordances and sensations that are discrepant with this. Herein lies the cynicism of the gamer and it is here too that we find the kind of 'fun' that is characteristic of video gameplay – a point to which I return in Chapter 3. This is important when it comes to situating the video game within the contemporary culture industry.

To work its magic, the video game has to be of a kind with the society of brands, consumerism and unbridled money-power that has produced it, something that is also true of contemporary art. The inner logic of the form is such that it invites people to play and in so doing opens up a form of experience that is resistant, but not oppositional, in relation to the dominant societal logic. This claim may seem paradoxical, since video games are published and distributed by some of the most important corporations in the globalized economy. Games account for about one-sixth of Microsoft's profits, for instance, and are growing as a proportion of their business. The video game industry is currently dominated by the three main console manufacturers, Sony, Nintendo and Microsoft, with PC gaming increasingly marginalized in the main markets of the US, Europe and Japan. These firms are global in the sense that they distribute their functions widely, with most physical production being done in peripheral, poorer countries of the world economy and switched between them to maximize rates of exploitation and profit (Kerr 2006: 77). Even within the rich countries, where design and development have been concentrated, Dyer-Witheford and de Peuter emphasize that much of the labour in the industry is subject to 'unwitting exploitation' (2009: 26) as young creative people are dragooned into long hours of intensive labour, devoted to the form they love to an extent that can be inimical to their own health.

Console manufacturers dominate the industry because the people who make the games need permission to produce games for designated hardware. This is controlled technically, through built-in restrictions on the machines; legally, through copyright laws; and informationally, in the sense that only approved developers are given access to the full range of specifications for new consoles. The latter clearly favours 'in-house' developers working directly for console corporations. However, industry publishers also have an important role since they alone can issue licences to developers. To develop a new game requires their approval and usually their investment. The cost of manufacturing a new game, which now runs to millions of pounds, is usually met by them. There has been a tendency over at least the last decade for publishers to have their own in-house development teams, partly motivated by the desire to reduce the risks associated with this. The number of independent game producers has declined during that period and it is increasingly difficult to break into the industry because of the high costs of developing and marketing a new game. There are clearly tensions within the industry between publishers and developers. The margin for creating interesting new games is being squeezed because there is a tendency on the part of media corporations to play for safety: high production costs are risks and a guaranteed return is preferable to gambling on a very high one. This is the economic logic behind the emphasis publishers place on securing rights to movies, sports events and other spin-offs from other media (Johns 2006: 169) and is also part of the explanation of the preponderance of 're-skins' of established games mentioned above. At the same time, the best hope an independent developer has of survival is to produce a game that is highly original and distinctive. Developers are the locus of creativity in the industry and securing standing in the gamer community with a 'hit' or even a 'cult' product is the likeliest way to secure publisher involvement in the future. The creative energies of the industry are located here, in these contradictions in its productive base. These conflicts over the forces of production are suggestive for the character of the products of the video game industry.

In their *Global Culture Industry* (2007) Scott Lash and Celia Lury update Adorno and Horkheimer's culture industry thesis. Since that argument was formulated in the 1940s, they argue, it has been superseded in a number of ways. Most profoundly, the economic processes that underscored the manipulative culture industry have altered, so that production is no longer tied to long-term cycles in the way that it was sixty years ago. Modern, lean time production means that the market for new cars, for example, does not need to have been prepared by TV adverts six months in advance, to ensure sales when the new model rolls out of the factory. Instead, people can customize their new cars using a computer in the showroom, or on the internet, and the instructions are relayed to a factory where it is assembled over the following few days. This does not mean that advertising is any less manipulative, only that the kinds of manipulation involved have shifted focus, Lash and Lury say, onto deeper recesses of the subject. We are drawn into and participate in the creation of the commodities we buy, through play. Authors who criticize video games as 'informational commodities' with negative ideological content (violence, sexism), such as Kline *et al.* (2003), overlook this, their position within contemporary 'distributions of the sensible' (Ranciere 2009). In contrast, Lash and Lury see the ambivalence of play everywhere. They argue that all contemporary commodities contain a playful element at their core. Technologies of 'virtuality' project a global commodity system that has extended its reach into all areas of life including art, intimacy and childhood, and subjected them all to the logic of capital accumulation. At the same time, however, the single improvement in our situation is that commodities now require us to instantiate and activate them through play. Lash and Lury call this 'getting ontological', because we bring contemporary commodities into being:

> One way of getting ontological with the object is in play, in the particular type of attitude, the special type of intentionality involved in play. In play we descend into the world with objects. (Lash and Lury 2007: 190)

In the play that has now become central to economic and cultural life – Lash and Lury call this the time 'when films become video games' – the invitation to play awakens residual possibilities for self-expression and the development of technique. Here we find a positive sense for the notion that video games are the ideal commodity of informational capitalism. At the same time this play is predominantly empty and repetitious. It is difficult to explain what you have been doing with a game without lapsing into tautologies. Tracing out the ambivalence of the video game as the locus of a peculiar experience of aesthetic form is the central task of the following chapters.

Notes

1 This ambivalence of gameplay is also brought out effectively by Dyer-Witheford and de Peuter in their analysis of the political economy of video games (2009: 213–14). They write of gamers playing with the possibilities of world creation and relate this to their own vision of a creative multitude (Hardt and Negri 2000; 2005) who could peel off from capitalism and begin to do this in reality.

2 Japanese players may extract more sense from the narrative because it contains cultural referents inaccessible to the Western player. However, my point is not about whether the story 'makes sense', but the importance of this sense to the play.

3 In his study of digital aesthetics, Andrew Darley writes programmatically that it is important to reject the 'hegemonic concern with hermeneutics' if we are to analyse games properly (Darley 2000: 5).

4 Williams clarifies this concept, writing that it is intended to grasp something 'as firm and definite as "structure" suggests, yet it appears in the most indefinite and least tangible parts of our activity' (Williams 1961: 48).

5 There would be no point, outside of highly specific technical settings, in trying to provide a purely physical account of someone else's speech, for example, along with all of its causal consequences; it is nearly always better simply to relate what they have said. This move also reflects a change in our own involvement in the situation, however, as we stop working towards a definitive, objective characterisation of the situation and move to the position of an agent who is involved in it (Davidson 1980).

6 I am thinking here of the distinction between a foul and a strong tackle, or the perception that a player is 'in possession of the ball', all of which may vary slightly between national contexts.

7 Unfortunately, there is something of an emergent consensus within game studies that aligns it with those cultural theorists for whom the norms of good interface design on digital artefacts are inherited unproblematically from the technical discipline of Human-Computer Interaction (H-CI). I have criticized this tendency elsewhere (see Kirkpatrick 2004, 2008). For H-CI, seamless integration of the technical and the communicative is an implicit goal or norm of all interface design. This approach to interfaces, including game interfaces, comports well with the attitude of contemporary cultural studies, according to which all

human behaviour has to be interpreted in terms of its meaning to those involved.

8   Galloway relates this to his idea of a gaming avant garde, or 'counter-gaming'. Progressive game designs 'should create new grammars of action' that will 'redefine play itself' (Galloway 2006: 125–6).

9   I am grateful to Aki Jarvinen for alerting me to the presence of Swink's important work.

10 'Mathematisation as a method for the immanent objectivation of form is chimerical.' (Adorno 2002: 143).

11 This is contrary to Pierre Bourdieu's assertion that Kant is trying to establish a pleasure or 'taste of reflection' that is completely inoculated against that of sense, resulting in the bourgeois 'pure pleasure' that has been paradoxically 'purified of pleasure' (Bourdieu 2010: xxiv).

12 This is an important difference with Roger Caillois, for whom the degree of differentiation of play as measured in the complexity of a culture's games is taken to be indexical for its level of development.

13 The seminal discussion of Freud's observations on infant play in connection with computers and the computer culture is provided by Sherry Turkle (1984).

14 In a similar vein, Jean Piaget writes that 'the function of symbolic play is to assimilate reality to the ego while freeing the ego from the demands of accommodation' (Piaget 1972: 134).

15 See Nordmann (2006) for a full discussion and an elegant synthesis of the two sets of views. I have tried to adhere to the logic of her resolution in the development of my own argument about video games.

16 This move within cultural theory (perhaps it is the growth *of* cultural theory) has been forcefully rejected by Žižek (1999) and Ranciere (2009). As we will see in later chapters, other developments in recent thinking reassert the importance of formally construed truth and its priority over convention-bound meaning. Refusing to analyse everything as if it were a text is not the same thing as denying that all artefacts operate in a social context. The manner in which cultural products are embedded in social context can involve multi-modal communication, much of it not assimilable into a linguistic, or semiotic model.

17 Indeed, according to Danto, Duchamp found it amusing that some critics suggested that he submitted the urinal for exhibition

because it had formal aesthetic properties, rather than as a subversion of form and other aesthetic categories.

18 David Roberts (1991: 63, 139) agrees that aesthetic theory has run its course in this sense.

19 This is one sense in which they are sometimes called 'virtual entities' by some theorists (Lash and Lury 2007; Shields 2003).

20 Adorno (1994) characterizes this as an alternative constellation that he designates as 'peace', in contrast to the paranoid rat-race that prevails in capitalist society.

21 Ranciere (2009) says modernist art theory makes a false move when its advocates stress a new relation between form and the material used in the artwork. He rightly points out that art's medium is defined by the aesthetic regime – anything that is hollowed out by art's 'text' is ready to contain an art image. The Adorno of *Aesthetic Theory* (2002) however, is already completely clear on this point.

2

Ludology, space and time

The game plays the user just as the user plays the game, and
there is no message apart from the play.

Espen Aarseth

This chapter situates the aesthetic approach to video game
analysis in the context of the emerging discipline of video game
studies. The first generation of video game studies was partly
defined by an opposition between ludological and narratological approaches. This chapter interprets some of the key points
of this dispute in terms of space and time as these feature in
video game aesthetics. The overall argument is that ludology
correctly identifies what is essential to the video game as a cultural object, namely, its character as a form of structured play.
At the same time, however, the discussion here acknowledges
the importance of more meaning-oriented video game analyses, which have forced ludology to reflect on the differences
between traditional games and their modern, digital variant.
This line of reflection raises legitimate questions about the
appeal of video games that cannot be answered from within a
perspective that insists games is all they are. Video games are
more than games in the traditional sense. However, scholars
who emphasize the story element in games jump the gun when
they assert that attention to meaning and to the story-telling
dimension of video games is the correct way to address the
deficit in ludology's approach. Closer attention to the formal
properties of games, in particular to the way they structure the
temporality of gameplay – its rhythms – opens up the possibility of a formal aesthetic method of video game criticism that

does not re-centre analysis on the meanings of play as projected by the game's ostensible narrative content.

The first section looks at how the question of what players do with games and the formal properties of this relation were first examined through the ludological critique of 'interactivity'. Focusing on Espen Aarseth's (1997) development of the counter-concept of 'ergodicity', it argues that the centrality of play to video games that emerges from this critique defines the problematic of video game studies as a new discipline. This leads, in the second section, to an assessment of work by Jesper Juul (2006), one of the leading exponents of contemporary ludology, in which he has argued that a defining feature of video games is that they are 'fictional worlds', which accommodate player progression in a way that was not true of older games. In his embrace of the concept of fictionality Juul may have conceded too much to those who argue that video games are best understood in terms of their story-telling properties. Re-interpreting the ludology-narratology dispute as an argument over the relative importance of space and time in video game experiences makes it possible to resist this move. Advocates of both perspectives end up converging on the idea that some kind of computer-generated space projects fictional meanings which organize either a virtual world (narratology) or a simulation (ludology). The third section focuses on virtuality as a way of thinking about space in video games and questions the importance of visual standards of virtuality to an assessment of the medium. The same reservations apply to the notion of simulation, which has been used by ludologists to grasp the kind of signification specific to video games. Once we concede that video games are partially defined through a specific experience of story, we tend to lose sight of the essential aesthetic tensions that define them. Repudiating the claims of virtuality and simulation over the video game establishes an opening for the aesthetic approach. Drawing on Foucault's (1983) analysis of Magritte's surrealist painting, the fourth section argues that video games do contain simulacral entities but that their proliferation is checked by the active role assigned to the player's body. The ideas of virtual space and simulation as defining features of the video game both neglect the role of the body as the site of the pleasures of video gameplay. Embodied rhythmic experiences are important factors in gameplay and these temporal factors determine the spatial character of the video game form. Drawing on the work of Alain Badiou (2005a), I argue that the way that video games play on our expectations creates an experience of 'time suspended in space' that the form shares with dance. This is illustrated in the fifth section, with reference to an analysis of *Max Payne* (Rockstar 2001). The chapter concludes by re-assessing the relationship between ludology and aesthetic analysis, arguing that ludology is the necessary starting point for a serious understanding of video games but that aesthetic theory rather than a rapprochement with fictionality is the obvious next step methodologically for the discipline it has established.

From ergodicity to ludology

To grasp the specificity of video games in aesthetic terms we need to identify the structure of feeling that distinguishes them from other kinds of object or artefact. For some thinkers, this difference can be grasped in terms of the notion of 'interactivity'. Scholars who understand well how film works, for example, find that video games seem a lot like films except that the audience participate in determining what happens in the on-screen drama. This active role for audiences can be called interactivity since it seems to reflect a new responsiveness on the part of the medium and implies a degree of complexity that makes the media object more like an interlocutor or co-participant and less like a finished work to be apprehended contemplatively. Similarly, scholars approaching matters from the field of literary studies find that video games have significant textual components, ranging from text on Heads up Displays (HUDs) to on-screen dialogue wherein game characters tell players the significance of game events in terms of a story that defines the game. Here again, interactivity seems to be a plausible term with which to distinguish video games from other media and in the work of Janet Murray (2001),

Marie Laure Ryan (2001) and others, the term is used to make this contrast. However, in an important intervention Espen Aarseth (1997) presents strong reasons for dissatisfaction with the term, which he finds too diffuse and insufficiently precise to grasp what is really important about the video game object. Interactivity, he argues, is actually a very vague term that aligns what is special and distinctive about the new form with pretty much anything in the world that responds and changes when human beings act on it (1997: 48). In so far as the term has any precision, it inappropriately aligns video games with things like Artificial Intelligence, which is partly concerned with the development of computer systems that can converse with humans on equal terms, or the science of human-machine interface design, which is concerned with ensuring that users of technical systems do not have to think about what they are doing (Kirkpatrick 2004). While it purports to differentiate video games as an object of study, interactivity actually deprives us of any handle on their specificity, the thing that makes them interesting and distinctive. Aarseth's preferred conceptual solution, in his pre-ludological work, was to introduce the notion of ergodicity, which he says is derived from a fusion of the Greek words, 'ergon and hodos, meaning "work" and "path". In ergodic literature, nontrivial effort is required to allow the reader to traverse the text.' (1997:1).

Aarseth's concept emphasizes the fact that the physical structure of the ergodic text is modified by its reader, or user, in ways that do not apply to other texts or media objects, but perhaps more importantly it also foregrounds the nature of the commitment that is required from the human subject of the text. Readers of books and films are 'safe' and their 'noematic responses'[1] are limited to eye movements or turning pages, but playing a video game, or navigating a cybertext, involves the risk of rejection by the text – you can *die* in games. It also presupposes a human agent who wants to use the object in an expressive way, to say something about themselves. When he invokes the notions of work and of finding a path, it is this struggle that, for Aarseth, genuinely defines the new medium. It is the particular character of the human relationship to the video game object that marks it out as distinctive, perhaps even unique; the way that the games are experienced is all-important. Ergodicity was an important step forward for video game studies because it took us towards the idea that this struggle, which Aarseth goes on to characterize as play (Aarseth 1997: 162), and not the more diffuse notion of interactivity, is the defining feature that marks out our experience with video games as against other artefacts.[2]

Aarseth's advocacy of 'ergodicity' became the starting point for modern ludology, the study of play and games. This view of video games situates them in the long history of games and prioritizes that lineage over more contingent associations, with visual or story-telling media. Video games are defined as games played with and against computers, or with and against other people through the medium of computers. They have gamic structures that distinguish them from other objects and other things that people do with computers and the task of the new discipline is to analyse these structures. The move to analyse video games as things that are played rather than as 'interactive' variants on established media forms also establishes video game studies as an independent discipline. Aarseth subsequently dated this to 2001, when the online journal *Game Studies* was launched. In the first editorial he proclaimed the cultural importance and newness of video games and the implicit conservatism of the methodological programme of computer game studies – games as such pre-date even Classical culture and, as a cultural innovation, the video game bears comparison with the Greek chorus. This is heady stuff since it announces the arrival of something both new and profound, which is a highly unusual combination in the sphere of culture, if not science.

The inauguration of game studies involved violence too. In the first years of video game studies ludologists waged a polemical war against 'narratologists'. The latter became a kind of catch-all term for anyone who wanted to study video games but who did not start from the centrality of play and gameness. Thinkers for whom video games represented a new way to tell stories, for example, were viewed as 'colonising' the new disciplinary field, notwithstanding Aarseth's own background in literary studies.[3] Video game studies was forged in the heat of a struggle between these two approaches. This struggle was highly typical of the kind of conflict that we associate with the emergence of new scientific discourses. According to Gaston Bachelard (1984), the founding of a new science involves the emergence of a new set of integral questions, or 'problematic'. These are most often a combination of questions previously addressed in other disciplines now brought together alongside some that were previously unthought of. The point about the new problematic is that once it is established it becomes clear to practitioners of the new science that its questions can only be addressed – in a way they only make sense – when viewed together. The problematic constitutes a worldview that orders the relevant part of reality. Bachelard famously discusses Lavoisier's discovery of oxygen in the 1770s, which was foundational for modern organic chemistry, as an example of the emergence of a new problematic. The difference between de-phlogistonated air and oxygen was not a difference of reference, but concerned the questions that each term was deployed to answer. The oxygen theory won, of course, but adherents of phlogiston held out for decades and the two groups denounced each other in the harshest terms. This kind of rhetorical violence is to be expected when a new set of questions is being asserted in the distinctive form of a new problematic. Such eruptions are rarely, if ever, peaceful transitions. Viewed in this way, the acerbic polemics of some ludologists can be seen as more than just the expression of a legitimate frustration with established scholars who did not grow up playing video games. They also reflect the emergence of a new way of looking at things, one that is grounded in truth but which as yet lacks any objective, especially institutional recognition.

The critique of interactivity can be read as a first attempt to secure the specificity of video gaming as a practice – its unique experiential properties – while refusing the horizon, or methodological worldview of any of the established disciplines. Ludologists like Eskelinen, whose work was mentioned in Chapter 1, maintain, sometimes quite forcefully, that video games are both too new to be adequately comprehended from within the perspective of established disciplines *and* part of a cultural sub-stratum (games) that is so old as to be beyond their reach. Video games are games and as such they predate communications media, including print and perhaps even writing. Trying to study them with the flimsy conceptual apparatus of 'media studies', or other recent disciplines amounts to a kind of intellectual imperialism but will also be a vacuous project unlikely to deepen our understanding.

It is important to recognize that the point of the dispute with narratology concerns the specific role and operation of meaning in video games and its difference from other media. In particular, ludology rejects the principle that video game-play is organized under, or explained by its meanings, or by the significance players invest in the practice if this is understood in those terms. Consequently, in his early writing Jesper Juul repudiated narrative theory's application to video games on the grounds that this theory introduces a temporal discrepancy that is essential to all reading but not present when playing video games. In narrative theory it is the difference between the time of narrating and that of the events narrated that is all-important. According to Gerard Genette, for example, the temporality of a written text always involves a 'metonymic displacement' (Genette 1980: 34) whereby we, as readers, allow the false time of the story to stand in for the true time it takes us to read it. This discrepancy between the time of reading and that of the events narrated is essential to the process of meaning-interpretation as it constitutes a kind of space where the reader interrogates and reflects on what she is reading. The idea that games 'tell stories' is simply incompatible with the reality that they are played in a singular time:

> In a verbal narrative, the grammatical tense will necessarily present a temporal relation between the time of the narration (narrative time) and the events told (story time). Additionally, it is possible to talk of a third time, the reading or viewing time ...
> ... the game constructs the story time as *synchronous* with narrative time and reading/viewing time: the story time is *now*. Now, not just in the sense that the viewer witnesses events now,

but in the sense that events are *happening* now, and that what comes next is not determined. (Juul 2001: 13–14)

If we want to study and analyse video games, then, we need to establish a methodological framework that is sensitive to this, their distinctive temporal immediacy, which is damaging to the mechanics of fictional meaning. This can be achieved only if we gain clarity on what constitutes a game. That will put us in a position to comprehend video games as the latest manifestation of the innate human need to play games. Taking this as his starting point Juul has drawn on some of the methods and rigour of analytical philosophy to clarify the concepts of 'game' and 'gameness'.

Gameness and its limits

Ludwig Wittgenstein's concept of language game is intended to explicate linguistic meaning with reference to social contexts of action and interaction. In the *Philosophical Investigations* (Wittgenstein 1992) he shows that the idea of meaning is not necessary to explain what people do when they say things to one another. Starting with trivial examples, including people passing bricks and tools to one another, he argues that behaviour determines our understanding of other people's speech and that what we are naturally inclined to think of as the 'meanings' attached to their words is actually a kind of extraneous metaphysical baggage that can profitably be excised from our thinking. He conceives his own philosophy as a kind of therapy to steer us away from the bad habits that result from carrying this baggage around. What we actually need to focus on in order to understand communication, he says, is the multiple kinds of game that shape contexts of action and interaction. If we situate our speech acts as counters in social games then we will be able to see how they work and it is this, not their meaning, that really matters. With Wittgenstein, then, the idea of game becomes a central tool of philosophical analysis. However, perhaps paradoxically, what a game actually is remains largely unanalyzed in Wittgenstein's thesis. For him, despite the

fact that the term 'game' enjoys this fundamental status and
enables us to tidy up the rest of language, it remains inherently
ambiguous. Consistent with the reasoning he applies to other
concepts, Wittgenstein argues that to understand what 'game'
means we need to see how the term works in context. However,
on this basis, he observes that each of its instances bear only a
'family resemblance' (1992: 32e) to one another that does not
withstand further analysis. Subsequent analytical philosophers
have questioned the emphasis on behaviour in Wittgenstein's
work and tried to examine the relation of speech to action and
decision, rehabilitating the idea of meaning[4] in the process.
His use of the term 'game', however, has not been a focus for
the mainstream of that philosophical tradition. Wittgenstein's
polemical purpose in invoking the idea of gameness was to
reveal levity and the absence of profundity where traditional
philosophy saw depth and meaning.[5]

Within philosophy it fell to Bernard Suits (1978) to reject
the idea that the concept of game was not susceptible to further
analysis as Wittgenstein had maintained. He argued that games
proper are specific action contexts, namely, those in which we
embrace a set of rules just in order to facilitate play. In games,
rules specify an end that is to be achieved and restrict the
means we can use to achieve it to those specified by the rules.
What distinguishes a game, as the term is normally understood, from standard contexts of action and interaction is the
acceptance by players of a specifically narrowed rule set with
which to achieve agreed ends. 'Playing a game,' Suits writes,
'is the voluntary attempt to overcome unnecessary obstacles'
(Suits 1978: 41). Hence, golf becomes interesting because we
undertake to try and get the small ball into a hole that is far
away using designated sticks. Before we play there is an understanding that balls in holes is the declared goal of our activity
and our common agreement not to just drive over to the hole
in our carts and drop our ball in is what makes it a game. The
rules here are constitutive of the activity and once established
they determine the acquisition of skills on the part of players.
None of this would be sufficient, however, without what Suits
calls the 'lusory attitude' that encompasses the elements of the

game (the goal as a state of affairs in the world as well as the rules) and commits us to *playing* the game.

Juul rejects Suits's notion of the pursuit of a goal by less efficient means as the defining feature of games. He argues that,

> this description is interesting but ultimately misleading. Suits's argument hinges on the fact that it is (mostly) possible to describe a game as the effort to reach what he calls a *pre-lusory* goal, a goal which can be said to exist independently of the game, and that there is always an optimal but disallowed way of reaching this goal. This idea is in itself quite problematic. (Juul 2006: 34)

However, Juul's reasons for finding it so are themselves confused. First, he claims that it cannot be true that this definition applies to video games because they are characteristically easier than their non-computerised versions (a point to which I return below). This leads Juul to maintain that,

> the concept of inefficient means completely breaks down in the case of video games. In FIFA 2002 (a soccer game) (Electronic Arts 2002) and Virtua Tennis (Hitmaker 2000) the video games are much easier to master than their real life professional counterparts are – namely soccer and tennis. (2006: 34)

This argument is confused because the player of a computerized version of a game is pursuing a completely different goal or end state than the people who play these other games. Indeed, it seems that a lot of assumptions are imported into the discussion when we talk of video games as versions or 'counterparts' of other games. The two objects and activities are completely distinct and we should not be misled by game packaging that projects a strong relationship between them – in aesthetic terms it might be more accurate to say that the resemblances of a video game to some real world counterpart are part of its charm, they do not touch on its substance.

In his argument Suits distinguishes the pre-lusory goal as a physical state of affairs (a ball in a hole) from the goal of play, which is that same state viewed and described in terms of the game and its rules. Juul seems to think that these distinctions do not apply to video games because we cannot see what it is that we would be aiming for outside of the system or frame of reference of the game. Juul asks, 'If we look at any video game how can we say that the player is using less efficient means?' (2006: 34). He seems to mean by this that in video game golf there is no distinction to be drawn between pursuing the ends in a ludic as against non-ludic way, since the game object is a game 'all the way down' and it does not allow a direct, unplayful route to the game's 'end'. For this reason, Juul maintains the lusory attitude is an inappropriate concept for video game analysis. However, Suits's notion of a lusory attitude has more life in it than this rejection allows. The different kinds of obstacles encountered by players and game refusers (Suits calls people who refuse to take the appropriate attitude 'spoilsports') may vary between real golf and computer golf but the applicability of Suits's distinction does not. That is to say, there is a physical machine state corresponding to a successful 'putt' and there are, in principle, a variety of means we can use to get there. The decision to *play* a video game and the attitude this entails remain fundamental to the game situation, just as Aarseth's reference to the centrality of players' intentions would imply.

Juul has other reasons for believing that video games differ from traditional ones, in ways that require a reassessment of the role of story or narrative meaning in them. Traditional games, like chess, work by presenting players with limited rule sets and some tokens. The design of the latter often carries some distant metaphorical association that may be useful at the start of play, which in the case of chess perhaps alludes to military conflict. Such metaphors may dispose players to engage one another and the game in a particular, agonistic way, although it is normally so remote and the convention that games can be competitive so ingrained that it is not really needed. These games provide players with what Juul calls emergence, which is what happens when a small initial set of rules generates a large and diverse set of possible and actual outcomes. Emergence is pleasurable because of the connection with pattern and form, ideas that were discussed in Chapter 1. Video games provide experiences of emergence too, but they also contain an unusual gamic structure, which Juul calls progression. Progression is the facility for sequential exploration of a series of states or scenarios. Juul draws the contrast in terms of the kinds of challenge each presents to players. He writes that there are:

> games of progression that directly set up each consecutive challenge in a game, and games of emergence that set up challenges indirectly because the rules of the game interact. (2006: 67)

Adventure games, in which players explore scenarios and solve puzzles in order to move between them, are games of progression, while games like chess and *Pong* (Atari 1972) exhibit the 'more primordial' structure of emergence. Most video games involve some hybridity of the two forms, but it is progression that distinguishes video games in the history of games.

Viewed in this way, traditional games are abstract: pieces in a chess set may be decorated to resemble armies, but any metaphoric signification is irrelevant to play. Play is enjoyable because of the emergence structure, which generates patterns, tensions and other aesthetic properties that are enjoyed by players of chess. Games of progression, however, do not work like this. They may contain a puzzle element, but their central dynamic is one of exploration and the kinds of pattern unlocked through this process are enjoyed consecutively, rather than experienced as a surprising outcome of intervening unpatterned states. The pleasures of progression are essentially those of reading a visual image, or knowing the significance that is attached to a representation. Adventure games are enjoyable because by solving the puzzle (not strictly a part of the progression) we are able to meet a new character, to find out something new about the game world, or simply to see something that we could not see before. These events carry meaning for players and so, according to Juul, we have to concede that this aspect of video games makes them *less abstract* than traditional games. In this sense, games of progression are games that tell stories. Juul argues that video games differ from traditional games with boards and tokens because they are 'half real':

> In having fictional worlds, video games deviate from traditional non-electronic games that are mostly abstract, and this is part of

> the newness of video games. The interaction between game rules
> and game fiction is one of the most important features of video
> games ... This interaction gives the player a choice between im-
> agining the world of the game and seeing the representation as
> a mere placeholder for information about the rules of the game.
> (Juul 2006: 2)

He is careful, however, to distinguish the experience of story-
telling we get in games from the one we have with media like
film or novels where story has long been integral. The concept
he invokes here is that of a 'fictional world', which he opposes
to the 'fixed stories' that we find in other media. Juul clarifies
the difference with reference to analytical philosophy, where
the idea of logically possible (coherent) worlds is used to designate systems of statements that are internally consistent yet
may correspond to no actual state of affairs. Possible worlds in
this sense designate open-ended, coherent structures that could
accommodate or include fictions, or stories. Conventional fictions are located inside such worlds, so that the events and
characters in Shakespeare's *Macbeth*, to use Juul's example,
are positioned in a wider 'world' that we imagine. Juul takes
from Marie-Laure Ryan, the principle that audiences use their
understanding of the actual world to 'fill in the blanks' (Ryan
2001, cited in Juul 2006: 123). This principle is usually supplemented by the imaginative conventions specific to genre.

The contrast between fictional world and fixed story distinguishes the game as a series of relatively static states projected
as scenarios by the interface, which makes for what Juul calls
progression, from narrative fiction, in which a series of events
are described. At stake here is a shift from the temporal distinctions that mark a conventional narrative (in particular, the
time of the story and the time of its telling) to a spatial concept
('world') and the process of exploring that space. Juul presents
the idea of a succession of spatially construed states as progression and acknowledges this as the basis for story in games. In
a sense his concession to story does not concede anything to
standard narrative theory; it just develops the idea of games
as spatially conceived states into a series.[6] In his critique of
Juul's earlier work, Julian Kucklich (2003b) already identified

a bias towards a purely spatial conception of video games and argued that the emphasis on gameplay to the exclusion of narrative elements shifts 'the focus from the temporal sequence of individual events to the spatial organization of the game' (2003b). Juul's newer analysis remains thoroughly spatial in its emphasis, even as it concedes a new role for fiction. Now we move between spatial configurations and this movement, he says, allows us to interpret the game as a fiction. Indeed, he implies that such movement is only conceivable if it is mediated by such a fiction-interpreting process.

Kucklich was dissatisfied with ludology's spatial conception of games because it seemed to him inconsistent with what actually goes on when players navigate their ways through the puzzles and scenarios games present. For him, this is always a meaningful process. He argues that 'a player does not necessarily gain access to the implicit rules of the game through playing, but ... he or she will find a way to interact meaningfully with the game, no matter what the actual rules encoded by its designers are. In fact, the player might even find ways to interact with the game that its creators did not think of'. It is, of course, true that players experiment with games and make them do interesting things, raising questions about the meaning of cheating in these games as against traditional ones (Consalvo 2007), but Kucklich presumes a strong role here for interpretative meaning in these processes, especially fictional meaning. The problem he raises is that sustained activity applied to a game seems to require a narrative or meaning element to explain why players seek to effect the relevant state transitions. Something like a lusory attitude gets us so far but it cannot explain the way that video gameplayers keep stepping outside the rules of the game and changing them, for example. For that, identification with character and immersion in some kind of storyline seem to be needed, to mediate, or explain the extra-ludic player activities – the things they do that do not fall under the lusory attitude. Meaning based explanations would situate their play in a larger, fictional or social setting and would explain their involvement in all of its aspects. Kucklich's point is that player activities, including perhaps even subversion of the game's projected or advertised narrative content, must be meaningful for people and these meanings must play some explanatory role. At the same time, they clearly exceed anything stipulated by the raw rules of the game. The fact that video games commonly include filmic and textual elements counts strongly in favour of such an analysis. However, as seen above, Suits's analysis established that similar oscillations between playing the game with a lusory attitude, which confers a distinctive kind of affective meaning, and manipulating its physical coordinates in a way that is free of those investments (perhaps to make it better) were already possible in traditional games. Moreover, Suits's distinction between pre-lusory and lusory attitudes accommodates our desire to play with both traditional and video games, without obliging us to assert a strong role for narrative meaning. There need be no stronger rationale for taking an interest in the game than the desire to play and to play better while, as we have seen, play itself is underscored by an attitude that requires no extraneous rationale. Clarification of Suits's idea of a lusory orientation might involve ideas about sensation and feeling that aesthetic theory says arise from a playful sensibility. In particular, pursuit of form explains what players do to secure progression better than attributions of meaning to the activity. This would relieve ludology of the need to accommodate 'story worlds' as a defining feature of the video game in the history of games.

If Juul's critique of the applicability of a temporal distinction seems to lose its force with the introduction of the idea of progression this does not create an automatic opening for the idea of fictional meaning or narrative. In the move between game states players' attention does move to extra-ludic reflection but their activities involve actions and reasoning that are also extraneous to story and these actions need to be understood as integral to the video game form as a whole. Alexander Galloway usefully characterizes non-story related actions as 'form playing with other forms … a play within the various layers of the video game' (Galloway 2006: 36). In this multi-layered play the human element must switch between discrete sets of rules, each bearing different kinds of relation to meaning, including some movements and activities that have no significance at all, captured nicely in Galloway's phrase, 'multiple vectors of agitation' (2006: 38).[7] The weakness of ludology, correctly identified by Kucklich, is not its lack of attention to fictional meanings but its exaggeratedly spatial conception of games as successions of 'game states'. Juul's notion that the game is a fictional world continues his earlier reification of the game program as a space, that is, he continues to treat it as if it existed prior to the player's actions with it, or as if the three-dimensional space on the screen really has three dimensions even if no one looks at it.[8] In fact, games only provide us with spatial *sensations* (the feelings arising from perceptions of space) when we play them in time.[9] The kinds of experimental or deviant activity players engage in commonly involves a break within *both* ludic and diegetic time.

The strongest contender for a horizon concept that organizes this disparate activity remains that of a 'lusory attitude' – the orientation to play that makes gameplay possible in the first place. This should be understood in its full ambivalence, as discussed in Chapter 1. A lusory attitude can be wry and detached as well as engaged and pleasure-orientated. Rather than assuming that the experience of studying an interface and looking for solutions to its puzzles must be mediated by a fictional narrative, an aesthetic approach understands these processes as intrinsically unresolved within the limits set by any established discursive framework. Viewed in aesthetic terms, this undecidability of the video game is a kind of call to the aesthetic regime. Some of Juul's earlier comments are suggestive here, as when he writes that 'the history of computer games is really a history of continually making computer games attractive in new ways' and then clarifies this by saying that, 'The development of any art form is at least partly to find that the emphasis *can* be shifted; that the details of everyday life can be interesting; that the painting does not have to represent anything; that the rhythm can be as important as the melody' (Juul 2003b). However, by introducing the notion of a non-abstract, fictional world as an integral feature of video games, Juul has developed his theory in a rather different direction, namely, towards convergence with those theorists for whom the video game is a form of virtual space.

Abstraction, virtual space and simulacra

In their influential book *Remediation*, Jay David Bolter and Richard Grusin (2000) situate video games in a larger history of visual media. They suggest that recent media theory has prioritized language-based paradigms and that assessing new media in terms of their place in the history of visual techniques has been neglected. On their account of this history, the development of new visual media always involves the interplay of two factors which they term the search for 'immediacy' and its subsequent loss in 'hypermediation'. Each innovation in the history of visual media has provided evidence that humans seek a standard of verisimilitude in their visual representations that matches reality itself. Hence, early phases in the development of a new technique are always discussed in terms that stress their superior capacity, relative to older media, to grasp and represent reality in its immediacy. This phase is as surely followed by one in which the new medium effaces immediacy by drawing attention to itself, in particular its technical basis. For Bolter and Grusin, this pattern explains why Renaissance painting, for example, ends up turning into the baroque. Often seen as a degeneration, baroque art takes Renaissance technique and exaggerates it so that we get paintings that spill out beyond the limits of their frames, murals that defy us to discern where the wall ends and the ceiling begins, and so on. These works draw attention to the means that have been used to create them and, in Bolter and Grusin's terms, they are an example of hypermediation. Curiously, the motivation for both these developments is the same:

> Hypermedia and transparent media are opposite manifestations of the same desire: the desire to get past the limits of representation and to achieve the real. (Bolter and Grusin 2000: 53)

Immediacy involves trying to create representations that are as good as the real, while remediation reflects a drive to represent the world in a way that includes representation itself. In connection with digital media, Bolter and Grusin argue that the phase of immediacy corresponds to the development of virtual reality, involving head-sets and data gloves. Virtual reality creates an illusion that acts on as many human senses as possible with the aim of creating an illusion that cannot be distinguished from reality. A key element of this is the creation of 360 degree models[10] – programs that implement whatever illusion we are trying to create in an illusory space that mirrors real objective, homogeneous, or Cartesian space. In reflection on digital art we find a similar notion of virtuality is operative. Since the discovery of linear perspective in the Renaissance, artworks have presupposed the position of a privileged viewer (Berger 1974). Visual spectacles and displays have been constructed with this viewing position, just in front of the canvas, in mind. However, according to Oliver Grau (2000), virtual art introduces a new principle within this history:

> The technical idea that is virtual reality now makes it possible to represent space as dependent on the direction of the observer's gaze: the viewpoint is no longer static or dynamically linear, as in the film, but theoretically includes an infinite number of possible perspectives. (2000: 16)

With the virtual art object the viewer enters the work and inspects it from the inside. The virtual affords us access to an experiential object with an infinite number of possible perspectives, corresponding to where we choose to position ourselves.

The spaces that result are re-mediated because the digitally-generated illusion, or simulation, is never complete. Instead, 'the computer always intervenes and makes its presence felt in some way, perhaps because the viewer must click on a button or slide a bar to view a whole picture' (Bolter and Grusin 2000: 46). These discrepancies draw attention to the medium itself, rather than us experiencing it as transparent. What distinguishes digital media in this history of immediacy and remediation, however, is that there is scope within them for a

particularly 'aggressive' form of remediation, which Bolter and
Grusin illustrate by referring to video games. If hypermediation normally effaces the immediacy of an illusion, in digital
media the intruding factors, like working a mouse or studying a drop down menu, can be used to compensate for the loss
of immediacy by 'involving the viewer more intimately in the
image' (2000: 28). This is important because it means that interactivity plays an important role in digital remediation:

> Unlike other examples of hypermediacy, this form of aggressive
> remediation does create an apparently seamless space. It conceals
> its relationship to earlier media in the name of transparency; it
> promises the user an unmediated experience, whose paradigm ...
> is virtual reality. Games like *Myst* and *Doom* are desktop virtual
> reality applications and, like immersive virtual reality, they aim
> to inspire in the player a feeling of presence. (2000: 48)

The phrase 'desktop virtual reality' is oxymoronic, since by
definition virtual reality should be indiscernible from reality
and being miniaturized and bounded on a screen are clear in-
dicators that the illusion is separate and distinct. However, for
Bolter and Grusin the reason digital media can remediate *and*
retain their immediacy – that is, continue to sustain the feeling
of immersion for the player and the sense of presence conveyed
by the illusion – is that what happens on either side of the
screen contributes to the development of the same illusion.
They explicitly describe this as 'mimesis', which, as discussed
in Chapter 1, entails a common meaning that orders events in
the virtual space and the actions and motivations of players.
Bolter and Grusin argue that the salience of new media in
social experience now collapses any distinction between illusions produced by such media and ordinary lived experience.
No longer privileged interpreters of experience who can distinguish reality from illusion, humans must instead judge what
happens according to whether it feels 'authentic' and respond
accordingly. On one hand, we know that all our experience of
the world is thoroughly mediated – no direct experience of
nature is possible any longer[11] – but on the other, 'immediacy
names the viewer's feeling that the medium has disappeared

and the objects are present to him, a feeling that his experience is therefore authentic' (2000: 70). This feeling of authenticity is all the subject of virtuality has to guide her through a world that is hypermediated but which feels immediately accessible to experience. The video game is assigned a privileged role in this distinctive account of what will be familiar to readers as our post-modern condition.[12]

Like Juul, Bolter and Grusin believe that the move to digital media involves a wholesale shift in the standard of representation that greatly reduces the role of abstraction. For them, this is comprehensible only in terms of a paradigmatic virtuality that, while not actually realized on computer desktops, is incarnate in the kinds of mimetic relation that people enjoy with computer programs, especially games. Drawing on Bolter and Grusin's work as their theoretical foundation, Geoff King and Tanya Krzywinska (2006) develop the notion that video games offer 'desktop virtual realities' that are uniquely present to players and in which people can become immersed. They also understand the idea of virtuality as primarily denoting a particular configuration of visual experience. What is important for a good game is that it should be immersive for the player and allow her to gain and maintain a constant sense of presence inside its world.[13] For mimesis to be attained controls should be as 'intuitive' as possible (King and Krzywinska 2006: 33) and a positive balance maintained between potentially intrusive factors like HUDs or stats screens and visual effects made possible by the virtual character of the camera we use to navigate the virtual world. Describing golf simulators, they argue that recent innovations have resulted in greater correspondences between controller operations and taking a swing with a real golf club. The result is an 'interface mechanism directly analogous, in its own thumb-scaled realm, to the real-world action' (2006: 148). The goal of such designs must be to make video games easier than performing the real-world actions that they are 'about':

> Too much realism of function would make sport and other games simply too difficult, and would diffuse the definition of core gameplay features ...

> Generally, the whole point of games is to be easier and, for most players, more fun as a result of the fact that they can achieve things they would find impossible in the outside world. (2006: 150)

The claim that video games are easier than other activities they represent or purport to be about is perplexing in that it is difficult to see what it is that most games are 'easier' than. Consider the large number of game sequences that just do not resemble any experiences we have elsewhere in our lives – like learning to fly on a huge petal in *The Legend of Zelda: Ocarina of Time* (Nintendo 1998). Even games that seem to have a real-world referent, like the ones where we guide fast-moving spacecraft, are not pleasurable because of a comparison most people never get to make. It is not even completely clear that driving a warthog vehicle in *Halo 2* (Bungie 2004) is any easier than driving a real jeep. The game of *Ikaruga* (Treasure 2002) is supposedly based on a scenario of flying a spacecraft but it becomes so abstract that it effectively gives up any such connotation, offering instead sensations of speed, intricacy and the thrills of fine-grained control.[14] In general it cannot be true that professional gamers of the kind that earn their living playing video games in South Korea for example (Chee 2005), have dedicated their lives to something that is, by definition, easier than a corresponding 'real' activity. Concentrating on the aesthetic aspects of gameplay enables us to see more clearly how the experience builds on a lusory attitude towards heightened sensations and experiences for their own sake, rather than towards virtual representation or simulations of other activities.

Applied to video games virtuality is a pseudo-aesthetic concept that is as imprecise and diffuse as 'interactivity', mainly because games simply do not present players with the kind of seamless representation that is implied by the idea.[15] As Eric Kluitenberg points out, it makes more sense to think about digital artefacts and the kind of engagement they solicit in terms of a 'hybridisation' of elements, including powerful visual displays (Kluitenberg 2008: 30). One of the striking things about the environments presented by video games is the salience of signs, ranging from the large pink arrows that appear over the heads of 'target' characters and objects in *Grand Theft Auto: Vice City* (Rockstar 2002), to the text in HUDs that has been a staple of most First Person Shooters since *Doom* (Id 1994). Hypermediation is a superficial interpretation of their actual aesthetic effect. The salience of written messages in particular within game 'worlds' has a strangely corrosive impact on the extent to which we find the visual illusion compelling as illusion, while it can actually intensify and lend focus to our engagement with the game object (as something else). For example, the arrows in *Grand Theft Auto: Vice City* focus the player's attention on those characters as elements that have to be 'played' (usually killed). There is a corresponding reduction or degradation of the rest of the presented scene, which now becomes just a backdrop when previously it was foregrounded and replete with coherent fictional significance. The switch of focus is a move into playing the game as an object, or cluster of objects, with priorities now set by action. It is a move away from concern with the fictional world as a setting.

This use of signing and textual elements is very common and not always effected in the comical way we find in *Grand Theft Auto* games. The effect on the salience of different features of the game world in the player's orientation towards the game is always the same. At the same time, the meanings we attach to the signs themselves is also altered in virtue of the fact that they appear within a fictional visual representation. We do not relate to text telling us that our 'health is low' or that we have to 'lure two cops to the lock-up and steal their clothes' in literal terms, as we would if we read them in a conventional fictional narrative. Rather, the significance they take on for us in the context of the game is narrowed to signify a range of actions we need to take with our hands (guided by our eyes and the rules of controller use) in connection with the game object. The effect of this discrepancy, between literal (fictional) meaning and significance in the game is often quite humorous and the gap between them is commonly filled or made up for with sounds, images and movements that are comical or stylistically cartoonish (a point to which Chapter 3 will return). From both sides, then, the video game's fictional world tends to be in a state of contraction, with its two key elements working against each other to mitigate any sense of unity or coherence consistent with the projected illusion that is the game world. On one side, the visual illusion, even when supplemented by tactile properties like the rumble controller or enhanced place for the body afforded by the Wii remote controller or 'Wii-mote', is undermined by the appearance of free-floating bits of text and random insertions onto the surface that bears the illusion. On the other, the inserted signs and texts are distorted in their significance, so that ordinary language itself gets dragged into the game and conventional significations become attenuated.

The dynamics of this can be illuminated with reference to aesthetic theory. Far from inaugurating a new naturalistic canon of visual realism, video games present a kind of callligram, of the kind Michel Foucault (1983) discussed in his seminal analysis of the surrealist painter Rene Magritte. In Magritte's famous painting 'Ceci n'est pas une pipe', a naturalistically rendered pipe hangs in mid-canvas, with the words 'ceci n'est pas une pipe' (this is not a pipe) underneath. For Foucault this defines a tension within the work. The pipe looks like a pipe, but the text tells us what we already know; it is only a drawing. At the same time, the text is also painted and so it cannot be read as a literal statement because it is in the work just as much as the painted pipe is. Textual and visual elements here work against each other, forcing us to question representation and its effects without reaching a definite conclusion. Foucault likens this to a particular kind of poem, associated with symbolism,[16] that combines textual elements (letters and words) arranged into physical patterns on the page. The calligram, 'brings a text and a shape as close together as possible ... It lodges statements in the space of a shape, and makes the text *say* what the drawing *represents*', and it, 'distributes writing in a space no longer possessing the neutrality, openness, and inert blankness of paper. It forces the ideogram to arrange itself according to the laws of a simultaneous form' (Foucault 1983: 20–1; Tanke 2009: 93–122). By using the calligram as a strategy to construct paintings that are puzzles, Magritte extends the programme of artistic modernism. The latter had been associated with abstraction; this being the most obvious way to oppose form to semblance, as discussed in Chapter 1. But Magritte discovered another way to achieve the same effect. Turning image and text in on each other, Foucault says, Magritte seems to offer a return to illusionism but his painting actually makes us question how such effects are achieved and especially the relationship between discursive and visual representation in traditional painting.[17] The effect of Magritte's work is to suspend the apparent intelligibility of the painting as a representation. The juxtaposition of textual and pictorial elements in a movement of mutual cancellation is continuous and open-ended making the virtual space of the painting infinite (Tanke 2009: 104). The pipes cannot be pipes but everything in the picture, from the pipe itself to the shapes of some of the letters in the text, keeps raising the issue of resemblance to pipes. What we find in Magritte's work is a proliferation of simulacra, an endless parade of copies, each of which is supremely well executed in accordance with the demands of visual realism, though it is impossible to say what they are copies of. The original, so to speak, constantly recedes on the horizon, leading Joseph J. Tanke, in his brilliant discussion of Foucault's essay, to describe Magritte's paintings as 'games of petrified similitude' (2009: 114).[18]

In the video game, the form is not simultaneous but distributed through time. The game designer presents us with a dynamic puzzle, whose fundamental tensions and properties are those of the calligram. It is not the designer who makes it clear that the elements cancel one another out, but the player who brings this to light by playing the game. Playing the game involves using points on the fictional horizon to orient us towards the correct moves, the ultimate effect of which is to reinstate our distance from the horizon. There is no resolution of our activity within which it is straightforwardly a fictional event, an event within the fiction. The experience is one in which our movements seem to be guided by yet are held apart from any actuated meaning. This makes it difficult to use the contrast abstract/representational to comprehend video games. Clearly, they are neither abstract nor straightforwardly representational and they also cannot be positioned anywhere stable in between. Just as with modern artworks, video games frequently involve us in a challenging, highly reflexive process that is world-constitutive rather than world-receptive, or even interpretative. Just as Magritte's work forces a proliferation of simulacra, copies without substance or weight, so video games offer us experiences in which simulacra proliferate, where we engage with objects that are never quite what they seem but which, nevertheless do afford us experiences that are coherent on their own terms, that is, as video game objects. Form here is in a play with semblance. The video game object has to appear to be something else, without actually performing the representational function of standing for any one thing.[19]

As Tanke points out, Foucault's analysis holds that the dynamic proliferation of simulacra within Magritte's work comes to an end, so to speak, in the bodies of the audience for the work. In the case of the painting this is because the proliferation of simulacra makes the work 'post-representational' in a specific sense, namely, that its images are no longer constrained to serve or be answerable to anything else. Instead, they take on a specific power over the real (Tanke 2009: 121). The effects of this power are to be measured in the emergence of specific forms of embodied subjectivity that are entailed in the work's production and reception. This observation inhibits Foucault's analysis from becoming that of Baudrillard (1994), for whom all sense of the real finally gets consumed by the proliferation of simulacra in post-modern culture. For Foucault, the art of simulacra does not surrender the functions of aesthetic art, in particular critique, edification and pleasure. The body arrests the production of copies, dragging them back down to earth and incorporating them as images in what Tanke claims are non-linguistic statements with concrete effects (Tanke 2009: 121). If this is true for paintings it applies with even more force to video games where, as Chapters 3 and 4 will argue, the involvement of the player's body is central to the aesthetic experience of gameplay.

The rhythm of suspended time

The structuring of time in video games is central to producing the feeling of pleasurable engagement that makes people play them. As Henri Lefebvre (1991, 2004) has shown, objective space and time are outside experience, because in experience there is always an active, human component. We tend to assume that there is a 'pure' time that can be accurately measured – the time of atomic clocks perhaps – but none of us ever experiences time that way. Time as we live it has texture and rhythm. There is always a sense of time having 'flown by', or, when we are waiting to see the dentist, of it dragging. Similarly, when we analyse our experience of space it is never the same as the space described by physicists. The homogeneous space we know is there is not the enclosing domestic space we experience in our living rooms (Bachelard 1994) or the daunting vaults of a Norman cathedral (Focillon 1992). This gap between the objective characterization of space and time and their lived reality is ineliminable and it means that just as all experienced space is produced and shaped by our activity, so all experience of time has a rhythmic, aesthetic dimension. To understand rhythm and its appeal in video games we do not need to invoke distinctions between the time of play and its contents, which was the problem with narrative theory, but rather to focus our attention on the distanciation mentioned above; the way that video gameplay as a series of actions is an effect of attraction (to the idea of the game) and restraint (we are never really 'immersed').

Aarseth's suggestion that we focus on the worked path taken by the player, to find its specific differences from other kinds of experience (since everything we do is 'interaction') does not suggest space; it points to rhythm or, more accurately, to what Alain Badiou calls 'virtual time'. Gameplay involves us in a to-and-fro movement with the game that is not adequately comprehended by analogy with merely spectating or even exploring a static fictional world. Our actions with the game involve a temporal, embodied dimension that is integral to, even productive of, the visual sensations of space we get from looking at the screen. Some games, such as *Blinx: The Timesweeper* (Artoon: 2002), *The Legend of Zelda and the Ocarina of Time* (Nintendo 1998), even *Mortal Kombat: Deception* (Midway 2004), which allows you to pause and 'meditate' in order to gain extra time to complete difficult tasks, actively exploit the rhythmic powers of video games. *Blinx: The Timesweeper* is perhaps the best illustration of this since it includes a whole system of controls that allow players to alter the flow of events as part of gameplay. The game includes a time-shifting vacuum cleaner powered by crystals gathered in the course of exploration. Different coloured crystals enable different time-shifting abilities, so that you can use the vacuum cleaner in 'pause', 'fast-forward', 'rewind', or 'record' modes. The first stops all other moving elements in the game, allowing your character to escape from tricky situations or act unhindered by other characters. Fast forwarding enables your character to move much quicker than anything else in the game, which can be useful but is also disorientating. Using 'rewind' makes all game elements other than your character go backwards through the series of event immediately prior to your activating the effect. This enables you to retrieve objects you had to leave behind, perhaps on the far side of a rock fall, and bring them back to where you started. Most interesting of all is the 'record' function. This allows you to record a sequence of play and then play it back, so that you can act alongside a spectral version of your character's first time through the sequence, and so perform two sets of actions at once. It is the only way to complete certain missions in the game: To solve some of its puzzles you have to imagine yourself acting in two different ways at the same time.

This is a very obvious example of how time and temporality can be structured to produce interesting play, but rhythmic variation is essential to nearly all video games. *Max Payne* (Rockstar 2001) has multiple rhythms built up out of several elements. For example, like many games, it alternates between gameplay scenarios and cut-scenes. The way this alternation is executed in *Max Payne* is very distinctive. Sometimes it feels almost seamless, as when you steer Max into a room, there is a change of camera angle and you are reduced to spectating on events. Most often, the move to a cut scene from play is accompanied by a sense of relaxation, even completeness, normally because you have just finished an intense play sequence and this has come to a conclusion. These transitions involve going through a door and finding that the screen goes black for a short period, after which you get the scene. Similarly, it is unusual for the game to simply throw you into a fight after a cut scene; there is usually some time to find Max's bearings, identify the elements in the situation that correspond to what you were told in the cut scene and so on. As each element is completed, its rhythmic interaction with the others combines to form a sense, along with the *noir*-ish narration and the comic book scenery, of what *Max Payne* is. *Max Payne* is an object with a distinctive feel, or aesthetic and this determines its character as an experience for players. At the centre of this is a feeling of expectation or anticipation that is worked and re-worked by the tensions and releases of play – exactly what, for Ranciere (2007), connects the various experiences of form in the aesthetic regime of art.

The element of repetition is the clearest illustration of the importance of rhythm to the medium. Distinct types of action repeat and recur throughout the course of *Max Payne*. For example, enemies are always encountered in groups and have to be killed one by one in a series of shoot-outs. When you kill the last member of a group he always flies through the air in slow motion. Playing the game, you come to recognize this as a cue that a given segment of action has ended. This results in a change of mood or physical orientation towards the game; it is no longer necessary to maintain an aggressive, concentrated stance. When it happens you can assume a different attitude, namely, that of poking around, exploring the game situation to see what you are supposed to do next. Exploring, fighting and watching correspond to feelings of tension, excitement and relaxation in the body of the player. They define the rhythm of incorporation specific to *Max Payne* – different games have different rhythms. *Max Payne* is a good example of this partly because it includes the principle of 'bullet time', which enables players to switch events to 'slow motion' as they steer the figure of Max into a roll-and-shoot maneouvre. The device is useful to get Max through difficult situations, enabling him to dodge bullets while his own shots continue to hit their targets. The rhythms of gameplay are not only a function of the game's visual elements. Each of the three core temporal modalities of *Max Payne* has its own, distinctive set of sounds. Exploring a scene, for example, prior to fighting, is largely silent. Cut scenes (which are watched) are accompanied by music and grainy speech, while the third mode, fighting, has all kinds of jarring noises including enemy voices, police sirens and other sounds from the environment, like TV or radio newsreaders, who are normally commenting on or filling out some aspect of Max's backstory. The aural element contributes to the rhythmic variation between elements that constitutes the game.

Within each of the three modalities described there are further rhythmic variations as well. The best example of this is the sense of challenge that rises to a pitch and falls away again after each encounter with enemies within a given sequence of play. Hence, early in a given chapter Max might have to kill three enemies, but by the end of the same chapter he will be confronting a much larger gang and as the player you will have to execute more moves within similar time spans. Things happen much more quickly than before. There is interplay here between the exploration and fighting modes. So, for example, while steering Max through his explorations of the environment, you find 'pain-killers', which, consumed at the right time, enable him to survive difficult confrontations. These are discovered in small quantities at first then later in large numbers in bottles that Max can carry around with him. The discovery of lots of painkillers is a sure indication that you are about to become embroiled in a fight, where you will need them and this triggers a shift in attitude towards greater concentration and focus, well in advance of actually meeting any enemies.[20] Through this kind of device a rhythmic alternation is established between the explore and fighting modes. This too varies. As you get comfortable with the move between looking for pills and fighting, so the difficulty of some of the fights grows. As you adjust your play to address this you find that the pause for exploration has narrowed, so that you move more quickly between more difficult fights. This creates excitement, a tension accompanies your focus on events and it grows as the game gets more difficult. Just as with a piece of music that builds itself up through the rhythmic interaction of multiple layers, so *Max Payne* generates tensions through the intersection of all these devices. Just as music can suddenly dissipate, leaving us relaxed or even deflated, so the tensions of gameplay can be dispersed in an instant when you finish a chapter in the game or Max loses a fight and gets killed. Reading a novel or watching a film, these sensations would be completely out of place. Even in racy genres where readers are supposed to be stimulated and the blurb writers refer to 'viscerality', feelings and sensations are secured through identification with characters in the fiction. In video games the action and the intensities of experience are much more like music in being relatively detached from these elements, to such an extent that we often need cut-scenes to remind us where we (our characters) are supposed to be in the game's overall 'story'. Such is the extent to which we are concentrated on play, its 'feel' and dynamics, and such is the narrowing of our focus onto game elements as signs not in a narrative story, but of the need to perform this move or that.

Within these fight scenes, there is also a rhythmic principle that we find in many video games and which often gets obscured beneath a general allusion to 'difficulty'. Difficulty in video games is very often about the mastery of a rhythm that is established between elements in the game object and becomes more complex as the player progresses. Fight scenes in *Max Payne* are a good illustration of this because of the contrast between those we find early on in the game in easy levels, and those encountered later. Early fights involve the player sizing up a situation presented on-screen and then responding with their fingers and thumbs on the controller, which is how they guide Max, point his gun and shoot. When we lose one of these fights we concentrate on the sequence that occurs just prior to Max's demise and try to get the right series of button pushes to ensure success. These practices are about calibrat-

ing our physical actions more precisely to the events unfolding
on the screen. The difference between early fights and later,
more difficult ones concerns the compression of sequences of
actions (recognition and response) into identical portions of
time. This is not just a matter of doing the same things more
quickly, but reflects learned mastery of increasingly complex
rhythms. It shows that *within the speed and dexterity of gameplay
there is always a hidden slowness*. Here, the art video games most
resemble is dance. As Badiou (2005a) points out, although
dance is normally choreographed physical action, this can
never be how it is presented. Each move has to present as its
own source and never as causally determined by its predeces-
sors. Something similar is true of video game action, which is
always structured by the program yet cannot ever feel as if it
is. This is a central aesthetic paradox of video games, hence
the controversy that still surrounds the idea of interactivity.
Badiou argues that dancers' movements always testify to a
force of restraint – they are attracted to something but hold
back from it. It is this immanent restraint that gives dance its
order and form. Dance, Badiou writes, is a kind of pure verti-
cality that is shaped by its attraction to an event that does not
happen – the event that would give its name to the meaning
of the dance. For Badiou only the naming of an event, what
he calls a 'cut', inaugurates time. The dance is the time before
time; time without a (horizontally assigned) place. Applied to
video games, this pre-temporal or virtual time explains the fact
that the repetitions and what we might call the many times of
gameplay rarely cohere with our sense of how long we have
been playing when we come back to 'real time'. Video gameplay,
like dance, is in Badiou's terms 'subtracted from the temporal
decision'; it is the play of time within space. In video gameplay
and dance alike, time is suspended within space. What we feel
in its rhythms is a pull towards a meaning the activity cannot
have. This is why the sensations of gameplay are so much more
intense than those of fiction – they are not pegged to or resolved in any particular meaning.

As far as the relation of these rhythms to meaning is
concerned, there is a strong connection here between the

gameplayer and aesthetic performance as this is understood in other contexts. Diderot's paradox,[21] is a much discussed idea from theatre studies and concerns the actor's assumption of a role to which they must appear to be thoroughly committed if they want to carry the sentiments of the audience. The paradox is that they can only achieve this appearance through concentrated attention to something else (namely, the performance itself). While an actor must know feelings intimately and express them sincerely to produce them in an audience, he cannot achieve this goal by sincerely expressing those feelings on stage but must have recourse to artifice. The best actors are not the ones who actually feel what their character is supposed to be feeling. This applies very much to gamers, who cannot identify too strongly with their characters, since they have to master the playing of the game. It illustrates a fundamental aesthetic problem with the idea of a straightforward (tension and paradox free) immersion in virtual space and fictional role play.

Ludology, narratology and aesthetics

The aesthetic approach to video games could seem like a further attempt to colonise them for another, alien discipline. Hence, while Aarseth rejects the notion that 'older, unmodified aesthetic theories' (Aarseth 1997: 23) can help us to understand them, I argue that the only way we can achieve his goal of understanding the contribution video games make to our efforts to communicate (1997: 17) is to develop established concepts of aesthetic theory in the direction of the new cultural form. From this standpoint, ludology's focus on play structured by ludic form means that it correctly identifies the heart of the issue as far as video games are concerned. Aarseth's assertion of the centrality of play to understanding what video games are has proved to be the most fertile move yet taken within video game scholarship. Play is an understudied phenomenon within the human sciences, indeed, part of the significance of video games lies in the fact that they cause a resurgence of interest in this topic. Playing games, pitching oneself against their rule sets and enjoying the results are the core activities of video gameplay. The reason video games appeal is because, as distinctive plastic objects, they allow us to have these experiences. However, ludology does not understand why these experiences matter. In particular, it has an ahistorical stance on play, regarding it as an anthropological constant so that its pleasures are always and everywhere the same. Play is viewed as anthropologically primitive, linking human nature to that of animals (Huizinga 1950). Similarly, video games are an extension of the game element in culture, which is as old as the species and essentially continuous even if it is subject to diverse cultural and historical articulations (Sutton-Smith 2001). Games are seen as rule-governed systems that structure play without negating its essentially purposeless character. They differentiate and organize play and their degree of complexity can even be seen as indexical for 'civilization' (Caillois 1958). For ludology, the history of games provides the context within which video games should be understood. Of all social and cultural forms, the game enjoys a privileged relationship to play and the video game extends and updates this tradition (Juul 2006: 16). The task of the ludologist, on this understanding, is to clarify what unites the diversity of play and games and to study specific instances of these phenomena in relation to this understanding.

To some extent ludology protected video game studies against association with postmodernism. It provided reasons to understand the video game and take its study seriously that had nothing to do with claims that all cultural practices were equally meritorious of such attention, or exaggerated arguments for the power of simulations effacing the distinction between reality and representation. As Ranciere (2007, 2009) argues, postmodernist thought reflects real changes in the aesthetic environment and in the history of the arts. But it too misunderstands itself when it posits these changes as constitutive of a break or radical rupture with modernity. The simulation emerges within the field of the modern and its presence is a part of the contemporary configuration of the latter as a particular experience of space and form. Postmodernism offers an ideological gloss on this that neglects its real dynamics, but serves nonetheless to orient us towards objects in a particular way, a way that is appropriate to them. This is related to Eric Kluitenberg's (2008: 175) observation that the phantasmatic is always a part of our relationship with technology. He points out, for instance, that mobile phones are rarely very reliable, yet used incessantly. His example illustrates how misrecognition, like the ideal of virtuality, can shoot through and enliven our relationship with a representation or an object while at the same time be repeatedly negated in the course of our experience. Part of the hybridity of games is their inclusion of misrecognition, which enables certain kinds of performance, and the play of this with correcting and alternative perspectives. From an aesthetic point of view, the play of misrecognition and self-correction are integral to the overall experience. To come at the video game properly is to approach it in this awkward perspective. The problem with analyzing video games on the assumption that the kind of virtuality discussed here is paradigmatic is that it assumes an organizing, integrating role for mimetic meaning that is not there. There is supposed to be an inherent connection between the moves of the player's hand and the ostensible visual narrative. However, sustaining this position in face of the disjoint realities of gameplay leads King and Krzywinska, for example, to exaggerate the significance of visual elements to video game aesthetics. Aspects of gameplay that do not centre on screen-based action are understood as merely instrumental activities carried out in pursuit of an aesthetic pay-off that is essentially visual. In consequence the real aesthetic dimension tends to get squeezed out altogether – it gets registered only as the (unanalysed) property of 'visual pleasure'. The sensations of video gameplay are not exclusively or even primarily visual but are contingent on the structuring of time as a mode of imminent action; as expectation and visual elements play a role in shaping this experience of form.

This book has already suggested that ludology conserves the formal element of games and that this gives it a natural affinity with the aesthetic approach developed here. However, in his avowedly narratological work, *More Than a Game: The Computer Game as Fictional Form*, Barry Atkins (2003) also

seems to discern the importance of aesthetic form to the appeal
of games. Atkins insists that games are 'game-fictions' and
provides elegant analyses of the story contents of several exem-
plars, which he acknowledges have been chosen because they
have strong 'narrative impetus' (2003: 20). At the same time,
however, he recognizes that this fictional content is often subordinate to what he calls the game's poetics: '… it is how they
are told and how they are read that concerns us here far more
than the content of their stories' (2003: 56). In other words, if
video games are more than just games it is clear that they are
also more than just fictions. Atkins denies, however, that the
element of form can ever subvert the 'coherent structure' that
fiction confers upon each game. Video games, he says, do not
become the jagged, fragmented aesthetic objects of radical modernism (2003: 48) because they are always organized by their
fictions. Discussing situations where confusion and dissonance
arise in games, for example, he acknowledges the importance
of such episodes (they are part of the fun and associated with
feelings like paranoia, which he rightly prioritizes over visual
aesthetic concepts) but insists that players find their way out
of these situations with reference to fictional meaning (2003:
142). It seems to me that in his recognition of the importance
of non-linguistic and non-visual cues to the unfolding of game
fictions (2003: 58) and his references to in-game movement
(2003: 70) and to dance (2003: 146), Atkins perceives the centrality of form to video game experience. However, he seems
to resist developing the idea because of a justified reserve concerning postmodernism. Exploring the affective tensions of
gaming for alternative unities and configurations *seems* to lead
directly into discussion of simulation (2003: 80), a reintegra-
tion of gameplay as a mode of virtuality indistinguishable from
the real. Reflection on the aesthetics of video games through
the concepts of form and semblance enables us to gain clarity
on their affective structure without imposing such false unities
on the experiences we have with them. In Atkins's terms, the
search for coherence in the game's fiction may be one part of
our pursuit of form within a game, but it is not sovereign.

Similarly, the real problem for ludology is not its neglect of meaning or even its exaggeratedly spatial conception of video games but its failure to recognize the role of suspended time in defining the specificity of video game spaces (their form). An aesthetic appraisal of the video game object can account for the state changes associated with progression without invoking a role for story or meaning, by aligning video games with dance. This argument will be developed in Chapters 3 and 4. A narratological position encases gameplay within a mimetic meaning, corresponding to the idea of the game as 'virtual environment' but this is implausible, being inconsistent with the physical reality of gaming and with the experiences of most gamers. Aesthetic reflection on games discloses that the elements of time and rhythm are as important as space in generating a distinctive structure of feeling associated with video games. The next chapter looks more closely at these tensions in the body of the player and how they are articulated to the game.

Notes

1 Using this phrase Aarseth invokes an association with phenomenology, in particular the idea that in an experience the subject and the thing experienced are fused in a single, intentional structure. Viewed phenomenologically, separation of the subject and object of experience is an analytical step that is always taken retrospectively. Husserl introduces the idea of noesis, or noematics, to grasp the central role of intention in the formation of any experiential whole (Husserl 1970, 1993).

2 This is important because in many ways the play is defined by the way in which it does not connect with the game, is held apart from it. The fact that we never really identify with our avatars, for example, is indicative of a restraint that is definitive for the actions of gameplay. Even if, as Rune Klevjer (2007) argues forcefully, our avatar is a kind of 'affective prosthesis' giving access to sensations we have in the game's virtual environment, still this differentiates it from a prosthesis proper, which we cease to differentiate from the rest of our embodied experience. The aesthetics of play and form are located in this difference.

3   As Gonzalo Frasca (2003b) later pointed out, this debate was to
    some extent a phoney war, not least because there were no real
    narratologists present. However, much of the ludological critique
    of narratology does apply to works by Barry Atkins (2003) and
    Julian Kucklich (2003a).

4   Commonly this has been done by examining the notion of rule-
    following more closely. For Wittgenstein, all language use is
    rule-following and different language games require us to follow
    different rules. We learn the rules by playing: 'In order to say
    something one must have mastered a language' (1992: 109).

5   For interesting discussion of Wittgenstein in connection with
    video games see Bojin (2008).

6   Progression can be thought of as movement between a series of
    partially played games, games whose rules have already generat-
    ed outcomes, as against the play from a set of rules that generates
    emergence.

7   Similarly, Steve Swink (2009: 304) distinguishes between con-
    textual meaning, or 'virtual sensation' and what he calls 'naked
    appeal': 'A virtual sensation has appeal when it's fun to play and
    tinker with in a completely empty space', that is, one that is un-
    cluttered by meanings.

8   I am using the idea of reification here to refer to attitudes and be-
    haviours that treat people or products as if they were objects we
    encounter as neutral, free of any affective taint deriving from our
    past engagements with them, either in our role as active produc-
    ers or as ourselves products of socialization. Axel Honneth (2008)
    highlights the role of forgetting in such attitudes, especially for-
    getting the affective dimension that underpins all cognitively
    understood social processes.

9   As with the concept of form discussed in Chapter 1, there is a
    paradox here. We have to use the concept of time to understand
    video gameplay as a rhythmic operation but (as with dance) what
    we find is that they spatialize time, or as Badiou (2005a) writes
    in connection with dance, they 'suspend time in space'. In other
    words, we need to view them as temporal in order to find the
    specific sense in which they negate the temporal in favour of
    space. The virtual character of game time is related to the fact
    that they do not signify, that we always withhold meaning from
    them, even though our involvement with them is based on the
    idea that they are meaningful. The fact that video game time is
    virtual also explains the tendency for players to lose any sense of

how long they have been playing since, in a sense, their activity has been timeless.

10   This is something that is also emphasized by Galloway (2006) in his discussion of games as simulations. I return to the issue of simulation, which also involves projecting meanings into games on the basis of a supposed coherence of their symbolic and procedural aspects, in Chapter 6.

11   According to Latour (1987, 2005), whom Bolter and Grusin cite approvingly, the modern scientific approach to nature was, no less than its romantic counterparts, premised on a particular set of social activities, especially the activity of 'collecting' parts, which happened in the seventeenth century and on which basis it was possible for science to conduct highly artificial experiments that confirmed its truth.

12   Bolter and Grusin do not mention what happens to truth in this scenario, but from their attachment to Latour we can assume that it ceases to hold any privileged place in relation to our meaning-making activities. For a decisive repudiation of postmodernism, including its claims to epistemological novelty, see Callinicos (1989) and for a less favourable account of Latour see Feenberg (1991) and Kirkpatrick (2008). Bolter and Grusin suggest that rock music threatens hypermediacy because it offers only the substance of a medium (music) with no diegetic world being presented. I think this is also true of extensive parts of many games.

13   'Distinctions between degrees of presence in games are closely correlated with differences in the visual perspective provided on the game world' (King and Krzywinska 2006: 97).

14   *Ikaruga* and similar difficult, abstract games are sometimes referred to as instances of the 'bullet hell' genre of video game.

15   It's worth noting that there is also no tendency immanent to the development of the medium towards more virtuality in the sense discussed here, indeed two-dimensional games like N and $N+$ (Metanet/Atari 2006, 2008) are still being made and played (Edge 2008). Pressures in this direction often come from misplaced concerns with marketability, as virtuality has informed the fetishism of digital commodities (Lash and Lury 2007). Bolter and Grusin's definition of virtuality is only one of several. Shields (2003) discusses a very different one based in the philosophy of Gilles Deleuze and relates this to video games. I have discussed

the ideological function of this breadth of application of the concept of virtuality elsewhere (Kirkpatrick 2008).

16 The first instance of this in modern poetry is Mallarmé's 1913 'Un coup de des' (Mallarmé 2006). The principle of organizing the physical page in accordance with the imperatives of the poem's symbolic content becomes even more pronounced in Apollinaire's 1918 (2004) surrealist poems.

17 Foucault says that for much of its history traditional painting assumed a kind of isotropism with language's powers of resemblance (Foucault 1983: 53).

18 Tanke writes that 'words, which conventionally anchor the image through commentary, here undermine it, converting it from resemblance to similitude' (2009: 111) and also observes that the shapes in Magritte's compositions are evocative of 'natural forms' that 'confer vitality on the work' (2009: 107).

19 Similarly, Swink (2009: 51) argues that in designing game scenarios a self-consistent abstraction is preferable to a faithful representation.

20 Sometimes this is a false indicator, so you get to the end of a chapter loaded up with pills. This causes you to relax. Conversely, that can sometimes be a trap.

21 Diderot's own eighteenth-century formulation and discussion of this can be found in his *Selected Writings on Art and Literature* (Diderot 1994).

3

Controller, hand, screen

The victim ... of a practical joke is in a position similar to that of a runner who falls – he is comic for the same reason. The laughable element in both cases consists of a certain mechanical inelasticity, just where one would expect to find the wide-awake adaptability and the living pliableness of a human being.

Henri Bergson

The previous two chapters have suggested that what really matters about video games and the key to gaining a proper-ly aesthetic understanding of them is what they feel like to players and how the structure of this feeling relates to prevail-ing cultural norms. Much of the available discussion of this issue has concentrated on the visual aspects of games because it has seemed obvious to many that video games are a visual medium. Part of the thrust of the current work is to try and counter this tendency. While they do constitute a development in the history of visual media, the way that visual experiences are deployed in video games can only really be understood if we position them alongside the other elements of the experience. Play is the central category, around which the organization of sensory experience turns. This chapter focuses on how the body is used in playing video games, especially the hands of the player, and in this way it illuminates the central place of the hand-held controller in the aesthetics of play with video games.

Spectatorship has been a part of popular entertainments culture at least since the eighteenth century (Stafford 1994) and in its main outlines the procedure has remained fairly constant: the viewer positions their body in order to watch a spectacle that has been prepared for them in advance. In the twentieth century this activity entered the home, with TV, but its core dynamic did not alter significantly. Video games do involve us watching, but what we see depends crucially on what we do with our hands and (more recently) the rest of our bodies. This articulation of hand and eye is not unique to the video game, but it is the point at which they break with the visual entertainment culture of the last two centuries. This chapter will concentrate on what is distinctive about what video gameplayers do with their hands. Paradoxically, this enables us to see more clearly how the visual and aural components of the video game function and how they contribute to the gameplay experience. Viewed through the lens of aesthetic theory, the unity established between these elements is constitutive of what we can usefully think of as the 'effect shapes' (Adshead 1988) of the video game, which are constitutive of the video game image. The central argument of this chapter is that the video game image condenses the tensions within the body of the player that are produced by the controller, screen and aural outputs of the game program. It is a form without a corresponding meaning. Clarifying this makes it clear why video games are more than just games, yet not quite art. We become aware of the video game image most often when it unravels in the form of a Bergsonian joke, which is why the best games are usually ones that make us laugh. In a sense, the effect shapes of video gameplay are always a joke in preparation.

The chapter begins with some further reflections on aesthetic form and its relation to art in the second half of the twentieth century. Discussing conceptual art, which does not foreground the action of the work on the human sensorium at all, it is clear that there has been a movement away from the shocks of modernism and towards a more subtle politics of form that is limited to the presentation of arresting, thought-provoking gestures that are defined as art largely in virtue of the spaces in which they occur and of not being anything else. This is in many ways a retreat for art and in some of its manifestations it involves overt points of convergence with the contemporary commodity and with brands. If contemporary art is predominantly relational and unconcerned with the energies associated with cleaving form from matter, these latter are clearly in evidence in popular cultural forms that have escaped the limits of being merely entertaining diversions. In light of this, the second section explores the applicability of Henri Focillon's (1992 [1934]) ideas about the hands in artistic creation to the analysis of play with video games. This section emphasizes the way that video gaming inherits a creative role for the hands from traditional art practices like playing musical instruments or creating sculptures. It leads, in the third section, to more detailed reflection on what we actually do with controllers. Movements and actions performed with them do not resemble actions performed in other contexts, despite efforts to interpret them in terms of mimetic relations of resemblance, or visual virtuality, discussed in Chapter 2. Articulated to other elements in the gaming apparatus, they are keys to sensations that create specific kinds of experience of space. This emphasizes the centrality of the controller to the experience of form and space in video games, as against the common association of these ideas with screen-based illusions. The fourth section draws on the motif of the Bergsonian joke to clarify the video game image. The movements we learn to perform with video games become skilful and adept only because we learn them and make them habitual. This exposes us to sudden changes: breaks with what we expected to happen of the kind that have been definitive of form in the modern artwork. The active role of the player's body in video games, however, means that, rather than mediating meaning, such dissemblance triggers comic moments in which we gain a glimpse of our own activity as something ridiculous. As such, it is both more and less than playing a game. This idea is presented through analysis of a specific episode in *Resident Evil 4* (Capcom 2005). Finally, the thesis is related to Walter Benjamin's argument that we can classify cultural forms with reference to the demands they make on the human body. This points towards an affinity, introduced in the last chapter, between complex play with controllers and dance as an aesthetic medium – the theme of the next chapter.

Form, vision and matter

With the rise of conceptual art in the 1960s, the idea of aesthetic form lost its centrality in art criticism. Instead of working on our senses to stimulate a feeling response, artworks were now concerned with the direct communication of ideas. In recent decades, the very idea of form has been largely abandoned by recognized artists. Scott Lash and Celia Lury (2007) provide a very interesting discussion of this.[1] A key source for them is the artist Robert Morris, who argued in a famous essay published in 1968, that 'the perpetuation of form is functioning idealism' (1995: 45). For Morris, form is an inherently conservative category of art appreciation because it interposes itself as an *a priori* of the creative process, imposing specific requirements on the artist who cannot, as a result, follow through on the modernist goal of revealing matter within the work. It is a false, idealistic premise according to which matter must always conform to a certain logic or order that will ensure it appeals to the 'optical' standards of traditional painting. Morris rejects the attempt to order the creation of artworks in accordance with such a tyrannical visual standard. He writes that, 'To think that painting has some inherent optical nature is ridiculous' (1995: 43) and, for him, repudiating this idea entails a rejection of form. Following in the tradition of abstract expressionism,[2] Morris argues that 'a focus on matter and gravity as means results in forms that were not projected in advance' (1995: 46) and are consequently detached from the idealistic investments in the idea that are present in traditional aesthetics. He emphasizes that allowing matter to speak, by leaving paint to drip, often involves little or no intervention from the artist at all and, in an outright rejection of the traditional idea of the craftsman unlocking form through a modality of action that is consonant with what is there in the matter, explicitly disavows tool use in artistic practice. Morris renounces form in favour of allowing matter to speak for itself.

In more recent work not discussed by Lash and Lury, Morris (2005) develops his idea of a post-form art through a series of drawings that he did blindfold. Claiming inspiration from the philosopher Donald Davidson, Morris maintained that 'drawing blind' within specified time frames (as against the conventional constraints of an envisioned diegetic or painterly space) enabled him to produce works (drawings) that conform to no enforced visual norms. Morris intends that the materials he uses, in conjunction with his physical movements, are sufficient to communicate. Next to one of the drawings, Morris places the following comment from Davidson:

> We must conclude, perhaps with a shock of surprise, that our primitive actions, the ones we do not do by doing something else, mere movements of the body – these are all the actions there are. We never do more than move our bodies: the rest is up to nature. (Donald Davidson, cited in Morris 2005)

The point seems to be that by painting blindfold Morris has renounced any specific affiliation with the optical standard of form previously considered essential to the communicative potential of art. In his work there is no play with resemblance; only matter speaks. Davidson's physicalist philosophy is invoked to emphasize the break with form as an idealist construct.

According to Lash and Lury, in conceptual art, 'the ideational space of a horizontal vector connecting the subject and object', gets substituted for, 'the material space of the painting' (2007: 68). When confronted with conceptual art installations, for example, we are no longer drawn into the work by our senses, but experience it as an event, a temporal field that communicates its meaning(s) as ideas. Endorsing this deliberate rejection of form leads Lash and Lury into a broadly positive appraisal of the most recent manifestation of 'anti-form', in the UK at least, the 'Young British Artists' (YBAs) of the 1990s, a movement that includes Damien Hirst, Tracey Emin and Sarah Lucas, among others. Their works are characterized by the uncreative reproduction of arrangements of objects found in mundane settings, like pharmacies or bedrooms, in gallery spaces. The works themselves are intentionally uninteresting and constitute what Lash and Lury call an 'evacuation' of the practices of traditional art. The significance of the works lies, according to Lash and Lury, in the fact that YBAs are personally associated with them in the mass media and, viewed in this way, individual YBAs are brands. As such, they add nothing and everything to the work, just as brands are the active principle in the contemporary commodity system, able to invest quite bland goods with a fetishistic sheen of desirability despite the fact that they add nothing tangible to the trainers, mugs or animated characters that are marketed in this way. Here the mediatized identity of the artist informs the art image – it is part of what the artwork is 'about'. Lash and Lury say that through the YBAs art becomes media, which suggests a 'meltdown of aesthetic value' (Lash and Lury 2007: 74). This is not a complete disaster because contemporary capitalism is also thereby rendered more playful.

Ranciere (2007) considers the claims of twentieth-century art to have renounced form misguided. For him the encounter with artworks is one that always involves an experience of space as shaped by a certain kind of action on the human sensorium. Viewed as a mediated delineation of space that connects the art image with politics and contemporaneous principles of societal organization, form is the dimension that connects the artwork to the structure of feeling determinate for life in a given cultural context. In recent art we find a move away from the specific optic that may have defined form for a time but this does not represent a break with form as such, even if it does correspond to a moderation of art's aspirations. What characterizes the art image for Ranciere is a play on resemblance and dissemblance, which takes the form of a rhythmic alternation with the expectations of the audience. Aesthetic form thus understood has nothing to do with materials or medium and it is not exclusively visual:

> A camera movement anticipates one spectacle and discloses a different one. A pianist attacks a musical phrase 'behind' a dark screen. All these relations define images. This means two things. In the first place, the images of art are, as such, dissemblances. Second, the image is not exclusive to the visible. (Ranciere 2007: 7)

Ranciere here clarifies the difference between mediation, which is carried out by art and is not centred on the visual element of its image, and mediatization. The first exhibits this play of dissemblance, which Adorno radicalized as the opposition of form to semblance, while the second contains none of these tensions but is focused solely on providing diverting spectacles. This is a useful way to draw the boundary between art and the experience of form on one side and entertainment and the culture of distraction on the other. On Lash and Lury's account of the YBAs, the aesthetic meltdown of art results from the fact that 'contemporary art is not so much conceptual as mediatic' (Lash and Lury 2007: 75).

It is in the confrontation of commodified art and playful commodity that we can clarify what makes video games more than just games. At the moment when art seems to renounce its play with resemblance and the experience of form, the video game offers a different kind of image within which we can find those things. Although video games are repetitious, the patterns we trace out on the controller with our fingers and thumbs involve much greater complexity and variety in our movement than any media commodity devoted simply to entertainment. The complex and rhythmic sequences mastered by players, then unlearned when new scenarios arise, are a long way removed from the 'hooks' of popular music, for example. In the way that they play with dissemblance and defy audience/player expectations, video games exceed mediatized entertainment in the direction of form. Video game form, like form in the art image, is not exclusively or even primarily a visual concept. It is certainly not tied to any particular optic. In 2006, for instance, Nintendo produced *Sound Voyager* (Nintendo 2006a), a game for the Game Boy Advance. What is distinctive about the game is the almost complete lack of visual feedback for the player. *Sound Voyager* only offers visual feedback in the early stages of the game. Once we have been introduced to a basic conceptual premise, according to which we control a central point on the screen and use the Game Boy control buttons to steer towards or away from other objects, we are left with a black screen. Using headphones, the player must work out what is coming by listening and assess the success or failure of her actions only with reference to aural information. The sounds in the game vary from the noise of a passing engine or crash of a collision to musical chimes that alert you to the presence of objects to be gathered. Success relies upon close attention to the sounds produced in response to player actions, rather than visual information. *Sound Voyager* invites us to question the idea that visual verisimilitude is important to gaming and its pleasures but notwithstanding this, and perhaps somewhat counter-intuitively, the game does offer its players an experience of space. Rather than opening up a three-dimensional illusory space in front of the eyes, *Sound Voyager* creates a sensation of movement and of shifting spatial relations in the back of the player's head. Sensations we are familiar with from other games, such as swerving this way and that; the sense of objects passing dangerously close, a perception of impending threat – all these feelings are normally carried in video games by a conjunction (perhaps unique) of manual operations and sensations in the hands on one side and visual data on the other. But in *Sound Voyager*, the same patterns, or forms, are traced out on our inner space. The essential pleasures of gaming, including humorous breakdowns caused by excessive attachment to learned procedures confronted by deliberate dissemblance and disruption of those expectations, are accessible in a non-visual form.[3] The form we find here resembles the 'effect-shapes' (Adshead 1988) of dance theory – a kind of motif connecting the positions of the hand around the controller with the screens and sounds of the gaming experience.

As we saw in Chapter 1, early twentieth-century modernist art attempted to radicalize the aesthetic image, opposing form to semblance and, in the *avant garde* movements of the 1910s and 1920s, actually repudiating their status as art. These movements inspired Walter Benjamin to anticipate a time when imagination might 'free itself' from art and channel its energies into political interventions that transformed the aesthetics of everyday life. The idea that form might migrate to unexpected areas of culture, taken up decades later by Adorno, must be attributed to Benjamin. Benjamin's thinking was influenced by changes to media when he was writing – he made radio programmes (Leslie 2007) and was interested in Soviet *avant garde* cinema (Tsivian 2004) – but also by developments within art, especially surrealism (Waldberg 1997; Nadeau 1978). One way of reading these movements is as an attempt to infuse social life and practices with the magic ingredient called form. Whereas Adorno identified this with the tensions contained within the modernist artwork and saw the latter as a site of resistance to the retrograde tendencies of modern culture, Benjamin argued that aesthetic interventions could burst into social space and impact upon the direction of historical development. In Benjamin's analysis the artwork has *aura*, which is a cultic property it inherits from ritual and sacred objects. As Susan Buck-Morss (1991) points out, aura results from a series of paradoxes in play in our relation to the work. The artwork is something we experience intimately, yet it is alien and other; it is immediately accessible yet it poses a challenge of comprehension and interpretation; the works are artificial yet the illusions they offer tend to efface their created character. These tensions give the work its charge and it is this power that can be used in political aesthetic interventions to lay what Benjamin thinks of as cultural depth charges with powers to illuminate the present and show us different ways forward.

In Benjamin's thought, the notion of a critically charged excess placed into the field of popular culture is associated with the concept of a 'dialectical image'. In such images we find the interplay of alternate temporalities, including disjunctures, eruptions and breaks, in which mundane reality can become infused with flashes of energy drawn from a radically different, parallel temporality. Buck-Morss characterizes this messianic vision in terms of a utopian collective remembering:

> collective imagination mobilizes its powers for a revolutionary break from the recent past by evoking a cultural memory reservoir of myths and utopian symbols from a more distant ur-past. Utopian imagination thus cuts across the continuum of technology's historical development as the possibility of revolutionary rupture. (Buck-Morss 1991: 116)

A key influence on Benjamin here, as Pierre Missac (1995: 115) suggests is art historian Henri Focillon, in particular the latter's notion of form as residing in a different temporality; a kind of *ur*-history. Focillon's theory focuses on and elaborates some of the specificities of this critical theory of aura or form that are most relevant to video game analysis and to understanding the experiences made possible by the video game. His theory points us towards the active role of the human hand in the history of form and this is essential to any understanding of the video game image.

Hands and touch

The controller occupies a paradoxical position in computer game studies. Although it is central to gameplay experience – it marks physically the difference between play with a game and merely watching a screen – it goes largely unreflected upon by gamers and in gaming literature. While other aspects of gaming paraphernalia, especially graphics cards but also limited edition coloured consoles and other fetishized hardware, are intensively discussed, controllers rarely receive the same kind of attention. There are exceptions to this, of course. There has been a lot of gamer discussion of and interest in the Wii-mote device; *Guitar Hero* (Red Octane/Activision 2005) has a guitar-shaped controller, and a 'chainsaw' controller was designed especially for *Resident Evil 4* on the GameCube. The difference is that other features of gaming and game design are routinely considered in game reviews, as varying with each game, while the controller tends to be bracketed as a constant of the hardware. But it is not constant in this way. Different game programs require us to do different things with the controller, to use its syntactic elements (pushing and holding down buttons, twisting levers and pulling triggers) in different ways and lots of work goes into matching game programs to the different controllers associated with each console. Clearly then, the controller is not just hardware, nor is it software and it is also not straightforwardly a transmitter of player intentions in the game. It is the most concentrated intersection of all these, the key elements in gaming. This makes it curious that the details of how this happens – what each game feels like in the hand, so to speak – are so rarely a matter for reflection.[4] It is perhaps even integral to contemporary computer game experience that we do not rationalize our actions with direct reference to controllers. No one talks about pressing 'X', then 'circle', then 'triangle' and no one feels that this is what they are doing, unless they are bored with the game, following a 'walk through', or using a cheat for the first time. Good play is about feeling and it seems that being able to feel what we are supposed to be feeling is, at least partly, a function of *not* looking at or thinking about our hands. At the same time, it is powerfully determined by what we do with them – an instance of Diderot's paradox, discussed in Chapter 2.

The relationship between hands and aesthetic experience is discussed by Henri Focillon in his *Life of Forms in Art* (1992 [1934]). Focillon places the artist's 'touch' at the centre of artistic creativity:

> The sense of touch fills nature with mysterious forces. Without it, nature is like the pleasant landscapes of the magic lantern, slight, flat and chimerical ... Without hands there is no geometry, for we need straight lines and circles to speculate on the properties of extension. Before he could recognize pyramids, cones and spirals in shells and crystals, was it not essential that man should first 'play with' regular forms in the air and on the sand? (Focillon 1992: 163)

Direct, physical contact with matter enables the artist to create form. In the process matter is shaped and through this a new experience of space is created. As Henri Lefebvre (1991) points out, space is not a neutral datum unaffected by human activities, but rather a plastic variable experienced differently depending on aspects of the organization of our activity: 'Organised gestures, which is to say ritualized and codified gestures are not simply performed in "physical" space, in the space of bodies. Bodies themselves generate spaces, which are produced by and for their gestures' (Lefebvre 1991: 216). Similarly, for Focillon, form and matter come into being together. Form is not to be

found anywhere without matter. And when it comes into being
it defines an experience of space:

> We must never think of forms, in their different states, as simply
> suspended in some remote, abstract zone, above the earth and
> above man. They mingle with life, whence they come; they
> translate into space certain movements of the mind. (Focillon
> 1992: 60)

Whereas for Kant form is a product of the interplay of faculties whose own conditions of existence remain obscure (Fenves
2001), for Focillon it is a kind of extrusion of pre-conscious
mental content, of that level within the mind that is below
conscious experience. Focillon seems to envisage a kind of
collective unconscious that unfolds according to an infra-his-
torical logic, outside of yet parallel to biological evolutionary
processes, which occasionally explodes into history and is often
associated with a new direction in the arts or in culture. When
this dimension of mind is extruded and so enters chronological
time, the result is aesthetic creation – the imposition of form
on matter. To understand how this works, Focillon urges us to
follow closely the technique of the artist. As a painter paints,
or as a pianist plays, he argues, we can discern a force greater
than their own creative conceit, it is 'the very technique of the
life of forms itself, its own biological development' (1992: 105).
Focillon argues that the elements involved here – the hand of
the artist; her tools; the material, and the form – cannot be understood independently of one another. In a sense, form *is* the
coming together of these forces in an object or performance. At
their point of intersection is 'the touch' of the artist:

> The touch ... conceal[s] what it has done: it becomes hidden and
> quiescent. But, underneath any hard and fast continuity as, for
> example, a glaze in a painting, we must and can always detect it.
> Then it is that a work of art regains its precious living quality.
> It becomes an entity, well organized in all its parts, solid and
> inseparable. (1992: 110)

In making itself invisible, the hand endows her creations with
a seeming permanence and solidity – a sheen or appearance of
independent life. Focillon concludes that 'touch is structure'
(1992: 110).

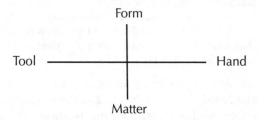

1 Focillon and the role of 'touch' in making form from matter and space

Focillon's model clearly assigns a privileged role to the artist who possesses the touch that cleaves form from the darkness of matter. However, if we want to understand the idea in its application to video games we need to reconfigure this relationship. Digital culture has been associated with a more creative role for consumers and players in determining what cultural objects will be (Dovey and Kennedy 2006; Lash and Lury 2007). It is changes to the interface of culture and technology over the past four decades that create the possibility of displacement between aesthetic art and entertainment. The plastic controller is the video game's strongest point of connection with the visual entertainment culture of the last two centuries *and* the point of its most radical departure from mere entertainment. In the panoramas (Comment 2002), phenakistoscopes and other devices of the nineteenth century, the body of the spectator is always involved, perhaps in the sense that you climbed onto a central viewing platform (in the case of panoramas), or cranked a handle, or inserted cards into a stereoscope. In the 1870s, such repetitive physical motions were necessary to enjoy the visual illusions of the day:

> The apparently passive observer ... by virtue of specific physiological capacities, was in fact made into a producer of forms of verisimilitude. And what the observer produced, again and again, was the effortless transformation of the dreary panel images of flat stereo cards into a tantalizing apparition of

> depth. The content of the images is far less important than the inexhaustible routine of moving from one card to the next and producing the same effect, repeatedly, mechanically. And each time, the mass-produced and monotonous cards are transubstantiated into a compulsory and seductive vision of the 'real'. (Crary 1992: 132)

The result of this physical activity is a stable and concentrated relationship between the eye and the resulting illusion. Communication of a visual meaning is always the priority, beneath which the rest of the activity is subordinate. There is no question here of dissemblance in Ranciere's sense. These machines do not play with our expectations, they move in accordance with them and they do not mediate in the sense discussed above. They conform to our desire to see an illusion, without comment. Describing the way video gameplayers repeat actions over and over to achieve desired performance in a particular gaming sequence, Dovey and Kennedy make a connection with other aspects of entertainment culture, including music and sports:

> no other kind of cultural consumption requires this kind of repetition. Instead we find it in cultural activities where musicians or sports players are called upon time and again to repeat actions in order to achieve a preferred performance or a kind of virtuosity. (Dovey and Kennedy 2006: 116)

The video game is repetitious in ways that we associate with entertainment culture and in that sense it is not unprecedented, as the quote from Crary illustrates. But at the same time, repetitious use of a controller is about mastering complex sequences that vary enormously within each game. To fully experience the form in a game we have to draw it out by playing well and we do this with our hands.

The connection between video games and playing a musical instrument is more than merely metaphorical. As Norbert Herber (2008) shows, playing a video game involves activating sound files that are increasingly calibrated to player actions and their effects on the global state of the game object.[5] The result is that players can sometimes even improvise musical effects as part of gameplay, although normally these aural effects are unintended, if satisfying. Much contemporary gaming is well described as music and sound wrought from a score that presents physical challenges to a player. *Elektroplankton* (Nintendo 2006c), for example, is a kind of musical instrument with a distinctive, visual interface. In that game for the Nintendo DS players 'poke' colourful plankton-like creatures with their styluses, or drag objects around on the screen in ways that that affect their behaviour. These actions produce sounds from the plankton, which seem to sing in response to different stimuli. Different kinds of plankton combined with different stimuli produce varied tones and sounds of different duration. Here and in other games we see greater variety in the relationship between players' hand actions and aural feedback compared to games in the last decade that had fixed, repetitive soundtracks. Now player actions and visual changes in the game combine with an evolving set of sounds, whose quality is defined by overall player performance at each point. However, expressive play, which in great performance mediates the meaning as it draws out the form, is not possible with video games. Great video gamers win contests with other players, they do not stage concerts with them. Hence, there is a paradox: In the complexity of their forms, video games exceed mere repetitious consumption and achieve something like form, yet, as programmed and mechanical objects the forms they produce do not accommodate expressive meaning as part of their fibre.

Dovey and Kennedy's choice of the term 'virtuoso' is suggestive. In music criticism the virtuoso is perfectly efficient but this is almost a defect (Scholes 1970). The term is often used ironically to suggest that the excellence is a bit empty and virtuosity tends to be negatively contrasted with interpretive play. Great performers relate to the form they are given and bring it to life, rather than just playing through it. This is why they can be almost as important as the composer to realizing the potential in the piece.[6] Form is something we can get better at cleaving from the game program. An adequate player of *Resident Evil 4*, for example, will be aware of various intersecting labyrinths

in the game and derive pleasure from steering their character through them. Rapid exploration of the game, according to
its logic of discovery or progression, facilitates a narrowing of
the intervals between the flashes of meaning, or moments of
recognition that come from familiarity with the game's visual
properties and the 'flickering signification' (Hayles 1999) that
constitutes the game's fiction. These sensations are only dimly
perceived by the poorer player, who loses the thread of the
story and gets lost in the labyrinth when he sees the same hall-
ways and corridors over and over. The elements of repetition,
labyrinthine complexity and rapid movement are, in Focillon's
terms, moments in computer game form and the same forms are
found across many, narratively-defined, genres of video game.
They are produced in the tension described here between, on
one side, movement of the hands to wring something out of
the dark matter of the computer and, on the other, feelings of
exhilaration and of pleasure associated with the game as a kind
of spectacle. In other words, an experience of form brushes up
against mediatized entertainment, in the space created by the
displacement mentioned above.

The controller

It is controllers that allow us to experience form in gameplay. The controller transmits the player's intentions into the
game and is correspondingly understood as an 'input' device.
Manoeuvreing through a game always involves digits pressing
and muscles and tendons straining. A complex and dynamic
forcefield is established in the palm, wrapped around the
controller, and it is changes of pressure and tension here that
seem to determine what happens in the game, giving us the
feeling that we initiate its events. Torben Grodal (2003) may
be on to something when he argues that this originates in an,
as yet undiscovered, neuro-physical correspondence between
contemporary cultural forms and our neolithic hard-wiring.
Viewed in this way, it corresponds to the notion of an infra-
historical, or *ur*-game, an underlying force that precedes even
the biological; is a kind of in-itself of biological phenomena.

Form in this sense cannot be grasped by inductive processes or experimental research but is real nonetheless. It seems to have been something like this that Benjamin had in mind when he wrote of 'languages issuing from matter' (1979: 122). Focillon calls the active principle here *mitosis*, the movement of form beneath the surfaces of history:

> In the same way that sand spread out on the diaphragm of a violin would fall into different symmetrical figures in response to the strokes of a bow, so does a *secret principle*, stronger and more rigorous than any possible creative conceit, summon together forms that multiply by mitosis, by change of key or by affinity. (Focillon 1992: 48)

The tensions in the hand are shifting and if we recorded the movements of fingers and thumbs against the plastic buttons we would find a series of crystalline representations of game action, which articulated to their corresponding events on the screen would constitute the game's 'effect-shapes'. In a sense, the important forces that drive the action of the on-screen game fiction are present in the tension between fingers, thumbs and plastic controller. There is a formal continuity between the configuration of digits and the structured, dynamic action sequences in the program and on the screen that is best understood in terms of an idea from effect shape analysis in dance theory, namely, the *kineme*, which grasps the role of expressive hand positions in relation to other parts of a dance (Adshead 1988: 47). Kinemes are rarely mimetic,[7] but are associated with other movements of the dance, like 'spatial levels, shape-flow quality, effort-flow quality' (1988: 49) and the formation and alteration of groups, all ideas that apply to the feel of gameplay. In studies of 'primitive dance' we find effect-shapes that mirror Focillon's forms, with 'simple reversal; cyclic; angular; curved; rotational, and looped' movements featuring in one account (1988: 44).

The controller and its resistances are those of the game and its objects. They are an instantiation of the game program in the hand,[8] which involves the creation of an intimate, narrow space of play. Play involves exploring and altering this field of

tension and it is here that the centrality of the hand and the
controller to video gameplay and to its form stands out as a
kind of obtrusion. When Steven Poole writes that the physical
skills learned in the playing of ancient, spear-throwing games
are 'exactly those skills exercised by modern target videogames' (Poole 2000: 174), he is obviously wrong, in the sense
that throwing a spear is *not* the same action as holding down
the 'B' button on a controller. He also conveys an important
truth about controllers, however. Something of the experience
of throwing a javelin – its tensions in the body; its discipline;
its conscious manipulation of weight and energies – gets con-
densed into the hand.[9] But the two things do not resemble each
other and this is essential. The form here is not that of a simulated action, but is a pattern present in the relation between
the kineme and the other elements of the game apparatus. Just
as painting is not contained in principle by a tyrannical optic,
so form in the video game is not straightforwardly articulated
to the semiotic field established by its visual signs. Indeed, the
function of those signs reduces to a series of 'yeses' and 'nos'
– you can do that, not that – in the course of gameplay. Our operation of the game as a machine, through the controller, grows
in complexity while the realm of communicated meanings actually diminishes, approximating binary efficiency. Form here
reaches a kind of blunting of its capacities, it is out of proportion to its meaning, which of course vitiates and ultimately
cancels its character as aesthetic form. It is in this sense that
form is essential to understanding video games, yet only ever
appears in them long enough to vanish.

The same forms are present when we play using a Wii-
mote. Superficially, using the Wii-mote is more like playing
a real game of tennis than other tennis-based video games in
which the player hits the ball by pressing a button on a joypad.
However, after playing for a while and getting better at the
game the most striking thing about Wii tennis is the dissimi-
larity between effective movements in the game and those of
playing tennis. This triggers amusement and prompts a kind
of self-consciousness. With video games the ironic distance, or
gap, between what the player is doing (with the controller) and

what the screen is representing is ineliminable. The subtlety of this corresponds to the reduced role for shock in aesthetic art, noted by Ranciere (2007). It is this space that accommodates the video game image.

Why, then, do we find such lack of reflection on controllers as compared to other aspects of the computer game interface (story, graphics etc) in the popular and scholarly literature that surrounds the medium? It is in the silencing of the controller that we construct the boundary between ordinary experience and the illusion we enter when we relate to screen imagery and other game feedback 'as if' they constituted an environment, or immersive world for play. Players initially learn to use a controller in connection with a specific game, finding out what each button does, learning about special moves, and so on. Learning generic properties of the controller is essential to becoming good at playing video games. When we feel we have learned enough of the controller syntax in this way – its basic terms – we try to speak for ourselves. But this process turns out to be limited to a clarification of game limits and rules; what perhaps seemed, on the basis of visual resemblances, to be a powerful simulation of experiential domains familiar from other contexts turns out to have highly restrictive parameters. As Ranciere says of the art image, there is a play with our expectations and dissemblance within resemblance. But with the video game image this is *all* there is.

Jodi, who make artworks derived from or based on video games have created an installation based on *Doom* (Id Software 1994) that, it seems to me, clarifies and plays on this difference (Jodi 2008). The user is given a standard Playstation 2 controller and a wall-sized screen that has images recognizable from the game. The room is also full of sounds that are from *Doom*. The strange thing is that the controller, while it produces some changes in what is seen and heard, does not enable us to affect it in the ways we expect it to. We are unable to gain entry to the game as a synthetic manifold. Instead, all its parts seem to be made disjoint, held apart from one another. The effect of this is to alert you, the subject, to your active role in synthesizing the game environment. This highlights the essential role of play in producing the powerful illusions of digital culture and technology, dereifying the game and reminding the subject of his or her own power. At the same time, the Jodi exhibit is intriguing and puzzling because we cannot get anything we are used to getting from *Doom* out of it. The space we occupy feels enlarged and public because we are in a gallery. In consequence, the exhibit restores the order of the traditional, modernist artwork: what interested at first was a resemblance to something familiar but what we take away is a new sense of the strangeness of that familiar thing. This alienation is caused by a thwarted expectation of space and action. In it we get a glimpse of the video game as the locus of a form that is largely missing in contemporary art.[10] At the same time, this glimpse is not a joke on our object-ness, but a prompt to reflect on our creative capacities. This mediation through meaning is what makes the Jodi exhibit a work of art and not a game.

Video game image

Learning to master the controller is responding to the other elements in the game but in a way that is quite out of step with them: if we reflected on it we would undermine the coherence of the game as an activity. We cannot not think about what we are doing with the controller if we want to succeed at playing the game, in much the same way that Woody Allen joked about being able to walk fine until he thought about how to do it (Allen 1971). This necessitates an oscillation of perspectives. In some games we are told quite early on to look again at the controller and when we do this it feels different than when we initially picked it up. An image of the controller appears on the screen and we look at our own hands as if from a new distance. This moment of alienation is important because it highlights the notion mentioned above, that we must sense the discrepancy between our 'real' actions and their translation into action 'in' the game. The sense of this and its subsequent repression constitute a central dynamic of video gameplay and it is particularly visible in some of the best and most-discussed elements of contemporary video games. To resume the example used earlier, in *Resident Evil 4* there are several crucial moments in the game when an image of the green button on the controller appears on the game screen,[11] with an arrow indicating that it must be pressed immediately. Events in the game move very rapidly in these moments and success turns on doing several other things besides just pressing the button rapidly, such as using the directional control to steer away from a boulder, to swim in a certain direction, or to aim a weapon.

When it happens the first time this eruption of a representation of the controller onto the screen is very amusing. The rapidity of game events means that we nearly always 'die' while the button continues to flash on the screen in front of us. While previously we have been intently focused on progressing through the game scenario, the appearance of the button and the sudden quickening of events conspire to produce a sense of ridiculousness. In the midst of playing the game, especially serious games with adult content, like *Resident Evil 4*, we are suddenly offered the spectacle of our own activity as something childish. We see ourselves pressing a brightly coloured plastic button on an infantile toy. The image of the controller here bursts onto the screen as a symbol of toys and toy-ness, a shocking reminder perhaps of the impulses that made us want to play when we were children.[12] These seem to be completely out of place when we are engaged in a repetitive, cyclical struggle for existence with an adult game (the game has a '15' age rating in the UK). The laughter has an element of nervousness in it, perhaps reflecting the fact that normally when we laugh at someone's childishness we are in fact offering a corrective to their behaviour, a point made by Henri Bergson (2007 [1940]) in his theory of the comic.

For Bergson, we become comical when our actions resemble those of a machine. Automatic or memorized parts of behaviour, perhaps the parts we do with least thought, are the parts of character that get seized on by satirists for this reason; they are the things we repeat because we are most sure of ourselves in them, but they suspend us over the space of ridicule. Similarly, the video game image that connects hand, controller, screen and sound according to the pattern required by the game program at any given time sustains the illusion of stability within a practice that is anything but stable. This is where all the elements of the Bergsonian joke are present in connection with most video games. When we 'die' in the game and throw our controllers across the room in frustration we become ridiculous to ourselves and others. The machine-like nature of our movements during play looms large and, normally, this, along with the knowledge that it was always going to end that way, is a source of amusement, which, while pleasurable also includes an element of discomfort. Laughter here, as elsewhere, includes a disciplinary component for Bergson, since it tells people when they are being ridiculous and ridicule is something we avoid. Viewed in this way, the accumulating tensions in the hand are a Bergsonian joke in preparation. They hold together a rigidity or fixity of purpose that gets us so far but then leaves us hanging. The more intense our involvement with a video game the greater the tension and the more we are exposed to comic possibilities of this kind. The explosion of the controller onto the screen in this incident illustrates its central yet concealed role, and the centrality of its concealment, in gameplay. The controller's role here is to keep the player physically attached to the game, while remaining out of view. Paradoxically, holding a controller is never a disinterested activity, even though no player will say that the controller is the 'interesting' part of what they are doing. Holding a controller always involves a physical tension for the player, even if we are just waiting for the end of the cut-scene (occasionally something that is cunningly undermined, as in *Resident Evil 4*, which puts us in control at moments when we do not expect it). But this tension, like the controller itself, and like the swaying from side to side that we all get into occasionally, is not conscious. We do not intuit it from the inside, as we would if we were swaying or tensing in other circumstances, but we do sometimes see it, as if from outside, especially when our attention is directed there by events on the screen. At this point we see how silly we look and this is funny – there is a release of tension – rather than pathological.[13]

This exteriority is also what ensures that the video game image is not an art image, because it is always cancelled out and prevented from being an image that mediates. According to Ranciere, play with expectations is something we can appreciate directly with the artwork – we apprehend it from within, as it were. This is how the art image communicates a meaning, or mediates. But saying that the video game image has the form of a Bergsonian joke entails that it can only be experienced as an obtrusion, even though it is usually ourselves we are laughing at. The point of the laugh is that in illuminating our excessive attachment to learned routines it makes us aware of the mediatic element in our activity. Its cruel reminder not to become stuck in character works because it shows us that we have already become object-like, less than human and therefore below the level of meaning-interpretation. In a sense the laugh is an invitation to lightness that connects humour to dance; it calls us out of ourselves towards play and indeterminacy. The conceptual artwork is mediated discursively in privileged spaces and this, in today's context, limits its ability to touch us; the video game presents us with experiences of aesthetic form but these turn out to be toy-like, even false, in that they do not communicate.

On the other hand, the effect of seeing the controller on the screen, with its humorous yet corrective connotations can also be read as an example of what Benjamin described as a 'dialectical image' (Buck-Morss 1991). Viewed this way, gamers participate in a cultural phantasmagoria, in which computer games are aligned with other contemporary technologies, being sleek, appealing and fetishized as commodities that are desirable for adults. Participating in this present – the world that game designers and console manufacturers project for us and as the 'future' for their businesses – presupposes that we have forgotten the real history that got us to this point. Consequently, we forget that the present of play is fraught with contradictions: Who wants you to play? Why is it normal for you to play? Why was it 'not normal' ten years ago for people your age to play? The forgotten history is a subjective one, of growing up with toys, learning to play, repudiating play to become an adult and then overcoming these conflicts to re-discover play in the highly specific cultural context that legitimizes it with video games for grown-ups. The objective history is also fraught, revealing an industry that shifts its demographics, deliberately misrepresents its consumers and tells whatever story about players is conducive to its own survival at any given time – recall how Nintendo and Sega fought each other to appeal to different age groups of children in the late 1990s (Kline, Dyer-Witheford and de Peuter 2003). When the toy-image of the controller appears on the screen, against the background of an attempted murder in *Resident Evil 4*, it is this real, conflicted history that breaks through, undermining the illusion of unproblematic play and its central value in our culture, straightforward 'fun'.[14]

The kind of tension described here – unreflected upon and subject to 'release' is associated in psycho-analysis with blockages and repressions. We can see that what is being repressed is the controller itself and with it the world of objects, including our own bodies. They are being excluded from our conscious attention and we are distracted by the illusion that is the 'game' and the range of feeling responses it excites. However, the act of repression described here is, of course, the false promise of the entertainment commodity, as discussed in Chapter 1. The coherence we fabricate from the flood of sights and sounds generated by game programs is held together, or bought with energy we save by not paying attention to what our bodies are doing. That there is a game, and that we are playing it; these are illusions the gamer works to produce and against which she or he struggles. We play against games not with them, and our activity is directed from the outset by the urge to bring it to an end, usually by winning. This work is done with the hands but the fact is not normally presented on screen. What appears on the screen only holds our interest (even seems to many to constitute a world) because this work of the hands is repressed, hidden from view. The experience of 'dying' in the game, perhaps caused by failing to hit the green button fast enough, causes a breakdown in the seamless experience of form. But, paradoxically, the recurrence of such breakdowns is what discloses its character *as form*. The tensions in the hand give rise to the pleasures of gameplay but we only really become aware of controllers when we feel the inadequacy that haunts the whole situation.

In these moments the controller is visible as a scratched, decaying object. It symbolizes the body in all its mute authority and, as such, it casts rays over the whole gaming experience. Here it becomes apparent that the repetitions and intensities of play have provided glimpses of another world. A kind of experience that contains something 'more' and cannot be understood in terms of representation or meaning is an opening to Focillon's time of forms and to the Messianic, or utopian time in Benjamin's theory. The appearance of the controller as suddenly visible in play in *Resident Evil 4* coincides with a kind of breakdown, consistent with modernist aesthetic interventions that draw attention to their medium (Butler 1993; Kirkpatrick 2003) and to the unseen and distasteful aspects of a phenomenon in order to re-contextualize it. In these moments our pleasurable experience of drawing out form from the dark matter of the computer game program with our bare hands gets detached from the illusion of smooth, continuous on-screen action and is repositioned as an activity that involves us physically. By seeing the game in this alternative context, which is that of embodied physical activity in contemporary culture, we are able at the same time to see more clearly the sense in which the video game is more than just another game.

Embodied activity and culture

This chapter has argued that video gameplay is centrally structured around a set of paradoxes that involve the controller. The controller is what connects us to the game and enables us to play but it is the part of play that we are least likely to reflect on. Gameplay is a physical activity that involves our hands using the buttons and levers and triggers on the controller, yet we prefer to talk about what we do with games as if we were 'in' them and not holding the controller at all. The sensations we derive from gameplay – how the game feels – all involve

the discrepancies we experience between what we do with
our thumbs and fingers and what we see and hear when we
play. Combining these things is integrating them in a unique
practice. The video game is a unique disunity – no discourse
connects pressing 'X' and jumping – and yet it is an activity
that is intelligible on its own terms. This is the function of
the video game image: it condenses the tensions of the player's
body with the other parts of the gaming situation in a synthetic
unity that holds the experience together and allows it to make
a sense short of meaning. The point of positioning video games
in this way is to comprehend them as involving aesthetic form,
as defined by Focillon. Through them the human body cleaves
form from matter that is, in itself, inert and unshaped. The
way that human beings carve out a place for themselves in the
world involves form before it can involve meaning or other,
secondary cultural truths. As Lefebvre points out, before we
fill space with our communicative utterances, values and ways
of life, we must first define it, delineate it so to speak. These
processes are historical and largely unreflected upon and they
involve the body, especially the hand, as a kind of infra-histori-
cal agent. Once they are established, forms and the practices
associated with them become folded into meaningful social
structures and ways of life. Underlying them, however, is a
kind of ur-ness, an affinity or correspondence of the human
and the rest of nature – there are patterns that recur in the different delineations of social and cultural space, just as sand on a
resonating violin tends to form into the same shapes. As digital
technologies have been appropriated and exploited by different social forces over the past few decades, we have become
habituated to thinking of them as affording us novel experiences of space – of 'worlds' and 'environments'. This space has
been carved from the dark matter of processors and screens by
hands and bodies and the video game and its controller have
been important tools in the process, alongside programming
languages and keyboards.

Controllers represent the bodies of players but also the
history and diversity of games. They contain redundancy, like

unused strings of DNA or organs that are no longer useful. They change slowly and if we ever looked at them we could see the history of games as a story of failed experiments, silly mis-adventures, boring failures, time wasted, as well as all the great simulations, hilarious adventures, and so on. Game graphics, in contrast, are endlessly 'new' and are caught up in the cul-tural project of distraction – they are always hyped as the 'next development'. Gamers use graphical improvements and other technical accomplishments as indexical for improvements in game quality, but those changes rarely represent a new structure of feeling or real innovation related to form. Here, mediation and mediatisation; art and entertainment come into antagonism within the development of the video game as a cul-tural form. Few reflect on controller design, yet it is here that many of the really interesting changes occur. The Wii-mote, for instance, has opened up the possibility of repositioning video games in the spaces of culture.[15]

The first feeling triggered by the Wii-mote is one of mild vertigo, because the tensions of play are not contained within the hand any longer. Some (not all) of the actions we have to do to play the game no longer have the controller to refer to, so to speak, and instead must occupy the empty space of the room we are in. We use more (a greater part) of our bodies to trace out the formal patterns that have to be enacted if we are to play the game but whereas traditional controllers involve a kind of condensation of the formal properties of the game in miniature, the Wii-mote generally makes the forms bigger and more abstract. This change in the phenomenology of control-ler use corresponds to the shift Don Ihde detects in the move from analogue to digital clocks. The conventional clock with hands communicates with us by establishing a kind of tension between the clock face, which represents blank, empty time, and the hands whose current positions signify only with the face as a background. The position of the hands is our position relative to time as a whole. When we move to digital clocks, which present us with a numeric representation of time, time loses some of its concreteness and becomes more abstract: digital clocks only tell us the time it is now, removing the current instant from any context. Ihde (1990: 68) links this to the historical trajectory of technology itself, which moves us towards increased detachment and decontextualisation of information. Driving a car with a digital speed display produces a similarly frictionless sense of speed, because the tension between the needle and the background, which here represents stillness, is no longer present. However, this change to the phenomenology of control does not change the fundamental character of our moves as forms because spinning one's arm when holding a Wii-mote (to 'serve' in tennis perhaps) makes the same kind of pattern (an arc) we would make with our thumbs using a lever on a traditional controller, only now it is drawn out in empty space rather than against the resistance of a physical object. These delineations of space are of different scale and proportion and they have different implications for the spatial experiences they produce. The intimate space of the hand-held is not exposed to the same gaze or subject to the same disciplinary incursions as are entailed by the empty homogeneous space traversed by the holder of the Wii-mote. The contrast here is between an intimate space of retreat or disconnection and the exposure of play to a kind of space that is more susceptible to power. This is one context for Eric Kluitenberg's recommendation that 'new hybrid spaces must be deliberately designed to create free spaces within which the subject can withdraw himself, temporarily from spatial determination' (Kluitenberg 2008: 211). It also relates to Ranciere's principle that form is a structuring of space that is always political in its ramifications (Ranciere 2009). By involving the whole body the Wii-mote makes possible games in which the space of gameplay may change in ways that are not yet fully understood, although it is surely no coincidence that the Wii has been associated with an increased interest in games among women and girls. The next chapter will return to this point.

Viewed in terms of dialectical image, incidents like the appearance of the controller on the screen can be seen as potentially progressive in relation to technology. Philosophers of technology have long observed that all technology seems to involve a kind of forgetting (Feenberg 2009). Presented with a new technological device, especially in the workplace perhaps, people do not approach it as a human creation whose fundamental properties might be open to modification or negotiation, but as if it were a kind of 'second nature' that had to be complied with. The entire history of invention and design that produced the artefact is concealed behind its 'finished' character. The significance of artefacts that invite us to play with them and to question their apparent unity and closure is that it may open them up to new questions, extending the to and fro of the design process itself into the working life of the finished machine. Playing with machines and gadgets always has this exploratory dimension and this is part of what video games have achieved in relation to computer technology generally (Himanen 2001). Indeed, the reason that we still have no real answer to the question of what computers are for is partly because each new generation of gamers never stops asking it, which is itself a function of the fact that all video games are a kind of opening up of the machine and begin the process of prising it away from the dominant historical narrative of 'technological progress'. In Benjamin's terms, the controller is the past active in the present and this makes it antithetical to the game as commodity, which is always 'new' and constantly defines itself in terms of innovation. Benjamin's notion that alternate historical trajectories can burst into the present, undermining our collective sense of direction is illustrated by the controller and the field of forces and tensions that are parcelled up in, or around it. The futurism and progressivism that gamers are involved in, whereby they fetishize the next technological innovation, the latest gadget, constructs straight lines out of the present. It is linked to a forgetting – of the diversity of games in the past, the good and the bad – which makes it possible to believe that the perfect game, the ultimate game is out there ahead of us. According to Benjamin, such straight lines only acknowledge physical mortality as an intersection, perpendicular, barely interrupting the overall direction of people 'moving forward'. However, if we listen to the language of things – in Focillon's terms if we experience their form – we can see multiple intersections, including openings onto alternative paths. This is not a question of lecturing people on the history of failed games. It is the search for a gaming aesthetic that would give us games that powerfully challenged contemporary social reality, especially the use we are making of computer technology under the hegemonic rubric of overwhelmingly visual concepts like 'virtuality', rather than merely re-affirming it.[16]

It is not necessary to endorse the concept of a 'dialectical image' or a messianic conception of history to appreciate the significance of the Bergsonian laugh as the central motif of video game aesthetics. Another way of understanding the video game image is in terms of its non-assimilable character in relation to the aesthetic regime. The combination of forces in it – Galloway's multiple vectors of agitation – require us to come at it awkwardly. More than a game but not quite art, the video game's most salient feature is that it never quite fits. Its aesthetic is a call to and a refusal of aesthetics and only in the light of this refusal can we see its aesthetic qualities. By putting the focus on forms made with the hands and the body I hope to have clarified the significance of controllers, including developments like the Nintendo Wii system, to the development of computer game aesthetics and culture. Unlocking and developing aesthetic form in computer games depends upon giving more power to hands to cleave form from the dark matter of the computer. New matter-forms, which depend on the invention of new controllers, will define new spaces for the playful body to inhabit. This relates to a politics of space and may include subversions of the always new (in this case, ever more photorealistic graphics) with images that help us perceive the neglected possibilities and immanent potentialities of technology, often suppressed by dominant design standards. It also points to a strong connection with dance, which similarly involves the embodied experience of form in territory that is outside the reach of discourse and involves alternate modalities of power.

Notes

1   They concur with the argument of this book in holding that play is central to the character of contemporary commodity-objects. However, they do not understand this in terms of aesthetic form.

2   The defining texts of this movement in American art can be found in Chipp (1968), see especially the writings of Clement Greenberg (Chipp 1968: 577–81).

3   Similarly, Rune Klevjer (2007: 158–60) discusses 'sound space' in games.

4   Dovey and Kennedy, for example, write that computer games illustrate our 'ability to intervene and control the computer through increasingly sophisticated visual interface designs' (2006: 2), which is at best a strangely partial truth. It is common for theorists to discuss user actions in digital environments in ways that elide the body apart from the eyes; see Lash and Lury (2007) and Burnett (1995), which I consider illustrative of the unbalanced approach to game aesthetics discussed in Chapter 2.

5   Swink (2009: 200) refers to 'chords' that result from playing these elements in combination.

6   Interpretation here should not be understood in terms of a hermeneutics of meaning – it is the function of critics to discuss what the piece 'means' in this sense. Interpretive playing is about enacting and realizing the form locked up in the score as a structure of feeling, while the virtuoso only follows its pattern with great precision.

7   Adshead describes a convention in ballet whereby arm movements are mimetic while dancers' legs produce other effects (1988: 51). Such mixed performances are also common in games.

8   This would have to be slightly reformulated in the case of small hand-held devices like the Game Boy or Nintendo DS and the dynamics of the process are altered significantly by the Nintendo Wii, a point to which I return.

9   Similarly, Steve Jones reports that the Wii-mote 'uses motion-sensing accelerometers to map intuitive player gestures into games' (2008: 17). This is not *all* that the device does, but it does describe the starting point for its operations.

10   According to Geert Lovink, new media arts are in crisis because they are too new and lack the resources of a tradition they can work against to produce meaning. Digital media, he writes, are in need of 'an older sibling' (Lovink 2008: 81) to guide them. The

Jodi work makes it clear that video games are the obvious candidate to perform this role. Art that cancels itself out confronts video games that are more than games at this limit point.

11 The green button appears on the gameCube version; on the Wii it is a white button.

12 There are other instances of such images in games. James Paul Gee (2003: 63) describes how in *The New Adventures of the Time Machine* a wave of light passes through the game world turning all the adults into children and vice versa.

13 This Bergsonian laugh is the image, in Ranciere's sense, that condenses form in the video game, which is why the best games are the ones that make us laugh the most, and this holds regardless of all other considerations (ostensible genre, etc.). We should not forget that for Bergson the exemplary form of this is the victim of the practical joke who, like the gamer, is the victim of an intrigue (Aarseth 1997).

14 This moment corresponds to what Espen Aarseth identifies as 'epiphany' in gameplay, while the more common dynamics of form and semblance discussed in the last chapter could be interpreted as what he calls the 'aporias' of the form (Aarseth 1997: 91–2).

15 At the time of writing a new wave of controllers is being marketed that replace the hand-held controller with the player's body. Advertising for the X-Box Kinect, for example, tells would be players that it offers 'controller free gaming' for 'full body play' (XBox 2010). Much of what follows on the phenomenology of the Wii applies to this kind of gameplay too, although some details may change. Of particular interest here will be the range of aesthetic effects that become possible as the disruptive presence of the player's body as a controlling element becomes increasingly foregrounded in game design.

16 Examples of such games are discussed by Alexander Galloway (2006), who understands the development of form in terms of an expansion of the algorithmic elements in game design as against the easily reproducible, front-end features defined by game engines and graphics.

Games, dance and gender

> Dance designates the capacity of bodily impulse not so much to be projected onto a space outside of itself, but rather to be caught up in an affirmative attraction *that restrains it*.
>
> Alain Badiou

This chapter develops an idea put forward at various points in the argument but not yet explored in detail, namely, that video games are a form of dance. Chapter 3 argued that physical movements, especially of the hands, were integral to our experience with video games, including sensations that are more commonly thought of as originating in, rather than just involving, the visual sense. This chapter will explore the incorporation of games into the embodied performances of their players in more detail. This clarifies further the position of video games in relation to aesthetic art practices by aligning them with dance and gestural communication. The aesthetic appraisal of video games here works to undermine a long-established view that identifies them as masculine. Feminist 'design critique' has assigned particular significance to the video game in explaining women's continued under-representation in technical fields and, in so doing, has focused on game contents, reading them off from visual and narrative elements games share with contemporary media. Judy Wajcman, for example, writes that, 'Many of the most popular games are simply programmed versions of traditionally male noncomputer games, involving shooting, blowing up, speeding or zapping in some way or another. They often have militaristic titles ... highlighting their themes of adventure and violence' (Wajcman 2006: 87). Feminist critique has analysed games as if, as with other media,

their content was the principal concern. However, as the paradigmatic developed form of gestural communication dance is
characterized by its eschewal of overt linguistic elements and
discursive meanings. Like dance, video games are caught up
in a paradoxical refusal of textual or discursive meaning, although anyone who has attended a dance performance knows
that something does get communicated. In both cases we find
there is an inherent ephemerality about this vanishing content
and that its very transience is somehow essential. Chapter 5
will argue that this limits the referential powers of video games,
even when they make explicit use of textual and verbal elements, to allegory. This chapter will suggest that understood
as an embodied practice, video gaming is deeply ambiguous in
terms of gender performance.

Lots of games now overtly involve the whole body and the
analogy with dance and the inscription of an established idea
of dance into video game design may even have become a bit
obvious. *Benami* dance mats, games played using the *Eye Toy*,
and Wii Sports (Nintendo 2006b), for example, all clearly
involve players using their whole bodies to play the game and
often dance is even mentioned as a metaphor for the practices involved. However, these examples are not central to what
follows. My emphasis is on the particular kind of manual dexterity that is deployed in video gameplay. As seen in Chapter
3, the hand cleaves a sense of space from the game program,
with the eye in a surprisingly subordinate role and this space is
a function of aesthetic form. Although Pierre Bourdieu (1993)
rejects the notion of form, it is useful in this chapter to draw
on his idea of habitus to explore the incorporation of computer
games into contemporary lived experience. This has implications for the question of gender and its relation to computer
gameplay. As we have seen, computer games are not straightforward objects in that our interaction with them involves
our bodies in ways that are unpredictable and not assimilable
into an analysis that assumes the process is organized under
a horizon of communicated or communicable meanings. The
main argument of this chapter will be that understanding the
relevant incorporation processes as a modality of popular dance

is illuminating with regard to the true position of video games in relation to the cultural politics of gender.

The chapter begins with some reflections on the parallel history of dance and video game studies, which includes discussion of the culturally subordinate status of both sets of practices and discourses. Dance and video games have been excluded from the academy and their status as serious arts has always been in doubt. The underlying reasons for this are similar too. Both dance and games involve the body in potentially transgressive ways and both involve gender politics. However, their subordinate status also reflects the fact that there is a mismatch between the traditional humanities focus on meaning and the way both dance and games refuse meaning while toying with it. Both practices create methodological difficulties. Meaning interpretation requires skills of exegesis and linguistic or textual analysis focused on ideas but dance and games present bodies in motion. Humanities disciplines may take an interest in issues of affect but they prefer the affect to make make sense, to fit with and correspond to some interpretable element that holds sway within a given work or between a work and its context. Moving bodies work on a range of affect that is not so easily accommodated within the practices of sense-making for which humanities methodologies have been developed.

The second section shows how Bourdieu's ideas are useful to analysis of the process of incorporation of computer gameplay into manual culture. His concept of hexis – habituated bodily routine – shows how embodied forms can be learned and even be constitutive for determinate social practices without being entangled in or mediated by meanings, although once established they do constitute sites where meaning investments can be placed. The third section relates this to the idea of the video game as a choreographic script for player actions. Many games provide training sequences that introduce moves to players. The cues to deploy these in game situations are not mediated through meaning but on the basis of recognition of forms. *Mirror's Edge* (Electronic Arts 2008) is discussed as a particularly good illustration of this principle. The next section builds on the idea that a profound change has occurred within contemporary manual culture, with implications for our understanding and performance of gender. Drawing on Nigel Thrift's (2008) idea of qualculation, associated with an enhanced role for the hand and for dance in knowledge acquisition and communication, it shows how dance with the hands takes on epistemic functions in video gameplay. The fifth section situates this development historically by offering an account of changes to choreographic practice associated with the move to the modern aesthetic regime discussed in Chapter 1. This positions the video game as a dance script in the history of dance's relationship to technology and the historical relation of gesture to discourse as understood by Foucault (1994). In conclusion, the idea that video games are a form of dance is related to the question of gender and technology. Drawing on Franko's (1995) study of modernist dance, it is suggested that the significance of the video game in contemporary technical politics of gender may be almost the opposite of what it is normally taken to be. Rather than consolidating the appropriation of computer technology by men, the video game is a site where the relationship of technology and gender is explored and renegotiated in performances that can plausibly be described as dance, with all the gender ambiguity that term entails.

Dance and art

According to Alexandra Carter (1998) the academic discipline of Dance Studies struggled to secure institutional recognition and was viewed with suspicion similar to that encountered more recently by computer game studies, until the 1980s. Prior to that, dance was not taken seriously as an academic subject. Indeed, many of the same anxieties and prejudices that seem to have been stirred by computer game studies were stimulated by attempts to study dance properly too. As the editors of a special issue of the journal *Topoi* devoted to dance put it:

> Unlike other domains of human expression, such as music, or visual art, dance has received very little philosophical attention, especially within the Western history of ideas. Is it too

evanescent? Too intimate? Too frivolous? Too chaotic? Too emotional? Too bodyful? The list of adjectives typically implemented to dismiss dance as a subject deserving of serious intellectual analysis bears a striking resemblance to those stereotypical qualities attributed to the feminine and/or the non-white. (Foster, Rothfield and Dunagan 2005: 3)

Both dance and play with a video game involve the body in potentially transgressive ways. Dance is expressive movement of the body. It is an art form that is defined by its essential transience: it creates an impression through figure and form in space, but is gone by the time you register it. It lacks the fixity or permanence of other media objects and refuses signification in a way that is quite distinctive. This leads Alain Badiou to argue that dance is a metaphor for the 'unfixed' or indeterminate within thought, or as he writes, 'the permanent showing of an event in its flight' (Badiou 2005a: 67) because dance is never fixed in relation to meaning. Badiou denies that it is an art, but acknowledges that dance-like operations are often unnoticed, yet essential, in the aesthetic arts. These comments position dance awkwardly in relation to the aesthetic art regime, close to where I have tried to locate video games.

Just as dance has not always been afforded the recognition it is due as an artistic medium, so the implication of dance practices in the visual arts has also been overlooked. The role of the body in art appreciation, for instance, is almost always limited to an account of the eye. The eye is drawn into the three-dimensional space on the two-dimensional surface, or it ranges over the surfaces of the sculpture. This understanding of the relationship between the viewer and the work is often highly illuminating, but there are occasions even in the history of painting when it is actually a distortion. Holbein's *Ambassadors* (1533) provides good examples of this. Holbein's painting demonstrates the painter's masterful use of techniques developed in Europe during the Renaissance. The picture first strikes you as a realistic representation of two men in a room. The painting has perspective so that the illusion is created of a space into which the eye is naturally drawn. It exemplifies the use of linear perspective in that elements in the painting – lines and form – are so positioned that in looking at the painting we experience it as if it were co-extensive with reality itself. At the same time, however, we are made forcibly aware that there is a difference and, in particular, that the room depicted is artificial, a representation, by the presence of a grey, elliptical blob in the foreground.

2   *The Ambassadors* by Hans Holbein the Younger (1533)

The presence of this object calls a halt to the initial activities of the eye and the first phase of viewing and analyzing the picture. We can continue to study the room, which contains many important clues as to the identity of these two men. They have the outward trappings of wealth, in the form of ermine robes, and scientific instruments of navigation, including a globe, are positioned on the shelf behind them, signifying their status as ambassadors. In offering us this view of the ambassadors in their parlour, Holbein's work conforms to the visual regime of representative art by celebrating the status of the ambassadors. It is subordinate to the requirement that it should be a painting *of* these men and it is a painting that enables its viewer to see it, to enter its fictional world, from a privileged position in front of the painting. However, the troublesome ellipsis does not conform to this model. It is an uncomfortable obtrusion that defies the conventions of naturalistic representation and comfortable viewing.

In order to make sense of the object in the foreground of the picture, the viewer has to withhold the normal investments placed in the visual sense. They must recognize that understanding this painting is not possible simply by looking at it. Instead, they are obliged to reintegrate their visual sense with other senses of the body. To see the object clearly requires that we move around physically in relation to the painting. It becomes a puzzle that we solve by moving through the space of our own immediate physical location, not by tracing out the contours of the fictional space of the painting with our eyes. We have to walk right up close to the painting and look down and across from about the mid-right point, towards the floor at bottom left. Only when we solve this puzzle can we see that the object is a skull. We have to dance with Holbein's painting if we are to get past its central puzzle. As such, it offers a template for understanding video gameplay not because of its place in a history of visual 'remediations' but because it involves bodies and eyes working together to generate an experience of form out of the encounter with a physical, public object. This movement around in front of the painting, which is essential to understanding it properly, is normally overlooked and the ellipsis is viewed as a *trompe d'oeil*, or a trick played on the viewer's eye. Slavoj Žižek's analysis of the painting, for example, correctly highlights the fact that when we are in the correct position to see the skull, 'the rest of reality is no longer discernible', but goes on to maintain that the lesson the painting has for us is that, 'reality already involves our gaze, that this gaze is *included* in the scene we are observing' (Žižek 1999: 88). That is, the painting presents two incommensurate views and alerts us to our presence, *as a gaze*, mediating between them. However, our presence is not that of a gaze, but rather of a body that steps up close to the painting to see the skull and steps back to see the room with the men. Our pleasure in this painting involves this movement. If we enjoy it this is, at least in part, because we are dancing with the painting.

There is an evident similarity between this activity and the experience we have with video games, as against other contemporary media that do not involve their players, physically in the work. Acknowledging the dynamic role assigned to the body in pre-modern art also helps us to see that the experience of space in connection with video games is not that of a single, diegetic illusion projected onto a two-dimensional surface. Rather, as we use our controllers to effect changes in the game state, we encounter a range of shocks and changes of visual perspective that correspond to these maneouvres. Deciding to consult a heads-up display for information, for example, involves shifting focus off one of the game's visual surfaces and directing our gaze onto another. The player's understanding of what is going on in the game and the pleasure taken in it are dependent upon all of these perspectives and, especially, the ability to switch about between them. Indeed, this becomes a key part of the rhythm of play. It marks a break with the calibration of body to eye that is presupposed in much of the cultural output of the twentieth century. The fact that you remain physically stationary while your eye and brain do the work was integral to modern experience. Lynne Kirby (1997), for example, defines what she calls the modern 'perceptual paradigm' as a culturally specific conjunction of a panoramic and mobile visual sense to a stationary physical self. This paradigm is common to railway travel and cinema, the defining technological media of industrial modernity.

As we saw in Chapter 3, the fact that video games break with this has implications for the way that space is experienced in them. In particular, it's not the two- or three-dimensional illusion that is offered to the eye on-screen that constitutes the

game space. Game space is produced in the articulation of hand
and bodily movements to different points on the game interface
at different times.[1] The latter includes the controller, as well as
screens, sounds from speakers, and so on. The intimate space
of the hands is usually central in effecting these shifts and our
practice with games involves intuiting, acting on and producing a formal reality (the reality of the game) out of actions we
perform with our fingers, thumbs and wrists. At the same time,
our bodies sway, especially when performing new moves, and
we move between states of high physical tension to those of
release and relaxation. These developments are not peripheral
to gameplay, with the real action taking place on the screen.
As we have seen, screens can be blank while the excitement of
gameplay remains. At other times, on-screen spaces and visual
sensations can be important, as we experience the feeling of
swooping across a ravine, or turning a sharp bend, for example.
The importance, however, is relative to the contribution these
sensations make to sustaining the more fundamental illusion,
which is not that of the on-screen or diegetic world, but involves the coherence of a form; the movement of the dance.

Habitus and embodied play

A particularly nice illustration of the principle that video
games contain dance moves is provided by *Pacman* (Namco
1980) and involves Pacman being surrounded by ghosts who
are bearing down on him along all the available paths. Only by
pirouetting on the spot can he wait for one ghost to turn off at a
junction, which opens an escape route. The player's body, especially their hand and arm, must transmit just the right forces
at exactly the right time to pull this maneouvre off successfully. Pacman is programmed never to be stationary so keeping
him on one spot requires rapid alteration of the directional
controls. This performance is normally accompanied by great,
Bergsonian hilarity, or at least relief, because it is such a feat
of poise and timing.[2] These patterns in our feeling response
require analysis; they are examples of kinemes, or 'dance hi-
eroglyphs' (Thrift 2008) that define the computer game as a

cultural form. It is interesting to note that Pacman's ability to change direction is the feature of the game that structurally differentiates him from its other moving elements – the ghosts. They can never perform a 180 degree about-turn but always move forward through the maze. This simple difference in capabilities is central to the core dynamic of the game in that it is what makes the chase amusing and what gives Pacman the chance of 'winning'. This kind of formal differentiation of the field of play, which establishes a boundary between our 'character' and the rest of the game program often goes unacknowledged, especially in discussions where it is assumed that there is an obvious correspondence between the semiotics of the appearance of our character on the screen and the margin of maneouvre that we actually have with it in the visually defined game environment. The rules of the dance intersect, intensify, depart from and sometimes subvert those of the fiction. The priority of form noted here holds even for ostensibly quite cinematic games.

In 'fighting' games like *Mortal Kombat: Deception* (Midway Games 2004), players control the movements of their characters using a circular pad. Pressing this way and that changes the direction of movement of the avatar on the screen. However, the relation between hand movements and on-screen developments is much more nuanced than this simplistic description makes it appear. A complex sequence of 'ups', 'downs', 'lefts' and 'rights' must be entered at exactly the correct speed in order to produce 'moves' by the on-screen avatar that have little or no intuitive relation to the 'directions' signified by the arrows on the pad. Sequences link to effects; directional inputs become detached from the direction of movement of the avatar, just as the speed with which one presses the pad loses any connection to its impetus or momentum. Indeed, if a sequence goes wrong, perhaps because it is mis-timed, the movements of our avatar may regress to a crude correspondence with the buttons we press, so that a 'left' press really makes her run towards the left of the screen, and this is both a sign of failure and a source of frustration. There is an interpretative gap here that is enjoyed by players, in the distance between the significance of on-screen events and what players know about their own and each other's hand movements – their dexterity. Observing players it is easy to miss their appreciation of one another's manual skills because when we hear people expressing their enjoyment, even amazement at what is going on, it can seem as if they are commenting on the on-screen action. However, this interprets gameplay as if it were organized under the rubric of a visual narrative. More often, players see a movement on screen and recognize it as the sign of mastery in the hands. After all, a cartoon effect like a fireball or a cartwheel is not that exciting in itself – we have been seeing those on screens since about 1920. Manual dexterity is central to computer gameplay. So how should we understand this activity and what value should be attached to it?

Pierre Boudieu's concept of habitus is useful to think through the implications of recentring our understanding of computer gaming as a cultural practice on the hands of players. His focus on embodied practices widens our perspective on the range of processes through which technology gets taken up and used by human beings. Bourdieu defines habitus as 'an acquired system of generative schemes' (Bourdieu 1990: 55) that we learn through early socialization processes. We learn habitus by copying physical behaviours; it is acquired unconsciously and present in the way we are disposed within our own bodies. He sometimes calls this *hexis*, which is the incorporation of learned physical routines that precedes and makes possible their investment with meaning (Nordmann 2006: 26). In a particularly telling passage he describes how the 'embodied belief' of habitus when confronted with a new situation is manifest as a 'rhythm', beneath the level of conscious meaning, and he likens this to 'the rhythms of a line of verse whose words have been forgotten' (Bourdieu 1990: 69). He continues, 'The constraints of rhythm or metre are internalized at the same time as melody and meaning, without ever being perceived in their own right' (1990: 74). If we want to understand how the video game insinuates itself into the field of social relations, including its relation to gender, then this will be the appropriate level on which to start the analysis.

To illustrate the relevance of this perspective to an understanding of gender and video game practices, consider the
explanations advanced to explain the relative popularity of the
Wii console among girls and women.[3] This has been attributed
to convergence of the allegedly enhanced capacity for accurate
simulation or mimesis in relation to real world activities like
playing tennis offered by the Wii-mote controller combined
with the production of a new generation of game programs
whose narrative or thematic content is more appealing, or at
least less repulsive to female players. However, this explanation
of the Wii's popularity is not particularly convincing because
of the failure of previous initiatives to feminize game content
(Laurel 1995; Nakamura and Wirman 2005) and the fact that
many of the games sold for the Wii are the same as for other
consoles. Moreover, if we look at the initial advertising of the
Wii, which might have been expected to have shaped its culture
of reception and incorporation, much of this was more overtly
sexist that any of the adverts for the XBox or Playstation 3
gaming consoles. Indeed, the Wii was marketed as a slim, ath-
letic woman to play with in adverts that contrasted her with a
more dumpy-looking, technologically savvy woman who represented the *X-Box*. Moreover, as indicated in Chapter 3, it is
also by no means clear that the Wii-mote really does enhance
the power of games as simulations. Many of the most popular
games for the console use the Wii-mote in ways that have
nothing to do with simulating a real world context of action or
performance. *Mario Smash Football* (Next Level Games 2007)
for example, involves flicking the Wii-mote and waving it about
in the air with our hand, actions that are not performed when
playing real football. Even if Wii tennis appears at first to offer
an experience like playing tennis in your living room, a few
minutes of play will soon dispel this illusion. If female players
are more attracted to the Wii this suggests that its coding as
masculine has been reduced on some level other than game
content, as conventionally understood. As we saw in Chapter
3, the real difference between playing a game on a traditional
console and playing with the Wii involves the experience of
space that is made possible by each apparatus.

The introduction of the Wii-mote shows that the different ways in which video games are incorporated by players alters their character as gendered artefacts. The introduction of controllers that interpret bodily movements of wider scope than just hand movements are more attractive to female players because they invite women into a space which, although far from liberating for them, is familiar.[4] According to Bourdieu's analysis of masculine domination, this is precisely the way that gender works through habitus. The 'manly man' or the 'womanly woman' are 'social artifacts' produced through a kind of deep dressage that 'concerns every part of the body' (Bourdieu 2001: 23, 27).[5] Bourdieu argues that over much of human history and across many different cultures there have been observable differences in the ways that men and women comport themselves. Disposing oneself differently within one's body inclines us towards some activities and deters us from others, purely on grounds of the kind of patterns of movement they involve. Bourdieu suggests that, historically, centripetal movement has been masculine and centrifugal motion feminine. This observation applies directly to the two kinds of controller. The traditional hand-held controller involves development of a concentrated set of forces contained in the hand and applied to a few specific points on the plastic device. In contrast, energies expended in using the Wii-mote are centrifugal; players sway and rotate in homogeneous, empty space until a given movement is played out, at which point they rest and then resume a starting position. In terms of dance theory, the kinemetic building blocks of each correspond to gendered habitus. Associated with each is a different experience of space. The first is intimate, closed space that is to some extent withheld from the world. This corresponds to the male attitude of concentrated energy maintaining an upright position and targeting a fixed point.[6] The second is the space of dressage; it allows the scrutiny of bodies in the open and is a space that is historically more familiar to women than to men. It is no coincidence that among the top-selling games for the Wii are products that are concerned with 'getting in shape', with personal fitness and exercise. It would be easy to decode these artefacts as gendered, through their advertising and the explicit cultural politics that links them with the beauty industry and the mainly female concern with weight loss and appearance. However, to understand how the games console came to be used for these purposes it is necessary to understand the technology in terms of the largely unconscious dynamics of its incorporation by bodies, the kinds of space that get produced when people use it and the sorts of sensation that people experience in connection with it.

Choreography in *Mirror's Edge*

Space remains central to our understanding of gameplay experience but how we understand this space is not quite the same as when we approach the representational space of a painting or photograph, or indeed the diegetic spaces of conventional cinema. Video game space is not primarily a space of spectacle or of story, although we commonly encounter these things as we make our way through it (most games do have screens and they use them to offer these kinds of experience). Rather, video game space involves the inner workings of form, extruded through the hands (controllers) and other bodily movements (processed by dance mats, eye toys) articulated to the game program and intersecting with visual, on-screen representations. The content of the latter is filtered by the player, so that what stands out in cinematic perspective, for example, in the representation of a street or a spacecraft, is not the same as what strikes us as important when we are playing a game that involves similar objects. This is why, perhaps, Espen Aarseth can plausibly assert that when he plays *Tomb Raider* he does not even see the supposedly heavily gendered body of Lara Croft[7] 'but through it and past it', since 'a different looking body would not make [him] play differently' (Aarseth 2004: 48). Similarly, in his work on game design Steve Swink (2009: 300) stresses the importance, when programming actions, of ensuring that players only see 'one idea at a time'. Game space is specifically structured by the needs of play and this involves form and rhythm. The peculiar nature of game space and the role of the body in determining our experience of it connect contemporary gameplay with dance.

The connection with dance is not one-sided; it is not simply that players dance with the game object in order to gain knowledge of it. Exploring a game also involves being scripted, or choreographed by the game. Viewed in this way, Janet Murray's (2001: 129) rejection of dance as a way of understanding gameplay because it (dance) does not accommodate agency is somewhat fallacious. It is often said that in games with very large, continuous and largely homogeneous visual spaces, players can enjoy a great deal of 'freedom'. However, it is important to emphasize that this freedom is a sensation – in Adorno's terms, it is 'merely expressive' – dance and gameplay involve bodily actions that are scripted by a choreographer or a program. In both cases, success is a matter of adhering our actions to these specifications – if you want the rush you have to move. The result is a fusion of the shapes and patterns that we trace out with our bodies in space with the movement of other objects to create an overall impression that, in some sense, communicates with viewers of the dance. Dance involves an element of coordination in movement that produces display. Gameplay involves the hand of the player learning the correct sequences of pressing and holding down buttons that are connected to and guided by experiences derived from visual and other sense data (from the screen and the controller). There is a clear analogy between the way that Colleen Dunagan learns a new dance move and the process through which a player learns to master a sequence in gameplay:

> Frequently, in order to learn a new dance movement, I find myself having to translate or transform the whole into a series of smaller actions that are familiar to me. Often in doing this, as I watch a demonstration of the movement, I assess the action in terms of what it feels like in my head. Developing a mental 'image' of the physical sensations assists me in analysing the step in terms of its similarity to other actions within my repertoire of physical possibilities. (Dunagan 2005: 30)

The comparison with identifying formally identical situations, which vary widely in terms of their visual narrative trappings, within game situations is fairly clear here. Players learn movements of their hands and associate them with formal sensations (swooping, diving, swerving, or just 'picking up') that recur throughout a game and to some extent carry over between games. These sensations represent possibilities for experiencing space with a given game program.

This is particularly clear in games that offer players a kind of 'training sequence' at the beginning of play. The player learns a sequence of moves on the controller that can be deployed when a certain kind of visually projected situation is encountered. To some extent, each time we find a situation like this in the game it is initially a puzzle and the challenge is to recognize it. We have to ask ourselves if it is a case for this manouvre or not and then we have to test the idea by trying it. Since it is difficult, we have to persist until we get it right. In so doing, we gradually master the move, much as a dancer learns a new sequence or position, so that when we encounter the right kind of situation later in the game we may get through on the first or second attempt. When we solve the puzzle, then, we identify in the visual space on screen a kind of receptacle or home for the moves that we have learned to associate with tensions and movements in the hand and the rush of feeling that accompanies it in this game. Using our hands we cleave a particular experience of form from the game program. This recurs in combination with a variety of projected visual settings on the screen but they are primarily just triggers for a kind of embodied sensation and an experience of form.

Mirror's Edge (Electronic Arts 2008) offers a good illustration of the principle that games are made up out of small units experienced by players as forms combined into complex wholes that determine the aesthetic character of a game, and it has an exemplary training sequence. In *Mirror's Edge* the left stick on the controller guides our character, Faith, through the game environment, while the right trigger determines her visual field, so you can 'look' at one thing while she moves past it or away from it towards another. During training a narrator's voice tells us that objects with 'interactive potential' in the game are often lit up in red. Looking at them with the right stick means that our actions will apply to them when that is appropriate. This applies to things like jumping up to grab hold of ledges – the L1 button on the X-Box controller makes Faith jump. Using the R1 button makes her perform a 180 degree turn, which we experience visually as mildly disorientating. The visual experience of *Mirror's Edge* is in 'first person' mode, which means that the screen displays game scenarios as they would be seen through Faith's eyes, including strange glimpses of her hands when we are running or hitting things, and occasionally views of her legs and feet when we fall down. Using the left trigger makes Faith crouch, so that she can pass under obstacles like suspended beams. The right trigger makes her punch. The triggers can be combined in sliding kick attacks. The training program introduces useful combinations of these elementary moves. Of particular significance to the game action, and a defining form of *Mirror's Edge* is the facility of 'wall walking'; to do this we make Faith run 'into' a wall and then jump. Some dexterity with the buttons is required to make Faith run up a wall on one side of the screen, turn towards a ledge on the other side and then jump across to successfully pull herself up onto it.

The scenarios in the game are images of slightly futuristic urban buildings. Faith leaps across roofs, balances on air-conditioning ducts, ducks under pipes and runs up and down fire escapes. She only occasionally ventures into public areas of the urban environment, the ones that are foregrounded in urban design. This is related to the central narrative premise of the game, which is that of a comfortably-off society that is intolerant of difference. The opening sequence tells us that Faith and her friends are 'runners'; they carry messages and packages for non-conformists who exist clandestinely, 'at the margins' of society. Aside from the presumed desirability of being marginal in a repressive regime, we are given no other reasons to identify with Faith (and no information about the contents of the packages) in the early stages of the game.

3   *Mirror's Edge* images © 2011 EA Digital Illusions CE AB. All
rights reserved. Used with permission.

Throughout the game Faith's passage through this environment is guided by the voice of a male character, Marcus, who
we see in cut scenes at the end of chapter one, and who has a
'com-link' to her ear-piece. He tells her to 'get out of there', or
to head for a specific rooftop. His information is gleaned from
banks of computer screens – a device familiar from numerous movie representations of the modern 'handler'. She is also
led around by a trail of objects highlighted in red. The latter
are not consistent with any principles of visual realism but, as
already argued, that standard is really quite incidental to enjoyment of this or any other game. Once the game has started
and we are given reasons for running and jumping about the
backwaters of the sprawling metropolis, we are involved in
identifying forms and using the basic controls above to activate and experience them. A sloping roof, for example, with a
glimpsed red object beyond it, means that we can 'slide' down
it. A gap at the bottom means we need to press L1 to jump or
Faith plummets to her death.

The more interesting game situations are all less obvious
than this, however. The fun of *Mirror's Edge* lies in recognizing
the relevant, formal aspects of a given situation and coming up
with the right combination of movements to get Faith through
them. For example, in the training sequence Faith is led by
another character, Celeste, through her first wall walk–turn–
jump sequence. The objects involved are on top of a roof and
resemble some corrugated iron and concrete blocks. Some

time later a similar arrangement of shapes – voids, reliefs and surfaces – are encountered inside a plush office building. Faith is trying to escape from pursuing police officers who are shooting at her. She has to run along the wall, turn and jump onto a balcony, from which she can make her escape. The resemblance between the two situations as first encountered is accessible only to a distinctive way of scrutinizing a visual image. This kind of scrutiny abstracts out the differences of context and meaning that can be invested in such representations (coded by varieties of texture, colour, writing, narration) in the search for formal patterns that denote a structural affinity between two situations. This becomes the basis for selecting appropriate actions, which allow the player to progress in the game. Progression is achieved by matching actions on the controller to these identified affordances of the game program. The processes of puzzle solving and action become increasingly intuitive as one becomes more familiar with the game and its forms, but both aspects – matching and performing the actions – get harder in later stages. What we have to do is identify the forms, or movements, that we learn and use in order to progress. In other words, the game is a choreography (or script/score) and our role as players is to follow its instructions. We cannot do this mechanically but have to respond imaginatively, using our senses, our memory, our intuitions concerning Faith's physical capabilities, and our understanding of our own hands as creatively involved in the execution of the game program. The process involves multiple senses structured around a feeling that gives the experience its form. Playing the game involves periods of tentative examination and testing out moves and forms, during which time the music is muted, even serene, but also periods of running and jumping across rooftops, over wire fences and so on, when it becomes a techno soundtrack and Faith is attacked by opponents dressed as militarized police or in the characteristic close-fitting attire and hockey masks of another runner (or a serial killer). Taken alone the visual cues would be confusing, perhaps even undermining for the experience. The lines of red that guide you in some periods of the game may at other times signify gun-sights, which swoop around Faith's body and have to be avoided by running. These vivid red lines are only marginally narrower than the 'zip wires' Faith sometimes uses to glide between blocks in the cityscape.

When it comes to experiencing form in video games, such rhythmic articulations of hand movements and sounds are key and assign a specific role to the game's visual representations. As Henri Lefebvre pointed out, rhythm has to be intuited; it cannot be seen, though it may be something we can listen for. Media of the culture industry squeeze out this kind of rhythmic variation, but this has consequences for the representations they provide, which Lefebvre characterizes as 'shadows' (2004: 31). Lefebvre calls for us to become 'rhythmanalysts', that is, we should learn to listen to things better and to comprehend the role of beats and their intersection in determining social aesthetics. Of particular significance here is a temporal experience that is neither cyclical nor linear but involves what Lefebvre calls 'appropriated time':

> Whether normal or exceptional, it is a time that forgets time, during which time no longer counts (and is no longer counted). It arrives or emerges when an activity brings plenitude, whether this activity be banal (an occupation, a piece of work), subtle (meditation, contemplation), spontaneous (a child's game or even one for adults) or sophisticated. This activity is in harmony with itself and with the world. It has several traits of self-creation or of a gift rather than of an obligation or an imposition come from without. It *is* in time; it *is* a time, but does not reflect on it. (Lefebvre 2004: 77)

This description of appropriated time as a time that forgets itself is what I have called virtual time (see Chapter 2) and will be familiar to anyone who has stopped playing a computer game and been surprised to find how many hours have passed since they started. Appropriated time corresponds to the idea of a time that is structured in accordance with form, or the rhythmic play with our expectations discussed previously, rather than social function or natural chronological time. Implied in Lefebvre's account is the notion that this may be differently distributed through social and cultural practices at different points in history – no medium or form is privileged.[8] Lefebvre notes that although in the modern era dance has lost its integral connection with music (Lefebvre 2004: 65) in the West, the possibility remains that dance and the rhythmic experience of form may resurface in connection with popular play experiences. This is significant for our understanding of video games, because they restore the rhythmic to the foreground of electronic entertainment media. This illustrates how tensions of the resistant artwork may be present in commodities of the global culture industry, which, as we have seen, is noted by Lash and Lury (2007) and Ranciere (2007), but it is also an opening to popular cultural forms of expression that may occupy a similar, ambivalent relation to the commodity – a possibility these authors overlook.

A dance aesthetic

According to Bourdieu (1993), as well as viewing new designs as responses to works within the same cultural sub-field, we should also understand them in terms of homologies they establish with developments elsewhere in the culture. What he calls 'positions taken' have to be interpreted in this broader perspective if we are to understand their proper significance for the field as a whole and for its relation to other fields and to their common traversal by the economy. If we view the activity of players' hands in this way it becomes clear that the design and use of video game controllers has been homologous with innovations across a range of cultural practices. Historically, what seemed like quite small changes in how people used their hands have been integral to paradigm-shifting practices whose significance was far reaching. Karl Marx famously observed that it took the whole of human history to produce the hand of the industrial worker of his time. Similarly, Frederic Jameson describes other changes that took place in the nineteenth century:

> With the invention of matches around the middle of the century, there begins a whole series of novelties which have in common

the replacement of a complicated series of operations with a single
stroke of the hand. This development goes on in very different
spheres at the same time: it is evident among other instances, in
the telephone, where in place of the continuous movement with
which the crank of the older model had to be turned a single
lifting of the receiver now suffices. (Jameson 1975: 75)

Such changes modify the aesthetics of social life, where the
hand plays a uniquely productive role. An important part
of the context for understanding the role of the hand and of
controllers as the locus of frenzied and experimental manual
activity is the contemporary culture of the hand, a domain in
which we have seen highly significant changes over the past
few decades.

There has been a largely uncommented-on change in culture
since the mid-1990s, associated with mobile phones as much
as with computer game controls. As these devices have modified our experience of intimate space (Fortunati 2002) and
lived time, so we have responded with increased attention to
digital dexterity and manual precision. We have incorporated
the devices into the rhythms of contemporary life via bodily
processes of tapping, stroking, squeezing and twisting. In this
process we have forged a kind of living space beneath the level
of linguistically mediated investments of the constructionist
kind. The cultural significance of these practices and tendencies is not yet clear but the argument here is that homologous
changes visible in such disparate areas as mobile phone use,
personal computing, even watching television are crystallized
by computer games in a form that presents them free of any
purpose. In other words, the computer game exhibits a distinctive kind of aesthetic form, or what Ranciere (2009) calls a
'division of the sensible' that is paradigmatic for our time.

If we adopt the description of computer games as a form of
dance with the hands it is possible to align them with other
recent developments that, taken together, constitute something of a revolution in manual culture. For example, on
video-sharing websites people exchange videos of their hands
dancing to Daft Punk's song 'Harder, Better, Faster, Stronger'.
The words of the song are written on fingers, wrists and palms

and the movies start with the camera fixed in position with a view of the hands at rest. As the song starts to play the hands come to life and present us with the words of the song as they are sung. As the pace quickens the feat of keeping the correct words on screen in time with the track becomes increasingly impressive (see Figure 5). Similar videos show screen shots of perfect (and sometimes less than perfect) performances using the *Guitar Hero* (Red Octane/Activision 2005) game program. Here, we do not see hands directly, but the record of their activity in the form of coloured buttons flashing at the bottom of the screen, as the player presses the buttons on the controller in synchrony with melodies predominating in the accompanying soundtrack. This may not sound like much of a feat. The *Guitar Hero* controller is a childish lump of plastic that seems to afford few of the expressive possibilities of a real guitar and, in several senses, this is indeed the case.[9] However, there is an evident skill required to keep up with and maintain accuracy in striking the correct buttons to perform a Dragonforce[10] song, for example, all the way through without mistakes. The skills are not those of playing the guitar; they are not even remotely similar to those skills, but anyone watching these videos can see that this performance is difficult. It requires discipline, rehearsal and mental focus and it requires all of these things be deployed for no end other than performance itself. Dancing with the hands has become a self-conscious mode of creative public performance in popular culture, for which players get peer recognition just as they do in connection with playing musical instruments and other traditional arts.

4   Stills from the 'Daft Hands' YouTube video

Another good illustration of this tendency is provided by 'Tap Studio', a musical game application for Apple's 'iPod touch' music player. The iPod touch is a wireless networked device that has a touch-screen interface similar to that used on the iPhone and iPad, which the iPod touch antedates. It is a hand-held gaming machine as well as a portable music player. Tap Studio is a game application that works with people's urge to tap along to music with their fingers.[11] Choosing tunes from your music library, stored on the iPod touch, you can make a record of your 'taps' to a particular song, The game provides three (or four) on-screen buttons and you hit and hold them with your fingers (or thumbs) in a sequence that corresponds to your feelings about the music. Once recorded, your 'dance' becomes a template or script, against which you and others can test your ability to reproduce that particular interpretation. Recorded 'taps' are compared for how well they comport with your own and others' sense of the affective qualities of the music. Using the networked properties of the device it is possible to exchange taps and for players to rate hand dances associated with particular music tracks. Here we see people dancing and choreographing manual activity within a culture of appraisal and criticism whose standards are clearly aesthetic. It is sometimes astonishing to find what people do with their hands in response to a piece of music and to find what 'works' and what does not. The game is also extremely amusing because in recording taps people perform remarkable feats of dexterity that are difficult to reproduce and attempting to do so frequently results in abject failure. Curiously, difficult sequences often seem to distract us from the music while we learn them, only for us to find that they fit the music well once we have mastered the sequences – a strong echo of the process of learning moves in a game.

Nigel Thrift (2008) argues that our collective experience of space and time is being reconfigured as a result of changes in which the hand enjoys a new priority. Thrift points out that we are living through a period in which number has taken on a peculiarly central and productive role in culture.[12] Increasingly, our experience is of or with objects and situations that, he says, are neither natural nor technological but are produced through unseen alterations at the level of the mathematically defined structuration of sites of experience. This process is altering the human sensorium, so that 'qualculation' – a novel sensibility that combines an active apprehension of data structures with manipulating and getting a feel for them rather than recognizing them as such – becomes the dominant social aesthetic. In this context, the hand takes on strange new powers; as Thrift puts it, 'the hand is changing its expectations' (2008: 102) and consequently, '"touch" will ... become a more important sense, taking in and naming experiences which heretofore have not been considered as tactile and generating haptic experiences which have hitherto been unknown' (2008: 103–4). Thrift describes contemporary play as 'a process of performative experiment' (2008: 119). In this context, dance takes on methodological, or epistemic significance – it is part of the way that we gather knowledge and understand the fundamental nature, or grounding conditions of contemporary society:

> dance has a particularly rich history consisting of experimentation with many genres and styles, which is of immense significance in trying to forge a symptomatology of movement which can help us both to understand and create expressive potential by gesturing to new ground. (Thrift 2008: 140)

Thrift's qualculation resolves an anomaly in our understanding of play with video games. One of the reasons many have sought to understand video games primarily as virtual spaces that resemble familiar scenarios and invite mimetic action responses is that players respond to them in ways that appear to be unmediated by thought about controls, or extended reflection on the differences between negotiating a real space and finding your way through a computer-generated one. For example, in sports simulation games players seemingly intuit how long they have to hold down a button to get a 'good throw' of a javelin. Is this because of the presence of visual clues in the game's interface? What if the content of the interface (the game's fiction) becomes more abstract, as in a game like 'worms' (Team17 1994), which also involves us lining up shots and holding down buttons for a period of time to determine the force of the shot? Never having been a militarized worm I can hardly relate to this (two-dimensional) scenario on the basis of any actual experience. At the same time, it is surely true that I do not sit with a stopwatch and time the difference between any two shots in my efforts to make them more accurate. Rather, I am engaged in a kind of physical testing out of the game's propensities, which is what Thrift has in mind when he suggests that dance – my rhythmic and pleasurable movements in connection with the game object – is performing epistemic functions. Dancing with the game enables me to develop a qualculative understanding of its properties as an object.

Thrift argues that in consequence new 'time-spaces' pervade and configure contemporary social relations. His account of these develops Lefebvre's notion of space and rhythm as variable rather than objective and as prior to and conditioning social and cultural meaning. In terms of its historic significance, Thrift argues that our transition to space-times based on qualculation has similar importance to the transition from oral to literate cultures. The 'object frameworks' Thrift has in mind enframe our experience of the world, but unlike Heideggerian enframing which 'throws' us in a specifically technological understanding, the new time-spaces are multi-dimensional. They are enframing, in the sense that we experience the world and relate to it only as it seems and it seems the way it does because of the work that they do. But they are also 'paratextual', meaning that we can alter them and create new configurations; they are surfaces but they are 'geo-physical as well as phenomenological', so that we can speculate on and work with their deep structure as well as their interfaces. The time-spaces of contemporary lived experience involve a kind of 'technological unconscious' and to comprehend what is going on we need new methods, including 'para-ethnography' that can take account of the dynamic, shifting elements that pre-structure meaningful experience. There is, he argues, an aesthetic dimension to learning in this new social situation and among the methods we have for gathering ideas and intuiting the constraints and possibilities of the new time-spaces is the method of dance (Thrift 2008: 91, 140).

As the term 'qualculation' implies, Thrift assigns a determinate significance to the rise of mathematics in his account of the new time-spaces (2008: 90–6). His account of this borders on technological determinism, since it is clear that, for him, the social diffusion of programmed objects including those that modify our physical environment without disclosing their presence, is behind the rise of qualculation as the new social aesthetic. However, while it is made possible by the presence of data structures and algorithms controlling computers, the 'melting' and 'flowing' nature of the new social architectures is as much to do with the way we have encased those structures in a revival of form. Although he does not use the idea of form, Thrift does suggest that the changes he describes are 're-naturalising' the world. Reified second nature is no longer mechanical, even if it is still artificial. One consequence of this new situation is that the human senses are reconfigured.[13] Sensing the new spaces will involve a heightened role for touch:

> qualculation demands certain kinds of perceptual labour which involve forms of reflexivity which position the subject as an instrument for seeing, rather than as an observer, in which a number of the mechanisms that we take for granted have been integrated into larger systems or into specialized feedback processes. Increasingly, subjects do not encounter finished, pre-existing objects, but rather 'clearings' that disclose opportunities to interfere in the flow. (Thrift 2008: 98)

There is, then, the rise of a new 'qualculative sense'; new kinds of perceptual labour which involve the subject's body as an 'instrument for seeing'. It is clear that video games generate just such an experience, in which body and eye collaborate to produce a space (a unique and shifting space that is formed in multi-planar intersections of intimate, body-occupied space and objective, three-dimensional representations on the screen) that reflects the player's ongoing intuition of the status of various, imperceptible data structures within the computer. In this context, dance is part of the way that we gather knowledge and understand the fundamental nature, or grounding conditions of contemporary society while play is 'a process of performative experiment'. (2008: 119)

Choreography and discourse

According to Michel Foucault (1994), early modern Europe saw language change from being just one item in the world, which was the 'primary text' (1994: 79), into the medium of representation standing between us and reality. This change in the structural position of language conditions what Foucault famously discusses as the emergence of discourse in the modern period: stretches of language that codify the world and human practices in accordance with knowledge/power. Dance was not immune to these changes. The development of pictorial notation for dance during what Foucault calls the classical age (roughly, the period from the French Enlightenment through to the 1860s) became more mathematical and, by the late nineteenth century, there was an increased focus on the disposition of forces within the body of the dancer. Positioning video games and video game technology in this historical trajectory makes it clear that the comparison with dance is not mere analogy but reflects a real development within the history of orchestrated movement and gesture. What Foucault writes about the productive character of the emerging sciences applies also to changes in dance practice that are associated with the Enlightenment, namely, this 'was not an age-old inattentiveness being suddenly dissipated, but a new field of visibility being constituted in all its density' (Foucault 1994: 132). In this field, dance was considered a primal source, an origin of linguistic communication. Eighteenth-century philosophers thought that, like language, dance originated in a practice of pure communication. The language of gesture was included in the pre-Babel myth. In the Enlightenment and the associated move to the aesthetic regime in art dance loses this connection with direct meaning and becomes a subordinate aesthetic practice, one that cannot measure up. In dance the element of resemblance remains less important than its grounding in sensation: we recognize the brilliance of a dance not simply through the visual impression its forms make, but because we marvel at the implicit strength masked beneath the apparent lack of effort in the physical performance itself. This tension is the play of dance. Although only presented with transient exterior forms, we are in touch with the interior of the dancer and this is integral to our appreciation. What we appreciate is the 'affirmative attraction that restrains' identified by Badiou in the comment that opens this chapter. Similarly, when we admire what another player achieves on-screen it is because we understand the dexterity of the performance and relate to it as if from within, as if her hands were our own and we aspire to emulate the performance when it is our turn.

Enlightenment scholars argued for a genesis of language from bodily movement and gesture with reference to an analogy between historical progress and ontogenesis. Early dance, which Condillac illustrates with reference to Ancient Hebrew and Greek cultures (Foster 2005), was still used to communicate ideas, including political and religious ideas. Just as language acquires autonomy from its roots in bodily movement,[14] so the facility of gestural communication became subtracted from dance and associated with pantomime and mime. It dropped out of dance completely in the eighteenth century. The dance for which Raoul Auger Feuillet developed his notation in the 1730s was a 'dance of steps', rather than a 'dance of gestures' (Foster 2005: 85).[15]

Feuillet's notation broke dances down into their component parts and specified for dancers how each one should be performed, much as the Enlightenment grammarians constructed tableaux of 'roots' that connected the disparate human languages. This resulted in what Foster calls 'foundational units' that could be combined and recombined indefinitely. In the nineteenth century choreographic notation became more mathematical. Carlo Blasis's drawings use the growing knowledge of mechanics to distill the essential properties of a position down to the lines of force it establishes within the body of the

dancer. He maps the trajectories of each dancer through space
with similar precision. Gabrielle Brandstetter gives examples
of the positions he recommends, like the arabesque:

> The arabesque is an extremely unstable pose. From a static point
> of view the body is in an unstable balance, which means that the
> centre of gravity is located in the highest possible position. This
> also means that the body 'carries' the greatest possible energy.
> (Brandstetter 2005: 73)

The transition from Feuillet to Blasis parallels the shift
described by Foucault from the Classical to the Modern episteme.[16] Feuillet's notation was based on a rigid classification
system based on observation, collection and cataloging, but
Blasis's is premised on reaching past surface appearances and
acting on forces internal to the dancer's human body. This parallels developments in the modern episteme, which Foucault
discusses in connection with a variety of disciplinary practices, including modern medicine. It gives rise to a conception
and practice of dance that, as Brandstetter points out, 'widens
towards modernity's aesthetics of perception' (Brandstetter
2005: 75).

Modern aesthetic dance rests on an understanding of the
inner forces of the body and its fascination lies in the fact that
"the dancing itself hosts a non-expressive communication
between inner and outer" (Franko 1995: 8). Modern dance
can be confusing to watch. It is a dance aesthetic, however, in
which the solo performer is central:

> In the swing of the turn, in the distorting dynamics of centrifu-
> gal force, disparate things and forms proceed from one another
> and into one another with no division: a transformation in a
> continuous flow of movement. At the centre, however, the
> Sylphide ballerina of Romantic ballet whirls around en pointe
> in a pirouette. She is the flywheel of this great general rotation.
> (Brandstetter 2005: 75)

There are multiple connections between the world of dance
and technology, from the modern conception of the dancer as
a finely tuned, balanced machine, which is implemented quite
literally by Blasis's notation, to the extensive use of video in

the 1980s to create a record of dance performances that could then be analysed (an important factor in the eventual development of dance studies (Carter 1998)). This continues in the digital era, with dance studies and choreography making use of programs that resemble video games to facilitate new kinds of performance. In work by the contemporary choreographer Todor Todoroff, for example, dancers wear devices that resemble game controllers on their bodies – their arms and legs – and these gather data from them while they dance (Chabot and Laloux 2009) .[17] These data are fed through algorithms that control projectors and sound systems, so that the embodied dance produces not only the appearance of the dancer's body but also music and images that are expressively related to it. Here, the idea that controller use is dance is made explicit and, paradoxically, it would seem that the dancers are more controlled than the average gamer (it holds them rather than the other way around), although this is not how the dance appears.[18]

Thrift argues that in contemporary culture dance is emerging as the primary mode of coming to understand and acting upon a new world. Of particular importance here is the idea that, while it is choreographed and constrained (enframed), the body is also creative in the time-spaces configured by digital technologies:

> This embodiment both signals beyond the present and re-works the present by exemplifying a totality rather than exactly specifying a class or category. In making another bounded world, the actors conjure powers and meanings that they despair of, which yet appear to derive from a location other than their 'ordinary' selves ...
>
> [Their bodies] ... delineate the immediate as a fragment of some different or new totality of meaning. (Thrift 2008: 116)

The notion that contemporary cultural practices involve the generation of worlds that the people making them at the same time despair of will be central to the next chapter. Viewed in terms of Thrift's argument, however, the video game can be seen as a revelatory event in the history of dance – one that discloses a new perspective on the underlying reality of the form.

The event has been recognized by choreographers, who have moved to embrace digital technology as part of their practice and have, in the process, transposed aspects of video gaming into the sphere of theatrical dance. This reflects a new salience for dance-like operations in contemporary culture, of which the video game is both a product and an integral part. Calling video gameplay dance should not be the occasion for imposing sense meaning onto the activity. The cultural history of dance just described shows how it develops in a space that is at a tangent to meaning–making practices. As part of contemporary aesthetic experience, dance is an element that cuts across other parts of the digital machine, dislocating them with movement.

Jon Dovey and Helen Kennedy (2006) suggest that biologically embodied player activity should be viewed as part of a 'cybernetic circuit' that also involves the mediation of a 'virtual body', which exists on the screen. Although they don't make this explicit, their idea of avatarial embodiment is a kind of hypothesis, without which the activity of gamers would, perhaps, defy interpretation.[19] The player of the game, they say, is involved in multiple 'feedback loops' with the game and 'these feedback loops require that we give a proper recognition to the avatar as an embodiment of the player's action and experiences' (2006: 108). Feeling embodied in the avatar must be part of what is going on for players; it is a necessary assumption if we are to interpret gameplay, to make it consistent with what people *do* in connection with computer games and other technologies. Although they acknowledge a central role for players' biological bodies in driving the machine along, they think that these embodied energies have no privileged position in the cybernetic mechanism:

> In the lived embodiment of gameplay there is no player separate to the interface and game world; there is a fusion of the two into a cyborgian subjectivity – composed of wires, machines, codes and flesh. (Dovey and Kennedy 2006: 109)

However, this vision of computer gameplay as a closed circuit in which the human element has been distributed is in tension with their claims elsewhere that what motivates the movement of the apparatus is players' pursuit of particular pleasures. They associate the latter with 'sweet spots' like those encountered in sports (2006: 116) and in players' pursuit of 'virtuosity'.[20] Paradoxically, this post-humanist conception of the computer game threatens to abstract games from their social context in the direction of what Bourdieu might have called a 'fictitious reconciliation' (Bourdieu 1990: 38) of actions that may have contradictory rationales. The cybernetic circuit is a theoretical fiction that threatens to swallow the practical, embodied logic of computer gaming, when what is needed is a framework that respects its intrinsic distance from other parts of the gaming apparatus and its capacity to generate displacements, which is integral to the aesthetics of the videogame. More sensations are present in the repetitive repertoire of a player's hands,[21] its successes and failures in terms of the progress of the game, the player's frustrations, habituations and pleasures, than are accounted for by Dovey and Kennedy's reference to the 'virtuosity' with which players strive for success. Interpreting this activity as flowing, rather than as a disjointed struggle waged by an individual who wants to achieve something with an object, is a reification of gameplay as a practice. In contrast, we should recognize that there is not one organizing meaning that suffuses the activity, but that its primary moments are just meaningless. Learning a routine in computer games involves countless interruptions, pauses and re-thinks, as well as repetitions ending in different kinds of failure. Once mastered, moves can take on different significance for a variety of actors – as part of a larger sequence later in the game where it might attract the admiration of other players, for example – but the core dynamic concerns these movements and their feel as embodied performance. This experience is not adequately comprehended by locating its actions within the technical intelligibility of a 'circuit'.

Aesthetics and gender

Approaching computer games as a form of popular dance enables us to identify a different context for the interpretation of gaming, one in which the activity takes its meaning from the intersection of gesture with the other elements of the experience. This has implications for the sociology of video gaming. In particular, computer games are not to be understood in a context formed by discourse because their core structures invoke a different kind of power, namely, dressage. When we position individual games in contemporary cultural politics we must take their algorithmic routines, their rhythms and sensations into account and not attempt to read off their 'meaning' from their textual components alone. In fact, the dance element in them sets up a distinctive and at times corrosive relation with these elements and this will be the theme of the next chapter. Viewed in this way it is clear that video games are, in important ways, dis-continuous with modern entertainment media or paradigms of reception associated with them. The body and especially the hands, have changed in relation to space and the video game controller, in all of its various permutations, illustrates the principle that we now have prostheses that enhance cognition (Thrift 2008: 102). The player who navigates game space does so not by committing to a visual space on-screen, but by working to produce it at the intersection of the intimate space of the hands and body with the multiple planes of the game interface. There are new, complex intersections of proximal, bodily space and the space of illusions traversed by the eye. The paradigm of a viewing eye and mobile visual field combined with a stationary body yields to one in which intimate spaces are formed by active hands that become information-bearing and mobile. Finally, in the new time-spaces thus constituted the kaleidoscopic nature of this game space, which has no stable location on either side of the screen, becomes a locus of form in popular experience.

Interpreting computer games as dance has particular implications for our understanding of their implication in gender. If technology has been viewed as masculine it is well understood

that dance is gendered as a feminine practice and remains implicated in contemporary understandings of gender performance.
The great modernist ballerina of the early twentieth century,
Isadora Duncan is often seen as paradigmatic in connection
with the politics of this. According to Mark Franko (1995),
Duncan's dancing technique involved a novel degree of reflexivity that enabled her to take dance to a new level, a
reflexivity that derives from aesthetic modernism. Dance
had been understood in terms of 'expression theory'; the
idea being that music creates an impression on the dancer
(affect) which is associated with a sensation (feeling), which
in turn explains, causally, the movement (gesture) of the
dance. This expressive conception of dance aligned it with
the traditional female properties of natural turbulence, excessive emotionalism, and a concern with display, and is
one reason for the ambivalence that has often been evident
towards dance, discussed earlier in this chapter. Duncan's
dancing superseded this natural-expressive model, substi-
tuting instead a concern with dramatic effect, produced by
the ordering of surfaces in a display. This display involved
fabrics and light as well as Duncan's overtly female body.[22]
Her dance repositions the body as a site of undischarged
feeling and of ordered presentation, which produces a
feeling response in the audience by making them aware of
tensions internal to the dancer. As Franko puts it, 'the dancing
self hosts a non-expressive communication between outer and
inner' (1995: 8). This is not a rejection of the feminine but an
attempt to stage it on equal terms to the public activities of
men:

> Consider that affectivity was traditionally sequestered with family
> and sexuality in the private sphere. In view of this, Duncan's
> containment of affectivity within what I have called sensation
> can also be interpreted politically. That is, Duncan's rejection of
> an overtly delineated affectivity ... is likewise a refusal to credit
> the inner/outer or male/female binary by occupying, literally
> dancing on, its boundary. Neither within nor without, Duncan
> critiques such boundaries. (Franko 1995: 16)

Duncan's intervention asserts the equivalence of the female with intelligence and self-control – a challenge to various kinds of misogyny. Feminist theory needs to take account of the presence of dance-like elements in contemporary culture, associated with the diffusion of digital technologies and controllers. If dance theory serves as a kind of archive (Thrift 2008) for contemporary social theory, we need to use it in order to explore as yet unplumbed depths of experience relevant to the constitution of gender differences and the reproduction of social inequalities based on them. It is insufficient to interpret games and game culture on the basis of superficial similarities with other 'masculine' media contents. A generation of young men have grown up dancing with their hands and the importance of this to gender politics has yet to be registered, still less explored.

This chapter has used Bourdieu's theory of habitus to explore the process of incorporation. To use a game controller one has to be prepared by past training in the use of hand-held devices that involve buttons, knobs and levers. Controllers resemble early learning toys in this respect and it is fair to say that these designs facilitate their insertion into the phenomenal world of the child. The most important habits that constitute the embodied learning of habitus are acquired in childhood and we can see that computer game controllers form part of a culture of hand use that has been established since the early 1990s, since games consoles became part of the furniture in most domestic environments in the rich countries. For the majority, the young adult habitus has been formed through engagement with computer game controllers and involves internalization of norms of correspondence between hand actions and a responsive, dynamic visual environment full of lines and colours, cartoon imagery and distinctive sounds. Players do not have to learn the basics of controller use each time they come to a new game because they have been culturally equipped for playing pretty much any game and the process of learning new moves, executed through complex series of actions with the controller is one that presupposes an embodied disposition.

However, as Beverley Skeggs (Adkins and Skeggs 2004) has argued in another context, the assumption that habitus meshes seamlessly with the world that has formed it and which it helps to reproduce is culturally conservative.[23] Aesthetic interventions in habitus induce disruptions and pose challenges to the learned expectations of the generative scheme of perception and response. The video game is a clear illustration of this since each new game can be critically assessed precisely in terms of how it stretches, extends and differentiates the *hexis* of the player. The better a game is, the more it complexifies the game space. Such continuous differentiation is located at the level of habitus but constitutes a challenge to the concept, in so far as habitus entails stasis and continuity. The fact that a field of cultural practice can be marked by complex and changing embodied activity that nonetheless assumes a degree of habituation amounts to a deployment of modernist dance principles in public space, one that subverts established spatio-temporal orderings. This process is ambivalent, loosening the hold of established norms of comportment and disposition on the one hand, creating uncertainty and misunderstanding on the other. Within this the video game is associated with performances that subvert conventional gender investments, thwarting expectations and blocking obvious identifications. In this context, theory has a part to play in determining what kinds of values get invested in the activity and which interests served in the field of distinctions that is emerging from video gaming as a cultural field. In other words, taking an aesthetic perspective enables us to see openings onto this field that would otherwise remain out of view.

Notes

1 Galloway (2009) understands this in terms of multiple interfaces *within* the game.
2 Similarly, in *Donkey Kong* (Nintendo: 1981) Mario backs up, advances and backs up again in anticipation of the course to be taken by different barrels as they cascade down towards him. The kineme is identical in the two cases.

3 There is little consensus concerning the extent to which women play computer games and estimates of the proportion of gamers who are female vary widely. One industry body claimed 40% of console game sales were to women (ESA 2009) but this figure has been treated with scepticism, with some pointing out that female consumers bought games for male partners and sons. There is evidence in this report and elsewhere of variation according to the kind of game played. T.L. Taylor (2006), for instance, suggests that women players may be proportionately more numerous in MMPGs than other kinds of game, while Kerr (2006: 107) thinks women may be more inclined to PC gaming than to consoles.

4 Viewed in this way, making computer games that appeal to women may be a kind of pyrrhic victory, on the same terrain Bourdieu (2001) situates many of the gains of the feminist movement, that is, they haven't touched the underlying reality in which masculine domination is grounded.

5 The thesis of extra-discursive dressage applied especially to female bodies and a key dimension to female oppression was elaborated first by Henri Lefebvre (2004).

6 As we saw in Chapter 2, Espen Aarseth (1997) tells us play is a risky enterprise involving commitment to a struggle, while Johann Huizinga relates it to an 'inner hardness'. These views are consistent with Bourdieu's (1990) comments on the masculine nature of play and games as places where men square up to one another.

7 According to the curators of the Game On exhibition (Game On 2002), Lara was originally designed to appear as a normally shaped young woman but in the course of a series of game design meetings her breasts grew and her form became so hyperfeminized that, were she real, she would be unable to stand up for any length of time.

8 Bourdieu notes (1993: 60) that new works can revive old normative standards within a given field. Video games issue a call to eighteenth-century ideas about aesthetic form in just this way.

9 Dominique Arsenault has provided a detailed analysis of the discrepancies between using the *Guitar Hero* controller and playing a real guitar (Arsenault 2008).

10 Dragonforce are a power metal band who specialize in very long, fast guitar solos. Their songs are available for *Guitar Hero* and well-known for being particularly difficult.

11 Other music game apps are also available, such as the 'Drum Kit' app.

12 Programmed objects of the kind that prescribe unit opera-
    tions are, of course, mathematical structures implemented in a
    computer.

13 This change is not itself without precedent, Constance Classen
    (1993) discusses anthropological and historical evidence of cul-
    tures based on alternate sensory configurations.

14 Language as discourse never secures full autonomy. As Foucault
    says, resemblance perdures as the unreflected upon ground of
    discursive knowledge: 'similitude is still an indispensable border
    of knowledge'. In this way it becomes part of what Foucault de-
    scribes as the 'historical a priori' of the Classical period: 'This
    a priori is what, in a given period, delimits in the totality of ex-
    perience a field of knowledge, defines the mode of being of the
    objects that appear in that field, provide man's everyday percep-
    tion with theoretical powers, and defines the conditions in which
    he can sustain a discourse about things that is recognized to be
    true' (1994: 158). The equivalent concept in relation to dance is
    surely sensation.

15 Holbein's painting can be read as symptomatic of this process.
    The forging of a new space of power, associated with the excision
    of a dance of gesture, informs its dynamic. The physical proc-
    esses of viewing are placed outside of the painting, where they
    can become quite funny, while the dominant illusion presents us
    with all the seriousness of perspectival depth (space).

16 We can also read this, as Brandstetter suggests, in terms of a
    movement of Enlightenment against baroque. The earlier dance
    notation made dancers into puppets, while this one will render
    them mechanically perfect. The first is consistent with an aes-
    thetics of ornate display, while the second emphasizes the virtues
    of precision and fidelity to nature (see Saisselin 1992).

17 I am grateful to Pascal Chabot for fascinating discussion of this
    issue.

18 Part of the fascination of Todoroff's work lies in the fact that it is,
    perhaps, a complication of dance's normal enigma, which is the
    appearance of freedom in a performance that we know is tightly
    controlled. The appearance of controllers foregrounds this
    enigma as the dancer struggles to establish a control we know
    they already have through an appearance of freedom we know
    is controlled. In both cases dance's aesthetic concerns a tension
    that we relate to through our bodies, rather than through the me-
    diation of a fictional narrative or as passive recipients of a visual
    spectacle. Similar tensions are present in *On Danse* (Montalvo and

Hervieu (2007)), where recorded images of scenes from the dance suddenly appear on the sides of brightly coloured, 6 foot high steps at the back of the stage. The dancers then drape themselves over the huge screen-steps and dance with 'themselves', making it impossible to tell just by looking where the 'real' dancer is and which of the assorted 2 and 3-dimensional spaces presented to your eyes is 'reliable'. *On Danse* resembles video gameplay in that it folds powerful visual effects into a performance that excites an embodied rather than a merely visual appreciation – the audience laughs, is encouraged to get to its feet and to make noise during the performance.

19   They argue it is necessary to introduce this idea 'for our consideration of embodied gameplay' (Dovey and Kennedy 2006: 107) but do not explain why or what the ultimate purpose of their analysis is. If the goal was interpretation then the assumption that people feel secondarily embodied might be a 'principle of charity in interpretation', without which their actions lack coherence. However, Dovey and Kennedy cannot invoke this methodological principle because as 'post-humanists' they do not assign any priority to understanding the human element in the circuit. The purpose of their consideration – its motivation and justification – remain, therefore, obscure.

20   In contrast, Thrift also maintains that contemporary artefacts present as 'specialised feedback processes' but emphasizes that human beings do not encounter them as 'finished', but rather as 'opportunities to interfere in the flow' (Thrift 2008: 98). His approach is also tainted with a post-humanism that means he cannot explain what motivates such actions.

21   As Patrick Crogan (2010) points out, this does not change with the introduction of the Wii-mote, which still has a button control pad to be used by fingers and thumbs.

22   Ranciere (2007: 97–8) discusses Loie Fuller in similar terms.

23   Writing in the same volume, Steph Lawlor notes that Bourdieu's views can seem to alternate between determinism and pessimism.

5

Meaning in virtual worlds

Truth, bodied forth in the dance of represented ideas, re-
sists being projected, by whatever means, into the realm of
knowledge.

Walter Benjamin

The argument of the last few chapters may have made it seem
as if the only thing that matters about play with a video game
is its form, in particular, how it feels to players. Yet at the same
time reference has been made to sensations of depth and movement associated with the screen and the controller and even
allusion to characters, like Faith, Max Payne, even Pacman,
and to specific fictional events in games, like being chased in
Resident Evil 4. It seems that even if the feel and form of gameplay are central to videogames, these other aspects are also
necessary; if we are not interested in our character and what
is happening to them then we will not be interested in playing
the game and if we do not continue to take an interest in the
unfolding of the game's storyline (however thin this is) then we
will not really be able to play because the things we are doing
(manipulating objects, creating changes on screen and listening to sounds) will not mean anything to us. My suggestion
has been, first, that not everything we do with video games is
or has to be meaningful; in some of its aspects play can involve
empty, technical routines. Also, there is an important disaggre-
gation of elements in the video game so that these moments are
articulated to physical movements and interpretation, or reflection on their meaning and holding these elements together
is something that players try to do because the organizing
unity of that activity is aesthetic form. However, it is clear
that meaning plays some role in this experience. Video games

contain cartoon imagery that signifies something to us and our activity with them is mediated through ideas that give each game its own specific identity. The focus of this chapter will be on the role these elements have in the overall experience.

Representation and signification do occur in video games – it is sensible, indeed necessary, to talk about video game fiction – but in a curiously muted way that has few cultural precedents. This chapter tries to clarify how this works and in so doing suggests that the meaning element of a game is something of a target for players in both senses of that term: in the course of gameplay we aim to construct something intelligible *and* devote a lot of effort to processes that are destructive of any kind of coherent meaning that might attach itself to our actions as players. All games offer some kind of metaphoric backdrop and a *purely* abstract game would be merely a complex, purposeless object, yet the storytelling aspects of video games can easily become excessive and upset their enjoyment. Cut-scenes, for example, can be illuminating and interesting but have a tendency to become intrusive and disruptive. The paradoxical way that meaning gets folded into games is related to the tensions presented in other chapters, which this book has argued are central to video game aesthetics. Video games are presented and marketed with much more emphasis on their story content than traditional games, as if it was what the games are 'about'. Yet, as we have seen, this is in tension with their gameness. On the other hand, games converge with contemporary story-telling practices at the very moment when these latter are most degraded in the sense that *their* fictional content is most weak and the element of play is strengthened in them. In other words, while there is convergence of contemporary play with mediated fiction, there is an equally significant move within fiction towards increased ludicity. These tendencies are related to one another in a move within the culture as a whole that exceeds either gameness or fictionality in the direction of form. The outcome of this move itself remains incomplete or undecided, which is the central difficulty for discussions of the video game object. It also informs any proper assessment of their political import, which is the topic of Chapter 6.

The first section presents the case for this convergence of ludic and fictional strains in contemporary culture. Drawing on the examples of the popular television programme, *Lost*, and *dot.hack*, a game for the PS2, I draw out a common organization of textual meaning in each of them which comports with what Henry Jenkins (2006) calls 'additive comprehension'. Instead of consuming fiction as a linear sequence of narrated events, additive comprehension involves playful exploration of a fictional world. A new reading experience is established in which gamic processes and those traditionally associated with fiction converge. The second section locates this convergence in what Angela Ndalianis (2004) theorises as 'neo-baroque' entertainment culture. In her analysis, contemporary fictional worlds resemble paintings, sculptures and dramas of sixteenth- and seventeenth-century Europe. They are open to multiple explorations, lack clear and non-porous boundaries with the real and prioritise displays of technical skill, even virtuosity, over profundity of content. In neo-baroque works, meaning is present in transitory flashes of illumination that are suggestive of a larger whole, or world that always remains out of view. The third section highlights the shaping effect of this cultural context on non-computerized games, in an effort to counter the notion that computer technology drives these cultural changes. Drawing on the example of the card game, *Magic: The Gathering*, it argues that the neo-baroque context shapes contemporary play, including video game technology. This section clarifies further the relation between repetitive ludic processes and a vertiginous sense of mystery, or of a meaning that is never quite brought into focus. Were it to be thus clarified, this meaning would negate play, in the case of games, and undermine the reading process itself, in the case of mediated fiction. Holding clarity at bay is the defining dynamic of the neo-baroque. As a cultural setting it also explains the over-representation of a certain kind of thematic content in popular fictions. The fourth section argues that the formal properties of video games limit them to allegory as a fictional mode. A concern with mysterious, fantastic and magical stories is necessitated by the limited referential powers entailed in the neo-baroque organization of meaning. Drawing on Walter Benjamin's (1985) study of baroque dramas, this is linked to the way that death is used in video games. The inability to construct tragic heroes, true individuals who would be defined as such by the manner of their dying, means that baroque dramas and video games alike incorporate death as mere mechanism or dramatic device. Unable to separate those it touches from their vital energies, death itself becomes a character, or an element in the play. The effect is ghostly, as death haunts the fictional world, punctuating but not ending the routines of exploration and play. The fifth section concludes by asking what it is that video games allegoricize, which leads to reflections on the cultural politics of video games as a form of mourning. The repetitions of video gameplay appear as an attempt to redraw the line between childhood and adulthood, to mark a distinction that video gaming and neo-baroque fiction alike would like to efface, but on which they are nonetheless completely dependent.

Fictional worldness

A characteristic shared by many contemporary media fictions is their 'worldness'. It is common to hear video games referred to as worlds. Sometimes this way of speaking is justified with reference to their social character – Edward Castronova (2005: 47), for instance, distinguishes Massive Multi-player Role Playing Game (MMPG) worlds from 'souped up video games' on precisely those grounds. However, the terminology of worldness reflects structural properties that unite contemporary popular media fictions and video games, in both their on and off-line variants. From the side of media fictions, these structural properties necessitate a distinctive reading process. From the side of games, the 'disconnected aesthetic quanta' discerned by Clifford Geertz (1991: 264) in connection with cockfights and other traditional games, become flashes of illumination. In both cases, the process determines a particular kind of content, which involves mystery, the fantastic and evokes (curiously) a sense of 'other-worldliness' that lends its flavour to specific events in the fiction and the gameplay.

The uncanny and even the monstrous tend to feature in the local representations, often as triggers that touch off a sense of deep meaning that cannot be expressed clearly or directly. This sense of mystery retains our interest in stories that are, read as a series of linear fictional events, usually not very good or interesting.

The popular fiction *Lost* illustrates the dynamics of this reading process. *Lost* began life as an ABC TV show but soon expanded to involve a range of on-line games and websites, a book, a board game and several YouTube videos that purport to have been left on the web by a character from the story world who never appears in the TV show. Each of these objects, including the TV shows, constitutes a kind of portal that gives us access to the *Lost* fictional world. This is a world that resembles our own and it includes familiar places, mundane technologies and cultural references that are not alien or fantastic. What makes *Lost* a world, as distinct from a story, is that in principle it is always there, open to fresh exploration and containing events and characters we have not yet found and do not find simply by following the dominant narrative thread. The *Lost* universe persists and we can add to it by doing more exploration. The web-based elements will cast light on events in the TV show, which most people would still consider central to *Lost*, but they do so not in a direct, linear fashion but rather by adding to our accumulating background knowledge. We do not follow events in *Lost* so much as we gather information about it and piece together snippets we have found in order to extend rather than deepen our understanding.

A group of characters are marooned on a tropical island after a plane crash. It turns out that the island is already inhabited by 'others'. This community seems to be in some way related to experiments carried out by a secretive corporation decades in the past. These experiments may be related to anomalies in the physical environment on the island, which include the presence of polar bears, monsters made of smoke and time travel. Read as metaphors, the issues raised by the programme, such as whether or not it is legitimate to torture captured others, are crude and obvious. However, there is a feeling of depth that is evoked by the way the *Lost* world is presented and the mechanics of world acquisition. Our curiosity is drawn to solving specific puzzles, like the presence of the polar bear on a tropical island, but the puzzles and anomalies are rarely, if ever resolved directly and clearly. We never actually find out what role was played by the corporation, for example, only that the actions of a faction that *may* have been connected to it may *partially* explain *some* of the things that happen! The mystery thickens even as small parts of it are resolved. This dynamic of partial disclosure accompanied by further mystery is what keeps viewers interested and keeps them playing with the *Lost* world.[1] Searching for *Lost* on the web, for example, we find websites that relate to characters in the programme as if they were real people – the 'rock star' Charlie has a web-page created by other band members, describing his disappearance. On 'You Tube' there are a series of videos that purport to originate on disparate websites and were collected by *Lost* fans. The videos document the efforts of a journalist, Rachel Blake, to track down the founder of the corporation, Alvar Hanso. Pieced together, these videos fill out part of the *Lost* backstory that can seem quite important but actually has few points of connection to anything that we see in the TV show. There is even a novel, *Bad Twin* (Troup 2006), that seems to have been written by one of the crash victims, although it also sits at a strange distance from the narrative in the TV show, being a fiction lodged within a fictional universe. It describes a corporation whose offices exist between floors in a skyscraper, concealed beneath the floor that is home to the Hanso organization, but this is incidental to the main plot, which is a stereotypical airport page-turner. Moreover, the nature of this play involves people incorporating the sense of mystery and contributing to the 'one step forward, two steps back' dynamic. In addition to the books, videos, games and 'official' websites, there are hundreds of unofficial sites and *Lost* discussion forums on the web where viewers discuss various hypotheses and share information they have gathered from these and other sources.

The worldness of the fiction invokes a specific reading dynamic, whereby the process of consuming *Lost* is playful and cumulative. Henry Jenkins, who mentions *Lost* but does not discuss it in much detail, describes the way we build our understanding of such worlds as a process of 'additive comprehension' (2006: 129) and relates it to a new kind of reading process:

> we are seeing the emergence of new story structures, which create complexity by expanding the range of narrative possibility rather than pursuing a single path with a beginning, middle and end. (Jenkins 2006: 121)

The fictional worlds of the contemporary mediascape are, on Jenkins's account, much more involving for their audiences than traditional narratives. In earlier work, Jenkins (1992) argued that it was a characteristic of 'fans' that they developed a kind of proximity to TV shows and other media products that others found disconcerting, even distasteful. Audiences for the new fictions are even more directly absorbed in them than was possible for 'Trekkies' and geeks of the 1970s and 1980s. Indeed, he says the additive logic of the new mode of storytelling requires audiences to be *inside* the media objects. This precludes the kind of distanced reading associated with narrative fiction, where readers interpret the meaning of a text as a representation. Now people are actively involved in producing the fiction, which Jenkins sees as a point of connection between video games and other contemporary media. The greater sense of involvement adds purchase to the idea that it is a fictional *world* we are dealing with in each case – we are in the world and our actions have consequences in a way that is not true when we read a traditional story. The meaning of the fiction is tied to the activity of exploring, moving forward to a new understanding and then finding that you have actually enlarged the sense of mystery. It does not lie in a deep interpretative exegesis of the textual meaning.

The Bandai series of games for the PS2, *dot.hack* (Bandai/ Atari 2003a; 2003b; 2003c; 2004) plays with this notion of worldness. The game has two fictional levels. When you start it up you are presented with a fictional PC desktop, from which you can access e-mails, consult fictional discussion boards and read the news concerning events in a fictional world. This, the game's primary fiction, is set in modern Japan and your character is a teenager who has just begun to play a game called *The World*. There is an icon for the game on your desktop and when you click it you find that you are propelled into a secondary fiction which is a simulation of an MMPG. In this world you are initially cast as 'Kite', an elf-like character who has few abilities and no friends. You are given the option of changing Kite's name, perhaps to your own, when you first enter *The World*. Your first encounter is with a more established character, Orca, who helps you to fight off an assailant and becomes your first friend. He gives you a bracelet at the end of this fight, the significance of which is unclear. Your first clue that all is not right with *The World* comes when you are subsequently informed that this character no longer appears in the game because its owner, an older player, has gone into a coma shortly after helping you. It is implied that this has something to do with his intense activity within the game and this discovery hangs in the background as you take your first steps as a player of, or in *The World*. To play, you use 'portals' to move between planet-like spheres, each containing some enemies on the surface and a multi-level dungeon beneath it. Killing enemies gives you access to spells and other useful items that you collect from them. You can trade these, or use them to modify your character and make it stronger, or just more appropriately equipped for fighting subsequent enemies. In this way the game simulates MMPGs, where these dynamics are common and where players are known to trade items like this (sometimes for real money) (Castronova 2005). During these opening plays you are likely to inadvertently port to a sphere that contains enemies whose power greatly exceeds Kite's and become easy prey. It becomes apparent that some kind of order is needed to guide your explorations. The game provides this, but not in the form of instructions or physical constraints – it is always possible for you to go and get killed if you want to – but by sending you messages from other players through the e-mail and discussion boards of the primary fiction. Agreeing with your friends to meet them on a specific sphere encourages you to pursue a particular course through the game's difficulty levels.

After some difficult encounters with enemies, you realize that the bracelet Orca gave you enables you to use a special power that you need to overcome opponents who are ostensibly much stronger than you. However, this effect, known as 'data draining' also has side effects. Initially, these are only implied. You read on the discussion boards of the primary fiction about power outages in the city near your home.[2] Then it becomes apparent that data draining is damaging the game world. Lines of code start floating across the screen, which flashes and falters as if you are about to lose connection. 'Sysadmin' contact you to warn that they know people hack games and that they view it as vandalism. You receive this information, however, at the same time as it becomes apparent that there is a deep instability within the game itself and that data draining is the only way you can progress to find out what is causing it. This will also enable you to retrieve Orca from his coma. Moreover, the discussion boards tell you that the corporation that owns the game has also extended its reach in the 'real world' of the primary fiction to construct a replacement technology for the Internet. In other words, you have to save the game in order to preserve safety critical infrastructure in the real world. *Dot.hack* is a profoundly repetitive game and its fictions (both of them) are in some ways trivial, even deliberately childish. Reading the discussion boards, playing the role of the young Japanese gamer takes up relatively little time; most of your activity is in *The World*. There gameplay is cyclical and predictable but punctuated by the need to navigate complex menus with hundreds of items in order to match the strength of your avatar to those of enemies in the dungeons you have to fight your way through. It is also periodically interrupted by factors that alert you to the imminent destruction of *The World*, which creates a temporary sense of its fragility and your precariousness within it. As in most games, losing fights results in death, which is followed by ejection from the game and in *dot.hack* this includes eviction from the primary fictional level. Each of these occasional jolts confers some kind of significance on your activity by prompting reflection on the larger narrative, although that activity is itself predominantly repetitive and empty.

In both *Lost* and *dot.hack* the local signs we encounter come to seem more incidental and superficial the longer we are engaged in the processes that are necessary to gathering them up; it is the reproduced sense of mystery that drives us on. The same core dynamic that sets repetitious, mundane and trivial characters, events and processes against a backdrop of unfathomable meaning and suspends us, playing on the triggers that link them, is present in and underlies our talk of 'worldness' in both contemporary media fictions and video games.

Neo-baroque entertainment culture

Angela Ndalianis (2004) describes a similar set of changes to reading practices in contemporary culture and she too makes the connection to video gameplay. She argues that this is part of a new phase in entertainment culture, which she calls the neo-baroque. The label is a response to similarities with the culture of the European aristocracy between the sixteenth and eighteenth centuries and she suggests that if the first baroque leveraged us into modernity the current, neo-baroque may well be a passage out of it.[3] The first baroque was a culture of excess in which the techniques of Renaissance art, for example, were taken to extremes. The illusionistic power of three-dimensional linear perspective, used to create awe-inspiring religious ceilings and windows by Michelangelo and Leonardo, was used by Pozzo and Bernini to create illusions that are technically accomplished but actually too full of effects to be enjoyable. Looking at a baroque mural or ceiling one feels disoriented. The limits of the painted scene overspill any set boundary, so that we cannot tell which columns are real and hold up the ceiling, and which are painted on. There is a feeling of being overwhelmed by forms as the painting lacks compositional logic. Instead of reading it in a convention-bound way, our eyes guided by the intentions of the painter to this point and then that, we find that there are many different ways through a baroque work. There is no starting point to which our eye is drawn and no conclusion, after which the painting as a whole makes sense. Instead, we are presented with a labyrinth, with no centre or clear exit.

For Ndalianis, contemporary media, including video games, manifest similar tendencies and she relates this to the presence of a neo-baroque cultural logic. A central theme for her is the proliferation of forms and patterns and it is no coincidence that she cites Henri Focillon, who as we saw in Chapter 3 was a historian of the baroque before he was a theorist of form, as a key theoretical influence. Neo-baroque cultural artefacts tend to have a labyrinthine character, which makes them sprawling fictional worlds, rather than linear narratives with obvious or intelligible plots. Their labyrinthine[4] quality is related to the fact that, like the ceiling discussed above, there is no privileged way through them. Engaging with a neo-baroque fictional world is not reading a story, but rather involves gathering evidence, assembling fragments and pieces of information that, when put together, illuminate a fictional world in a way that reflects one particular way through it. This 'way through' is always incomplete in the sense that the fictional world does not have a privileged reading; it requires each reader to find their own way. Stories in neo-baroque fiction are, 'not centred or contained within one enclosed static structure (as in one film or comic book). Instead, stories extend beyond their formal and media limits, encompassing rhythmic notions that intersect characters and stories across media' (Ndalianis 2004: 36). There is an interweaving of fictional levels and of the fictional and the real that can be disorientating.[5]

We have already seen that in *dot.hack* there is an intertwining of the game's fictional levels that conforms to this neo-baroque principle of overflowing boundaries. Similarly, in each episode of *Lost* we are presented with (increasingly implausible) elements of backstory for each of the individual characters, each of which casts a few rays of light but at the same time actually deepens the central mystery, often because characters turn out to have met in what they sometimes refer to as 'past lives'. Even video games whose story content is obviously not their main element, like the fighting game *Mortal Kombat: Deception*, exhibit a similar tendency towards gratuitous complexity at the fictional level. The 'conquest' mode of that game offers a kind of story that enables us to meet all the characters who, in the main part of the game, we can choose to be our avatar or as opponents. Each of them shows us different fighting routines, which we learn by copying and repeating sequences. Before we do this, however, each one tells us a highly convoluted back-story that explains their participation in the fighting and the reason they are interested in fighting alongside you or against you. There are 26 of these stories and they are long, told in great detail, and quite comical in their pointlessness. For example, Liu Kang tells you:

> The sorcerer Shang Tsung had killed me and consumed my soul. I remained trapped within his being, tormented by his evil, along with many other victims of his vampiric soul drain. Through Shang Tsung's eyes, we witnessed the battle with Raiden, who sacrificed himself to stop Onaga. Raiden's blast destroyed Shang Tsung and our souls were free to ascend into the heavens. I remained in Outworld, however, to aid my friends in the fight against the Dragon King.(Midway 2004)

These stories rarely, if ever, inform gameplay and if they did it would be a truly extraordinary feat of memory if anyone, after hours of fighting, remembered anything about them in any case. They constitute a kind of excess of representational content that corresponds to the diminished role played by fictional meaning of the traditional, interpreted kind. This should not mislead us, however, into thinking that audiences are thereby overwhelmed and reduced to a more passive, consuming role. On the contrary, such excess demands an active response, even if the pay-off for such activity is not to be had in the form of a good story.

Ndalianis also identifies repetition as a key property of neo-baroque fiction. In place of a linear order that confers meaning through singular interpretation, neo-baroque artefacts involve an 'aesthetics of repetition' (Ndalianis 2004: 69). She discusses the example of sequels, which are increasingly common especially in connection with blockbuster movies. They save media producers money, but the modern sequel is also an integral part of the new mediascape because they involve audiences in a new way. Whereas in the old culture industry of the 1960s or 1970s sequels were inevitably disappointing attempts to tell another story with established characters, now they are an opportunity to revisit fictional worlds from alternate perspectives, repeating our actions over and over as we test out hypotheses and integrate each iteration into our wider sense of what is going on. Video games generally are illustrative of this, as we have seen in previous chapters. In *dot.hack* repetition is integral to the logic of the game and its world. Three different versions of the PS2 game (there are four in total) were released in the same year and there are no fundamental differences between any of the four games. Each contains hundreds of spheres with just a few minor structural variations among the dungeons. The appearance of enemies varies somewhat, but in its basic architecture the game does not change. Playing the game is itself deeply repetitious. We port between spheres, we fight enemies and we make our way through dungeons. Even fights with enemies take on a circular, repetitive character. Kite's strengths lie mainly in the area of casting spells that keep stronger allies alive, which means that the best strategy in difficult levels is nearly always to run around the perimeter of a dungeon avoiding harm and charging up our friends when they need it. It can take fifteen minutes of this kind of activity to overcome a powerful adversary.[6]

Ndalianis goes further than Jenkins in helping us to understand how such repetitious and essentially empty actions can form part of an active reading process. For her, the navigation of neo-baroque labyrinths requires repetition and virtuosity. At its heart is an experience of assembling meaning that she clarifies by contrasting its syntagmatic and paradigmatic levels. In the first, sequential elements of story are present – as when we receive an e-mail or watch a cut scene in *The World*, or when we watch part of an episode of *Lost* – but, 'players are also encouraged to participate with the work on the paradigmatic level via multilayered intertextual references' (Ndalianis 2004: 73). Through this process, audiences, or players, recover from their

initial disorientation and construct order for themselves out of
the neo-baroque's 'complex and expanding spaces' (2004: 69).
In *dot.hack* syntagmatic reading and virtuoso play converge in
the massive array of menus and choices that have to be made as
you progress through the world. As it becomes clear that using
data drain too much can result in 'game over' you are forced
to learn the role of an experienced MMPGer in *The World*,
which involves understanding the elemental properties of different enemies and relating these to your choice of weapon
and defence arrays. It extends to tactical decisions in the heat
of battle and even affects which 'friends' you take with you
on which mission. The process of consulting menus and, for
many players, on-line guides, takes us deep into the complex
architecture of the game. Hours of doing this, however, bring
us to the realization that we are enjoying it as a game – we
forget that it is a game within a game. The other vantage point,
of a fictional character who is trying to save the world, feels
very remote from the activity of simply playing. Nonetheless,
the motivation to play in *The World*, which is repetitious and
time-consuming, is derived from the primary fictional role. It
starts as a childish desire to play a game, becomes a mission to
save a friend and then changes into a vague desire the save the
world. This sequence is as vertiginous with regard to meaning
as the endless spiralling around in dungeons is closed off and
empty. What gets missed out in Ndalianis's 'reading' metaphor,
however, is a sense of the way the struggle to bring paradigmatic and syntagmatic elements together feels. The tensions
between them situate the video game within a baroque modality of signification and are at the same time an experience of
form. The signing processes involved here are contingent on
and secondary to the game's formal procedures, which create
and sustain a sense of distance, a delineation of space between
the two poles of meaning.

According to Ndalianis, there is scope for great virtuosity
in the way that syntagm and paradigm are integrated.[7] Neo-
baroque works are gratuitously complex and often this is about
showing off the technical skills of their creators, but they also
invite virtuosity from their audiences:

Computer games introduce a new dimension to the neo-baroque principle of virtuosity. The player's interaction and more active involvement with the game space suggests a role of creation. The unraveling of the maze of the computer game can, in a sense, exist only when the player plays it ... players produce their own distinctive form of gameplay. Because of the complex programming, no game can be played the same way twice. (Ndalianis 2004: 106)

In the labyrinthicity, virtuosity and repetitious nature of their performance, video games like *dot.hack* are powerful illustrations of the neo-baroque hypothesis. However, largely lacking from Ndalianis's account is a sense of the limitations set on meaning by this reading process, and this is central to our concerns here. Emphasizing the virtuosity of play and the importance of an essentially subjective meaning making process leads Ndalianis to overlook the antagonisms at the heart of the baroque object, which inhibit its capacity to communicate. Neo-baroque worlds are assembled from multiple sources, each of which involves a series of laborious processes in which we chip fragments of meaning away from a larger source that remains enigmatic and distant. Within each of these artefacts there is a swirling vortex that carries us into meaningless repetition and this stands off against a slide into a complete excess of meaning; meaning on a scale that cannot be processed.[8] The play of these artefacts involves us surfing the resulting wave. The central conceit of *dot.hack*, which is the split and intertwining of fictional levels, and the way it is played are particularly illustrative in this respect. Playing *dot.hack* involves assuming a fictional role as a teenager in modern Japan. To be that character, of course, is to want to play in *The World* – what could be more important to them? – yet playing in *The World* immediately diminishes the significance of the primary fiction. Moreover, doing it effectively means you have to be prepared to use data drain, which ultimately destroys *The World*. This tendency of the secondary fiction to corrode the purchase of the primary one, while remaining completely dependent on it, is an allegory for video game fiction in general.

Form and fictional content

If the neo-baroque context shapes the form of contemporary games, this also has consequences for the kind of metaphors we tend to find in them. Commonly, video game fictions are fantastic; they make reference to magical powers, mythical creatures, gargantuan battles and often depict extreme violence, sometimes using quite gruesome, albeit cartoon, graphical imagery. The salience of these themes is commonly attributed to the upbringing of game designers, their education in games like 'dungeons and dragons' and, of course, their masculine preoccupation with violence. There is doubtless something to this but it tends to overlook similarities at the level of content with the first baroque, which also exhibited a concern with magic, the fantastic and a playful culture of death and spectral apparitions at a time when, presumably, much of the cultural baggage of today's game designers was not formed. Common to both is an excess of pattern over meaningful content. Computer technology lends itself to creating patterns, but this does not explain the preponderance of form in contemporary culture. Rather, the relation of video games to particular kinds of content is shaped by cultural forces that are reconfiguring games, stories and technology. There is more than a hint of technical determinism in much discussion of video games, for example, Jesper Juul (2006) states several times that the increased emphasis on fiction in video games is a function of the computer's growing technical capacity for visual storytelling and Dovey and Kennedy (2006) make similar remarks. However, the decision to use computers, in particular video games, to tell stories is something that requires a social and cultural explanation, perhaps especially when most of the stories are so strange.

Games always have some relation to meaning. The role of metaphor in chess is paradigmatic here in that in the design of the pieces and their names we get the idea of two royal households confronting one another in a battle. As we saw in Chapter 2, this meaning is both useful to leverage an attitude (of competition), especially in novice players, yet very distant from the core activity of playing the game and nugatory in its effects on it. Such a minimal layer of meaning glosses many formal and technical activities engaged in by human beings (Feenberg 2002). In the contemporary cultural context this layer seems to be increasingly called upon to lend its energies to structured play. Consequently, we find new non-computerized games have some of the formal qualities Juul (2006) associates with progression and even some older board games have been reconfigured this way too. The salient feature of these games is less an enhanced role for meaning-making as a dimension of gameplay than a disposition towards a specific kind of play with fictionality. The configuration of contemporary games involves an opening to fiction, but one that is routinely blocked off in the course of play. The result is a sense of meaning that suffuses the scene of play, with little or nothing in the way of plotline or narrative actually informing the play process. An example of a relatively new game that illustrates this is the card game *Magic: The Gathering* (*M:TG*) (Wizards of the Coast/ Hasbro 1993).

M:TG was invented by game designer Richard Garfield in 1993.[9] It achieved cult status in the US and became a multi-million dollar industry, based on sales of cards and game-related paraphernalia.[10] There are approximately 10,000 *M:TG* cards in circulation, although it is difficult to be precise since new cards are added so frequently and older cards are withdrawn, or 'banned' by the games regulatory agency, the Duelists' Convocation International. *M:TG* cards contain vivid artwork featuring characters and items drawn from stories set in the fictional world that is the *M:TG* 'multiverse'. These stories are elaborated in over 20 *M:TG* novels, which amount to a vast epic involving enormous expanses of diegetic time, including at least one period of post-apocalyptic millennia during which nothing much happens. To play *M:TG* you need to construct a deck of the cards, or a 'library', that you think will enable you to play successfully against (or with) other players similarly equipped. The game has a distinctive core mechanic involving two kinds of card, 'land' cards, whose function is to generate 'mana',[11] and spell cards that contain statements bearing consequences and setting new conditions for the game state. Land cards are 'tapped', signified by being turned on their side, to 'pay' for spells. Spells include magical creatures, 'instants' that have a one-off impact on the game state and 'sorceries'. Creature spells and sorceries reconfigure the game environment, tipping the advantage this way and that. When they enter play they instantiate rules and conditions that can be combined by players into attacks, strategic combinations, defensive maneouvres and winning strategies. One way of winning the game[12] is to take points from your opponent by using spells to break through their defences and strike their 'life total' (each player starts the game with 20 life total points).

Spells are interrelated in ways that cannot be anticipated by game designers or players. As more cards enter play in any given game the situation becomes increasingly complex because cards have effects that modify values and effects of other cards and their relations to each other. There are cards that contain special 'win' conditions, for example *Battle of Wits* contains the text: 'At the beginning of your upkeep you win if you have more than 200 cards in your library'. Clearly, someone with a larger than average deck (most players choose to have decks of around 60 cards) would have reason to include this card, simply on the basis that it improves their chances of instantaneous victory. At the same time, however, many 'instant' cards, which can be played during other players' turns, give players the power to counteract spells. So *Battle of Wits* might be countered by the instant card *Counter Spell*, which, in common with several other instants, has the effect of sending spell cards to their owners' graveyard, a pile of used cards that sits adjacent to the library. Significantly, there are many conditions in the game under which it is possible to retrieve cards from the graveyard and far from signifying an exit from play, the graveyard is linked to the active parts of play by an evolving set of rules and conditions specific to any given game. Similarly, other cards in play, in particular 'sorcery' cards, stipulate additional, contingent rules that modify the entire game environment. For example, *Layline of Singularity* makes all non-land spells 'legendary', meaning that only one copy of them may be in play at a time. A player whose deck relies heavily on getting multiple copies of a single creature spell into play will need to counter this, perhaps by playing *Mirror Gallery*, which cancels out the legend rule. This, though, will have further effects, allowing opponents to play more than one copy of their legendary creatures. Clearly it is important to check the range of effects in place before adding new spells to the mix, because you may inadvertently harm your own life total, or gift a powerful spell or effect to one of your opponents. This, however, is difficult to predict and with each turn, the complexity of the situation can increase as the stipulations on one card interact with the strictures on another and the fields of force generated by their combination.

M:TG cards have a common structure that allows players to scrutinize them and make preliminary judgements as to their calibre. Some experienced players pride themselves on being able to spot a good card quickly, but there is normally debate between players as to the merits of any given card. Novice players frequently give themselves away by mistaking a card with high attack power for a 'good' card, when this can actually be of little significance to how the card will perform in play. The *M:TG* card is a signifier in this sense – it tells players what it can do – but it contains information relevant to multiple levels of gameplay and these can be in tension with one another, so that seeming strengths can be undermined by weaknesses that emerge in the course of gameplay and vice versa. Players interpret data pertaining to each of these levels and relate this information to their knowledge of other cards and to their intuitions about how the card will actually function in game situations. They think about how the properties of a card might be set to work in conjunction with those of others with which they are familiar. Playing the game is centred on the creation of a complex filigree of rules – a labyrinth – and involves no deep engagement with the *M:TG* fictional multiverse. However, the labyrinthine rule set that is generated in the course of a game of *M:TG is* consistent with Juul's (2006) idea of progression. The most striking characteristic of *M:TG* as a game is its emphasis on the reflexive modification of the rules in play at any given time, which means that we regularly move not between moments in a single emergent structure but from one complete rule set *plus emergent properties* to the next.

Changing the rules of a game as part of playing it or, more accurately, generating new constraining rules out of an initial set is a part of many games and can concern the creation of exceptional states associated with specific events. A foul in football, for example, invokes a whole new set of restrictions on play that punctuate the initial set-up and its flow of emergent properties or states. What defines progression, for Juul, is the ongoing periodic shift between totalities of rule-determined states within a given game. As we saw in Chapter 2, this is what supposedly necessitates a narrative dimension, which surfaces as a way of holding the game together as a unified entity. Even free kicks in football do not modify the underlying rules – the ball remains spherical and the objectives remain the same. In video games these features can be changed, as when players of *Half Life* (Valve 1998) discover that their enemies are not who they thought they were, or when you move from exploration to mission mode in *Grand Theft Auto*. However, with *M:TG* nearly every move we make – each spell we cast – reconfigures the rule set and imposes a different meaning on each of the card-signifiers in play at that point. Even the core dynamics of the game, the order in which we do things to play – is often altered in the course of a game. What Juul calls the 'setting up phase', which should establish a basis that remains constant throughout gameplay, is itself subject to revision and reversal by spells that reconfigure the very logic of gameplay.[13] A goal of play is to establish networks of rules that allow us to do things, often without direct implications for our opponent (creating combos that allow us to generate large amounts of mana, for example). The reflexive modification of its rules, often for reasons that seem to be purely aesthetic – there are beautiful patterns to be made in this game – is what the game is about. Consequently, playing to win is only one way to approach *M: TG*. Others play for the fascination of seeing what effects cards will produce, or simply to enjoy the patterns that emerge and re-emerge from the shifting rule structure.[14] Here we see progression but with no correspondingly enhanced role for linear fictional narrative mediating player actions. As the discussion here has highlighted, this unusual game has evolved alongside a massive fictional edifice and it is plausible to suggest that the game would not have the appeal that it does in the absence of some sense among players that this complex sprawling 'multiverse' is there. There is a kind of affective relation between the in-game properties of the creatures depicted on cards and the way that they are described in the novels. The following account from a *M:TG* novel illustrates how some of the convoluted dynamics of play described above make their way into the related fiction:

> At the rear of the Thran lines, elves unleashed spells. Desert scrub brush grew rampantly, miring sand crabs and minotaurs alike. Artifact engines rusted away to dust, but so too did Dwarven axes. Summoned creatures appeared – ferocious bears, giant spiders, timber wolves – but none were a match for these sand crabs; none were meant for desert battle. Only the scuttling avenger folk in their filthy multitude made any headway. They and their specialized hex-irons and crowbars could strip an artifact in a gasp. Of course, with sand crabs, those who stripped the machine were also stripped by it. For every sand crab disabled, scores of scavengers died. (King 1999: 8)

The different attacking properties of elves and other creatures here resonate with the properties of cards bearing creatures of that type in the game and the way that their offensive properties combine to produce an environment, in the way just described, is also dramatized here into a fictional narrative. In a way the fiction rationalizes the convoluted and mind-boggling practices of play, but it does so at a distinctive distance. No one thinks or talks about this kind of scenario while they are actually playing the game.[15]

Death and allegory

One implication of this is the inherent inapplicability of traditional ideas about character to entities encountered and played with in video games. Character traits are fictional but as played an avatar is only a set of functions, opportunities and constraints. More immediately perceptible attributes like the way that they look, or the sound of their voice are short-lived in their relevance for the gamer. The player experiences the character they control as a set of causal propensities (things it can do and that can be done to it) and limitations, not as a separate third party for interpretation or an extension of themselves in any meaningful, or emotionally significant sense. Character in games can never be more than comic, on Bergson's understanding (as discussed in Chapter 3) and this reflects the fact that in them the uniformity of the machine and the expressiveness of the human individual are pressed up against each other.[16] It also explains why Juul is correct to preclude the emergence of particular genres in video game fictions. Tragedy, he says, would be especially difficult because 'tragedies are about events beyond our control that are then transformed into something more meaningful through the tragedy, but games are mostly about having power and overcoming challenges' (Juul 2006: 161). Overcoming the challenges is normally about survival and escaping death and this difference from tragedy is a clue to how signification really works in video games.

In his study of the German baroque 'mourning plays', Walter Benjamin (1985) shows that in these works meaning only ever appears in order to appear – it flashes but then degrades and vanishes. The only mode of signification or meaningfulness that applies to these plays is allegory. His observations apply well to video games and explain the 'strange legibility' (Jameson 1975: 72) that video games possess for us; the unity they possess that fits no established cultural template. The mourning plays, in common with much baroque culture, have proven difficult to classify historically; they lack the formal finesse of great plays of the tragic era. George Steiner, in his introduction to the English translation of Benjamin's study, describes them as 'esoterica' and emphasizes the extent to which they exist in a historical world apart from traditional stories. Like video games we struggle to see the intention of an authorial genius in them,[17] perhaps because they were assembled in accordance with manuals which described how to put together a solid Aristotelean drama (Benjamin 1985:

58). Benjamin observes that 'their form was not shaped by any sovereign spirit' (cited by Weber 1991: 475). Video games are also now designed by teams working from manuals and under the strict constraints set by the capitalist marketplace (Kerr 2006: 87–9; Shields 2003: 114; Atkins 2003: 62).[18] The expressive potential of both is limited in ways that extend to characterization: in the mourning plays stereotypes predominate, for example, all kings are tyrants or martyrs, with nothing in between (Benjamin 1985: 68).

The mourning plays are consistent with Maravall's (1986) general characterization of the baroque as shallow and manipulative. This led scholars before Benjamin to view the plays reductively, as if their significance was exhausted by their social function and, as just implied, this is, in a sense encouraged by the plays themselves which are self-consciously structured just as dramas 'should' be, in accordance with Aristotelean dramatic principles – an instance of the point made above about the baroque as recycling classical techniques in degraded form. As we have seen, according to some scholars video games can also be read quite straightforwardly as 'social texts' with scant attention to their formal aesthetic properties. Benjamin's study, however, queries this approach, not with the aim of making claims for the aesthetic virtues of the mourning plays but rather because without attention to these properties, which unite them, we view them simply as part of a baroque culture of diversion (Saisselin 1992) and this reductionism does not explain properly why people watched them. Benjamin emphasizes that despite the seemingly inferior quality of the mourning plays as plays, the experience of form may still be stronger in them than in better dramas and that this aesthetic aspect, which he links to space and movement, demands independent analysis (Benjamin 1985: 47–58). He goes on to link this explicitly to ballet and says the plays take place in 'a spatial continuum which one might describe as choreographic' (1985: 95). The similarities between these properties and those of video games are striking, but not surprising. As already mentioned, the baroque was a gaming culture. The plays all depict courtly scenes in which a plotter initiates a conspiracy, just as Aarseth

(1997) describes video gameplayers as victims of an 'intrigue'. The strongest similarities, however, concern the centrality and treatment of death in the plays and the importance of allegory to understanding how meaning works in them.

Those who write about video games as if they were primarily meaningful texts rarely discuss the salience of death in them. This is strange because it is in the way that they use death as a mechanism that we find the most important clue about how meaning works in video games. In traditional games a player's failure might have resulted in being told to 'miss a turn' or 'go back to Start'. These options were and are available to the video game designer too; nothing in the formal concept of progression, for example, necessitates this use of metaphoric death to punctuate the rhythms of play. Death is the point of contact between form/rhythm and meaning in video games. It can be rationalized in terms of the fictional content of games, which often concern violent struggle, but the suggestion here is that the movement is actually the other way around: the salience of the death metaphor drives the development of the kinds of fiction that we associate with neo baroque excess.

In tragedy proper the death of the hero is central. They embody a virtue that pitches them against destiny or fate and in showing their demise, the play offers an idea of transcendence. In overcoming inevitability they are destroyed but we, the audience, are given a vision of the human as elevated, higher than mere things and capable of moving beyond the reach of causality. As Jesper Juul notes in the citation in Chapter 2, tragedy is beyond the reach of video games and it is the hallmark of the mourning plays that they too do not attain that status, indeed their failure to do so is the reason they have been viewed as inferior to both classical and modern dramas. At the same time, the mourning plays are centrally concerned with death. Their heroes die but it is not the life-defining event of tragedy, partly because the characters themselves are not drawn with sufficient depth. The individual hero is not sufficiently differentiated from the order of things – nature and objects – to determine a transcendent function. Peter Fenves clarifies the nature of individuality proper and its relation to naming, with reference to infinity:

> from the beginning finitude enters into the infinitude of language under the insignia of the proper name. It is the 'point' at which the infinitude of language fleetingly touches on the finite. (Fenves 2001: 217)

Each person has a name that differentiates them from others but in themselves proper names do not make this distinction sufficiently well. Possession of a proper name actually signifies our potential membership of an infinite number of predicate-bearing classes, or sets. Hence, our proper names single us out as an individual but this operation only works because of the infinite one that can never be performed. A Google search reveals other people with the same name as you but no list will succeed in enumerating the properties any one of those individuals might have, which actually specifies them as just this particular one. Recognizing the uniqueness of any individual turns on having this glimpse of the awkward to grasp, impossible infinite which conditions their finite singularity.[19] The greatness of tragedy lies in bridging this gap through the power of poetry, or the poetic image.

With characters in video games and mourning plays alike, no such individuality is presented. The poeticizing of the relation of eternal or infinite values that enables the individual to determine a transcendence of their circumstances is lacking and consequently, while death defines the tragic hero by arresting infinity with finitude and making his name the sign of something greater (think of the significance that attaches to the name of Hamlet), the death of a video game avatar lacks this significance – 'Kite' could be anyone; it is just a name. What Benjamin writes of the hero in mourning plays applies directly to video game characters:

> If the tragic hero in his 'immortality' saves not his life but only his name, the characters in the mourning play lose, with death, only their named individuality but not the vital force of their role. Undiminished, they revive in the world of ghosts. (Benjamin cited in Weber 1991: 488)

The death of the tragic hero is always a verdict in the sense that it rehearses the meaning of their singular existence, but death for video game characters is never fixed; it is a judgment delivered or as Samuel Weber expresses it in his study of Benjamin, 'death is no longer the line that separates finite being from itself' (Weber 1991: 491; Benjamin 1985: 66). Just as in video games, characters in mourning plays reappear and repeat their actions. This does not mean that the death is meaningless, only that the hero's life was meaningless. The enigmatic character of their death becomes the most eloquent part of the drama. Death reduces the character to the level of another object and is itself now contained within nature, where it transforms all of life into something spectral, infusing it with the strange mixture of superficial lightness and remote profundity that underlies much talk of 'the virtual':

> death now leads nowhere, and least of all toward any sort of (transcendental) beyond. Death remains, as it were, enclosed in the field of immanence ...
>
> Instead of defining identity, death returns as the shadow that splits life into a life that consists largely in passing away, and a death that has nowhere to go but back to the living. (Weber 1991: 494)

In video games the signification of the name is never more than a finite set of characteristics that have been defined as functions within a technical system. The only individuality that can ever attach to the name is an accumulation of items from the game world and a history of accomplishments drawn from a pre-determined, finite menu of possibilities. The name of the avatar never signifies more than this and the only true vitality that it possesses comes from its player. In the course of playing *dot.hack*, our name dies repeatedly. The consequences vary depending on where our character is at the time. Perhaps the commonest occurrence is also the most annoying: having struggled our way through a difficult dungeon we find that we are low on spells, weakened and confronted by a particularly powerful 'boss'. Death here has the consequence of throwing us out of the game – we see 'Game Over' in red letters on the screen and since there are no 'save' points inside dungeons we will have to repeat everything we have done and may have lost a variety of items and improvements to our skill level. We know that for Orca the consequence of such death seems to have been that he has entered a coma, in the fictional real world, and this is vaguely worrisome if we have been playing for a long time, especially in later parts of the game where the world fizzes and cracks and seems as if it is breaking.[20] Nevertheless, the striking thing about 'death' here is its containment within the fiction, its failure to touch the real capacities of our character. Even in video games where death deprives us of all our acquired assets it never means that our character is no longer available to start again or loses the functional capabilities it had at the start of play.

This use of death in video games is the key to the kind of meaning that they can offer, that is present in them. This is allegory and its importance is that it separates signs from referents and deploys them in, usually repetitious, sequences where they form part of a 'masquerade or spectacle' (Weber 1991: 497) and take on altered significance. On one side, they are mere machine, automated emblems in a world bereft of signification but on the other they hover over a vertiginous excess of potential meaning. The move discussed above, whereby superficial fictions work by evoking unsolvable mysteries is the defining motif of allegory, its core mechanism:

> In allegory, things are cut off from what they seem to represent, or rather, they signify precisely the non-being of what they represent. Whatever is presented allegorically has no being apart from its being represented. (Weber 1991: 491)

According to Benjamin, the allegorical container and its internal dislocations arise in response to the absence of nature. The salience of allegory in seventeenth-century cultural production can be understood in terms of the changes to representation discussed in Chapter 4. As language ceases to be just another layer of representation in a thoroughly meaningful world (Foucault 1994), so nature stops being something that language can mimic – resemblance recedes to a point beyond the horizon of coherent language use. The result is a crisis of meaning-making and a retreat into the kind of encapsulated performance we associate with the baroque. Complexity and gratuitous demonstration of technique seem to stand in for any attempt to communicate and thematic content shrinks to the kind of strange, morbid contrivance that Benjamin finds in the mourning plays. For this reason, Benjamin contrasts allegory with aura, which, as seen in Chapter 3, is a property of the artwork proper. In aura 'a mysterious wholeness of objects becomes possible' (Jameson 1975: 77), but in allegory such wholeness is unattainable, only its intention remains.

Play and mourning

As it stands, though, this argument leaves video games as bad stories, open to interpretation and inherently ambiguous. This is not really how we encounter them and the reason for this is that the concept 'game' mediates our relationship with them;[21] they are things we expect to play. At the same time, the person who insists that is all they are is an extremist; we know that video games are popular entertainment media, that they must be meaningful fictions. No straightforward grasp of the second point is possible, however. Either way, it is as if we needed to 'go wrong' in order to get it right about video games. The ludic here can be viewed as an instance of the infinite that, according to Peter Fenves' (2001) reading of Benjamin, can only be (unsuccessfully) grasped from what he calls an awkward perspective. The sense in which video games are games is originary, it is the dimension of video games that cannot be experienced except as 'a movement of restoration' (Weber 1991: 472). The sense of an infinite or eternal force that cannot be apprehended directly yet is essential to clearly identifying experiential singularities – singularities it also cancels out or prevents from becoming clear – is how Walter Benjamin understood the failed operation of meaning (its vanishing character) in baroque drama.

This is the key to repetition and its function in video games. Repetition is a defining feature of the video game which, as we have seen, constantly eats away at their capacity to tell meaningful, self-consistent stories that live in the minds of players. The many deaths of the form impose countless repetitions of sequences of action whose meaning is consequently vitiated. Such repetition is the attempt, described above, to reconnect the spatial emblems of the game to the abyss of profundity. It is our attempt to arrest our fall, to infuse meaning to what we are doing now and in so far as it succeeds, repetition fails: if we find ourselves thinking we *are* Kite in a dungeon, we will lose the fight. All we can do is repeat our actions to ward off this moment and, according to Benjamin, the underlying meaning of such action is a kind of attempted remembering characteristic of mourning (Benjamin 1985: 137–9). The reason so many critics target the 'joyless pleasure' of video gaming is that the underlying sentiment of such repetitious action is connected to a kind of melancholy that animates baroque and neo-baroque alike. This dance is not one whose content can be apprehended or comprehended cognitively; it is the rhythmic eruption of a half-remembered origin or a repeated attempt to find the idea that gives, or should give, order to our experience and meaning to the world. The person who is mourning rehearses events in the world of memory, trying to get from them something that will give sense to the world they are currently in, by reliving imaginatively events that perhaps had little significance at the time but are now, in connection with the void that looms large, evocative of meaning. This is why Jameson writes that the baroque is a mood rather than a meaning and that,

> allegory is precisely the dominant mode of expression of a world in which things have been for whatever reason utterly sundered from meanings, from spirit, from genuine human existence. (Jameson 1975: 71)

Players are often drawn to games by their ostensible stories but if they want to play them they have to switch their attention and focus on the rules. In deciding to play a game this is a decision they have already made. Consequently, players can disregard elements of the projected fictional world that would constitute unacceptable inconsistency in other contexts, elements that would make them 'poor' as fictions. Players negotiate games as functioning plastic objects with programmed properties that regulate what can and cannot be done with them. Discovering new properties and adapting them to different situations within the game is integral to emergence in video games (just like learning new moves in chess). To achieve this we have to break with the fiction to explore and examine the game as an object. The fiction never disappears altogether, but it is worn very thin especially by the repetition of these processes. The structure here mirrors the one encountered in *Lost*. As *Lost* is a story that cancels out its meaning so that gameness obtrudes in it, so video games are games that rely on fiction yet constantly corrode it so that only awkward fragments remain.

The appeal of games resides in the complex implication of play with rule structures (an activity that is meaningless in itself) with the shards of projected fictional meaning that we find on the game interface. Patterns in this relationship, associated with bodily activity, account for its pleasurable character, which cannot be dissociated from its frustrations, especially the moments when we find our progress is blocked by a sequence of events that always seems to result in death. Following this kind of event are the inevitable long periods of repetition, when we master a sequence of moves essential to evade that boulder or kill that monster. During these it makes little sense to postulate anything other than a constantly receding role for fictional meaning. This is not a matter of the game giving us a choice between fictional or gameplay modes – that is too static a way of describing what is happening. Rather, the game projects an interesting appearance and then requires us to play against it. Our task as players is to pursue the difference between the illusory fiction and the game as rule-bound object, often until the first is almost forgotten altogether.

In repetition the mourner calls on memory in an attempt to resurrect what has been lost. This is impossible but it transforms the present nonetheless, not with the actuality of the past but with its appearing to appear. The mourner cannot live in the present because all his efforts are directed to reviving the past and this activity alters and shapes his and our experience of the present making it more and less real. This mourning is a kind of refusal of death's ability to separate us from ourselves and its consequence is that the past haunts the present. This is why baroque dramas are full of ghosts and spectres; why cards in *M:TG* can come back from the graveyard; why John Locke can be resurrected in *Lost* and why the many deaths of the video game never result in actual deletion of our killed character from the game world.

What is it that video games mourn? In *dot.hack* we discover that the source of the difficulties in the world centres on an action of its creator, a programmer called Harald. When he made the game he found a way of transporting the soul or essence of his dead daughter, Anna, into the game. This was a way to bring her back to life in perpetuity. But the fundamental transgression involved created an instability that ultimately jeopardizes not just *The World* but all the real world's computer systems. There is a kind of pathos when we encounter Anna as a spectral figure all in white. In saving *The World*, and the world, we have to destroy this, its essence, and so she 'dies'. Her death remains enigmatic, since the game contains, after the final credits, a long series of additional dungeons with the promise that she has in some sense migrated there and can still be found, although her presence is no longer the threat that it once was. This story is an allegory for the mourning of video games, which is surely centred on the changing position of childhood as a time of innocence in contemporary culture. This is not about the passing of childhood, often bemoaned by cultural conservatives, but concerns the distinction between childhood and adulthood. Video games are still marketed ostensibly at children and teenagers but they contain adult themes and the average age of gamers is rising all the time. As Adorno pointed out, one function of the artwork was to turn us back to play, to make us see the childishness in our desire to 'grow up'. Obviously, only an adult can appreciate this message and the play of the artwork is a play with this paradox:

> Art brings to light what is infantile in the ideal of being grown up. Immaturity via maturity is the prototype of play. (Adorno 2002: 48)

Now this play occurs in the video game but its message is blunted. If the artwork was a call to our humanity and a prompt to greater maturity and autonomy, the video game mocks our inability to achieve these things and invites us to rehearse the childish in a defence against the taunts of an unattainable adulthood. In the seriousness of play we mourn our inability to advance from infantilized consumers to free citizens. This brings us to the question of where video games, understood as aesthetic objects, stand in relation to contemporary cultural politics.

Notes

1 In the UK the first series of *Lost* was broadcast on Channel 4 in 2004 and was accompanied by a 'point and click' game on the TV company website. This game has since been followed by more than one *Lost* board game (Hasbro 2004) and video games in PS3, XBox 360, and PC formats (UbiSoft 2008).

2 Other stories on these boards are ostensibly trivial but have similar themes to the one being described here. For example, there are humorous reports of a genetically modified apple that tastes like a potato, which end in the disappearance of the scientist responsible and his enigmatic note, which reads like a code for opening a new portal in *The World*, although it does not actually work. Similarly, there are reports of big-foot sightings in Oregon but these become a story about scientific cover-ups and deception.

3 Her text is ambivalent towards post-modernism; at times it seems that the neo-baroque is what post-modernists were trying to say, at others it is a rival hypothesis.

4 Actual mazes were a feature of the baroque garden popular with the aristocracy of this time (Saisselin 1992).

5 It only rarely attains the anxiety levels achieved by players of 'Majestic'. This was a real on-line game involving mobile phones and 'real world' websites that trod the boundary between game and reality in the months prior to the terrorist attacks on New York in 2001. The game was withdrawn early in 2002 (see Kolko and Taylor 2003).

6 This kind of circular pattern in play, which involves running around the periphery of a dungeon or battleground can be quite

hypnotic and is common in video games. Many *Zelda* boss battles, for example, also have this formal characteristic.

7 This also illustrates the limitations of the reading metaphor – reading is not a practice susceptible to virtuoso performance.

8 I have in mind the many apocalyptic visions we find in games and other popular media, including the end of the world, total system collapse, global pandemics and planetary conquests.

9 His company, Wizards of the Coast Inc. became a subsidiary of the games giant Hasbro in 1999 and Garfield now works for that company as a designer. For Garfield on designing games, see the short piece in Fullerton (2008).

10 There is surprisingly little of this. It extends to storage boxes for cards and 'life counters' that are optional for play, but does not include branded items unrelated to gaming like T-shirts.

11 Land cards come in five different colours which correspond to and are referred to in terms of aspects of the natural environment, so white mana is represented by 'plains'; blue by 'islands'; black by 'swamps'; red by 'mountains', and green by 'forests'. Images of these kinds of natural setting in the Magic multiverse, form the artwork for these cards, which lack the individuality of *M:TG* spell cards.

12 The game is constantly evolving and new 'win conditions' are one of its emergent properties. According to one authoritative count there are currently 28 ways to win the game.

13 If *M:TG* was chess we would find that the rules of movement for specific pieces could be altered by our opponent's and our own moves.

14 This has led to an interesting player typology that has been developed and published on the *M:TG* website. It characterizes players in terms of their gaming strategies but the resulting classification ranges more widely than this. Hence, while 'Spikes' play to win and build their decks accordingly, 'Timmys' are more likely to choose cards that appeal aesthetically, while 'Johnnys' are drawn to those with interesting effects. 'Vorthos' are more attendant to other media dimensions of *M:TG* – they enjoy the artwork, collect the cards and appreciate the fictional universe of *M:TG* more than they enjoy playing the game (Rosewater 2006).

15 The enhanced role of labyrinth and progression, again without any marked increased in fictional role playing touching on the processes of gameplay can also be seen in new versions of established games, such as *Cluedo: Reinvention* (Hasbro 2008).

Traditionally this game had a simple 'beggar your neighbour mechanic': the information relevant to solving the murder mystery was distributed about the board (the rope, revolver etc. were placed in different rooms) and in the players' hands (the cards were dealt at the beginning). Players of the new edition of the game have to construct the information basis for their enquiries in the course of the game. The board, for example, comes in pieces that have to be added as players explore the house, while cards have to be obtained by exploration and by gathering 'event' cards. In the new configuration progression displaces emergence, but there is no enhanced sense of being a fictional sleuth. Similar mechanics are common in new games, such as *Mid Evil* (Twilight Creations 2005), which also features graveyards and characters rising from the dead.

16 There is an analogy here with playing a musical instrument: Many comedians have made careers out of deliberately playing badly.

17 Frederic Jameson writes that what we find in them is the procedural expression of a 'disembodied intention in search of an object' (Jameson 1975: 60).

18 Shields includes this in an implausible list of 'barriers' to treating video games as seriously as other cultural phenomena, like films and pop music.

19 Interestingly, dot.hack contains an allegory for this in the form of the 'infinite diversity theorem'. This theorem is the discovery of the creator of *The World* and it is supposed to quantify over the efforts and intentions of individuals as these relate to the reach or extent of their outcomes. This algorithm underlies the programming of *The World* and partly explains how the game is able to reach beyond itself to have effects on the real world of the primary fiction. *Lost* also includes a sequence of numbers that are important in a number of the intersecting backstories that feature in the TV show, with one character having used them to win the lottery. Further investigation of the *Lost* universe reveals that there may be a connection with the 'Valenzetti equation', which lies behind many of the theories explored by the Hanso foundation and predicts the end of human civilization. In his study of the original baroque, Maravall points out that in seventeenth-century Europe growing awareness of the power of mathematics went hand in hand with an enhanced place for 'magic' symbols and a visual-spatial aesthetic that drew heavily on them. Pointing

out that 'all the very typical aspects of baroque culture relate to gaming' (1986: 192), especially cards, Maravall argues that baroque culture was centrally concerned with converting magic symbolism into a dense web of visual entertainments that would guide the population by involving people actively, rather than by traditional methods of issuing orders backed by static authorities (1986: 68).

20 We may feel this more intensely if we know about the Korean player who died while playing a game not unlike *The World* of dot.hack (Chee 2005).

21 Similarly, Ranciere writes of the importance of aesthetic education to mediating contemporary forms taken by images (2009: 27).

6

Political aesthetics

Art and politics are ... linked, beneath themselves, as forms of
presence of singular bodies in a specific space and time.

                                                    Jacques Ranciere

This chapter will try to situate the video game, now understood as a cultural object with distinctive aesthetic properties,
as a presence in contemporary cultural theory. The point of
doing this is to contribute to the development of a comparative
cultural criticism of video games and to ask what kind of video
game, if any, might be considered socially beneficial or progressive. It will examine some of the positive aspects of computer
gaming as a socio-technical practice, some of which have been
overlooked in recent theory. At the same time, however, the
chapter will reflect further on the limitations of the video game
as a cultural form and highlight some of the ways in which it
is symptomatic of a culture of mass powerlessness and cynicism. These negative traits are much more important than any
alleged association of video games with addiction or violence
(Funk *et al.* 1999; Dill and Dill 1998; Carnagey and Anderson
2004) and their solution, if there is one, can best be addressed
by a technical politics (Feenberg 1991, 2002) that operates
within the development of the medium itself. One point of the
chapter is to ask what kinds of goals might be appropriate for
such interventions.

Until recently cultural theory has tended to view all cultural objects as texts or component elements of discourses that
contribute to the production and reproduction of identities.
The process is often understood in terms of Louis Althusser's
(1984 [1970]) notion of 'interpellation'; a kind of hailing of the

human individual by a social structure. This hailing secures
the recognition of the subject and, in the same process, produces them as the kind of subject that responds to that call.
Understanding society and culture in these terms leads to a
strategic conception of discourse and social relations, according to which identities are produced, subverted and re-made
through cultural-political interventions that disrupt the workings of language as it sorts experience. This approach has
enabled theorists to understand TV shows, movies, novels,
even art installations on the basis of a certain literalisation
of their content, albeit one that takes into account the social
instabilities and conflicts essential to understanding them in
context. As already argued throughout the current work, video
games are not susceptible to being read in this way and even
reading them 'in context' does not help social or cultural theory
to grasp their significance. The meanings of individual video
games tend to be fairly obscure and uninteresting except in
their generic features, in particular the many deaths of gameplay. Their real sociological significance lies in the dynamics
of their corporeal appropriation by players and understanding
how this meshes with the cultural context is the key to understanding their meaning. As Raymond Williams (1961) pointed
out, a period in cultural history may be marked, even defined,
by a particular pattern affecting bodies in space, the feeling
of the world to the people of a given place and time. Calling
this the 'structure of feeling' of a period, Williams grasped the
delicacy, even fragility of the aesthetic dimension but also its
robustness as an explanatory dimension of social change.

Video games are integral to the contemporary structure of
feeling; they are an important example of how social relations
are becoming increasingly dance-like and animated by a distinctive set of rhythms. A recent and important attempt to
grasp these processes is to be found in the work of Ian Bogost,
who has pioneered the idea of a comparative critical framework
for the appraisal of video games that is attentive to the formal
aspects of their social and political implication. The first half
of this chapter will be given over to a critical assessment of
his work. On the basis of this engagement I am able to clarify

my own view on the political potentials of video games. The first section, therefore, describes the key elements of Bogost's approach, which centres particularly on the idea of 'unit operation', a concept that broadly corresponds to what can be described as the form of video games. The next section examines Bogost's attempt to articulate the notion of unit operation to meaning, which he has attempted through the concept of a rhetorics of persuasion. Some reasons are suggested for refusing this articulation and preserving the concept of unit operation as an original specification of the mechanics of form in contemporary media. This leads, in the third section, to an assessment of Bogost's use of the French philosopher Alain Badiou. Bogost's notion that unit operations are necessarily meaningful takes a very different route than post-structuralist and post-modernist thinking about representation and difference, passing instead through Badiou's notion of set theory as ontology. I argue that engagement with Badiou can be productive for computer game studies, not least because of the applicability of his ideas on dance to video games. Ultimately, however, video games present a problem for Badiou's system, namely, that the game is an eternal form which secures no recognition in his philosophy, even though he claims that such forms are the conditions that make philosophy possible. The fourth section draws on some of Badiou's ideas to suggest that the emergence of the video game as a cultural form constitutes a kind of cultural truth event, with ludologists as the subjects of that truth. This lends a slightly different sense to the idea that video games may have political implications and reflection on this point concludes both the chapter and the book.

Unit operations

Ian Bogost has developed a novel methodology with which to understand how meaning works in video games. He envisages his approach as a theoretical framework for comparative video game criticism and suggests that the range of such a framework may reach well beyond games into other areas of culture. This is because of the diffusion of what he calls 'unit operations'.

Unit operations are defined procedures that express meaning. We encounter them primarily when working with computer programs that have been made using object-oriented programming languages, like Java. What is characteristic about these languages as against older, linear ones is that they allow programmers to create discrete blocks of functionality that can be combined with others of their kind to build programmed systems. Each such program behaves like a discrete object when it is run, with its own rules and algorithms that control its interactions with human users and with other parts of the program. Programs written in this way can inherit features of other objects defined in the programming language as members of the same class as them. Each object created in java, for instance, is a member of such a wider class. It is possible to build programs that are tailored for specific commercial operations largely by importing and modifying existing objects. This kind of programming allows programmers access to a kind of evolving language of sophisticated machine responses, whose meanings as projected at the user interface may vary quite radically between contexts. For Bogost, part of the significance of object-oriented programming lies in the fact that programmers no longer start at the top – with a specification of what the program must do, which they then conceive and implement as a whole – but can instead work their way from the ground up, combining objects into a coherent usable program. This method of working has been formalized in textbooks on software design, which is now almost always an iterative process that involves consultation with program 'end users' throughout. The modern programmer, Bogost writes, is the 'bricoleur, the deft handyman who assembles units of pre-existing meaning to form new structures of meaning' (2006: 50). This is so much computer science, but Bogost's point is that the cultural salience of programmed objects requires us to rethink all other areas of cultural activity, including criticism itself, on the model of unit operations.

Unit operations are little blocks of programming that condition a human response. Each one is both a formal specification of an embodied action and a unit of expressive meaning. Unit

operations are encountered in video games all the time, as
rules that constrain and facilitate the constituent elements of
gameplay, like characters or manipulable objects. According to
Bogost, it is the patterned nature of our experience with these
rules that ensures they take on meaning. The precise significance invested in a given operation is a matter of subjective
interpretation:

> meaning emerges where authors or users create or recognise pat-
> terns ...
>
> Pattern creation or recognition systems ... usually take the
> form of unit operations that perform one kind of action on data,
> resulting in some judgement about its worthiness as a *particular*
> pattern. One person's signal is another's noise. (Bogost 2006:
> 29)

When a computer program gets run, or instantiated by a user
on her machine she has to respond by working with it and this
involves recognizing the pattern and adopting its procedure
as her own. Bogost's account of procedures tends to assume
meaning is essential to the way a program choreographs player
actions. Turning to video games, Bogost observes that, as we
saw in Chapter 1, many current game programs actually share
a common basis in coding terms, namely, the game engines
that control things like the environment, dynamic properties
of objects and their relationships, and so on. Unit operations
are 'in' game engines, like common tropes in literary genres.
However, while genres are conceptual and transcendental with
respect to specific story contents, unit operations are neither.
They have 'cores' that correspond to 'units of gameplay' and
these cut across such literary distinctions subverting their applicability to games. It follows that games which have the same
engines are connected in ways that exceed the scope of traditional media concepts. As Bogost writes:

> *Quake* and *Half Life* are different in some ways, but they share
> the same material basis: the same core code. The low-level rou-
> tines that render objects, manage collision, fire projectiles, and
> model physical interactions between characters and objects are
> fundamentally, explicitly identical. (Bogost 2006: 62)

In other words, while genre distinctions might seem to be imposed by obvious similarities between game imagery and that of movies, or easily interpreted storylines and those of novels, or whatever, the reality is quite different. Games with the same engines collapse literary notions like metaphor and analogy 'into encapsulated unit operations'. At the level of procedurality, or what people actually have to do with the games to perform their unit operations, video games are more like other video games with the same engines and the same programmed objects than they resemble other cultural objects, or indeed games with similar ostensible thematic content. The way that Bogost describes this, as a kind of collapse of the literary material within the work is compelling. It implies that seeming analogies, metaphors and so on in games are corroded from within by the logic of their appropriation and the constraints that this reading imposes on games as meaning communicators.

Notwithstanding this, Bogost insists that video games *are* representations and it is as such that they are critically interpreted by players and can take on meaning for them. For him, the mode of representation that is appropriate to video games is simulation. Bogost works with Gonzalo Frasca's (2003a) definition of simulation as a sign system that represents both a situation and a model of behaviour.[1] What distinguishes ludic simulations from conventional narratives is that the former require human agents to inhabit and work with them in order to describe or represent because, 'Unlike narratives simulations are not just made up of sequences of events, they also incorporate behavioural rules' (Frasca 2003a: 227). The outcome is an 'unusually first-hand' form of narration for the person who uses the simulation (Bogost 2006: 98). It is through incorporation by players that video game simulations take on meaning. The unit operations in the simulation are interpreted by players and embodied by them in their behaviour so that, 'instantiated code enters the material world via human players' faculty of reason' (2006: 99). This, 'the most important moment' in the videogame is where the player of the game enters what Bogost calls the 'simulation gap'. As we saw in

Chapter 2, working with a video game is not the same as using a perfect simulation – a copy of an unattainable, real original in the post-modern, Baudrillardian sense – rather, it involves the player in a contradiction. To play the game we respond to the seeming simulation by acting on it, which involves a tacit acknowledgement that the simulation is not a complete representation. At the same time, working with the simulation and implementing its unit operations is a kind of affirmation of the model and a denial of its intrinsic biases. According to Bogost, when we play a game we are in the grip of 'simulation fever'; we oscillate between accepting and rejecting the simulation, we refuse it and accept it at the same time. Moreover, this is the key to how the form works, since it presupposes this human reaction in its very design. Bogost describes the simulation gap as that between 'the rule-based representation of a source system and a user's subjectivity' (2006: 107).

Bogost's focus on the unit operational level of video games enables him to move towards a fuller understanding of the multi-dimensional embeddedness in culture that is characteristic of the video game. Games, he says, do not 'telegraph' their meanings in the way that natural languages or social customs do. Rather, they, 'create complex relations between the player, the work, and the world via unit operations that simultaneously embed material, functional and discursive modes of operation' (2006: 105). Video games mesh with our lives and our phenomenal engagement with the world on all these levels. In performing unit operations we participate in simulations that may resonate for us in all kinds of ways and this is the key to their meaningfulness for us. This is a rich and suggestive account of how video game form may interact with the rest of life in modern societies, but it is not balanced by any corresponding recognition of the inherent blunting of reference and diminution of semantic content that, it seems, must result from such a polyvalent and profoundly embodied mode of insertion into the web of social and communicative relations. Through the ideas of simulation gap and simulation fever Bogost grasps the essential role of the player's action in bringing simulations to life and positions the game in our physical, material and cultural existence. But he does not recognize any deficit, any price to be paid by the medium for the unique breadth of connecting points whereby it inserts itself into our experiential fabric, a breadth that is held together by the player's attachment to form. As we saw in Chapter 5, the price of such engagement is that the video game also suffers from expressive limitations – it is not that clear what they mean; they cannot mean that much.

Rhetoric and persuasion

As procedural expressions video games can be used to communicate political ideas. Bogost (2007) cites numerous fascinating examples of games, many of which he has himself made, that supposedly project political messages. To clarify how this works, Bogost articulates the notion of unit operation to rhetoric. Rhetoric is the art of using language to persuade, or of speaking in such a way as to win people round to your point of view. Such speech is not necessarily cogent and rational discourse. It answers to a different standard of truth, namely, that of beauty in an oration (see Skinner 1994). Bogost argues that video games are especially capable of projecting arguments that are compelling in this, highly particular sense. In order to achieve this interpretative position on games, he articulates his interesting and valuable idea of unit operation to the principles of the *ars rhetorica* – the classical art of rhetoric.[2]

Bogost's discussion begins from the standpoint of the game author. Writing a game, he says, is different from writing a book or a piece of music because while those kinds of production result in *artefacts* or things that represent processes, only the creator of unit operations, programmed segments that must be undergone and acted out by their users, creates 'processes that represent processes'. The difficulty he faces in developing this proposition is the one that we have encountered previously, namely, that the complex of action and undergoing that is characteristic of video gameplay bears little obvious or mimetic relation to any other spheres of human activity or endeavour. For this reason, attempts to interpret video games as communicative media that transmit meanings to players, or allow players to explore and express meanings through the games, have focused too much on what turn out to be relatively secondary features of the games, in particular their 'narrative content' as this is manifest in on-screen action or through textual components of the game interface. Bogost's (2006) approach, however, is several steps ahead of this game. Through the notion of 'unit operation' he has understood better than most the actual relation between physical actions of gameplayers and the programmed components that make up the game as a technical artefact. Moreover, his notion of simulation fever draws out very clearly the inherently problematic nature of games as representative simulations: the idea that players strive through their actions to close the 'simulation gap' is a close relative of the core thesis of the current work, that video games are games played with the problematic nature of meaning-making itself. However, Bogost's emphasis on rhetoric menaces the insights of the earlier work. Video game unit operations, he now maintains, constitute 'procedural rhetorics', which he defines as follows:

> Procedural rhetoric is a subdomain of procedural authorship; its arguments are made not through the construction of words or images, but through the authorship of rules of behaviour, the construction of dynamic models. In computation, these rules are authored in code, through the practice of programming. (Bogost 2007: 29)

Unit operations in video games are procedures that game designers and programmers make available to players. The player responds to these procedures as one responds to an argument, namely, by hearing it out and responding to it. A characteristic feature that links video games as procedural arguments to the tradition of classical rhetoric is the notion of the *enthymeme*.

The enthymeme is what is known as a 'rhetorical figure'; it is a distinctive form of a verbal argument. Commonly, an argument has the structure of a syllogism: major premise; minor premise and a conclusion that follows from their conjunction. An example, relevant to many video games might be: big guns are more powerful; that gun is bigger than the one I have now; therefore, that gun would be more powerful. What is characteristic of enthymeme is neglect of the major premise. It makes oratory more seamless and flowing if key points do not have to be reiterated but can be assumed because the audience is relied upon to 'fill them in'. This is why enthymeme is a principle of rhetoric, the art of speech, rather than logic, which is concerned to preserve truth. A speech writer trained in philosophy might be inclined to check the validity of all the arguments put forward in a speech, by setting them out as syllogisms. But a good speech writer will be less concerned with this than with writing a speech that is compelling and persuasive, not because it appeals to the rationality of its audience but because of the presence in it of a variety of elements understood by classical rhetoricians as contributing to the beauty of an oration. Bogost's idea is that, viewed as procedural arguments, video games hold out similar figures to their players. Viewed in this way, player action has a role in driving the development of the game that is similar to that of the audience for a speech. As players, we supplement the procedural argument in a way that makes it rhetorical, rather than merely logical. We can understand this in terms of previous discussions concerning the character and quality of video games as visual representations. Players discuss the quality of graphic images in games and, as Bogost points out, they are perhaps excessively interested in how new games look. However, when it comes to actually playing the game what really tends to matter is less whether a gun looks like a gun, or a door really opens, than understanding and identifying with a goal, or recognizing that repeating a move is the right way to proceed, even where such things have not been explicitly formulated anywhere on the game interface. It is in this sense that games involve enthymemes and, for Bogost, this is what distinguishes their unit operations from those of other kinds of software and ensures that their procedures are 'procedural arguments'. This is what makes them rhetorical. Rhetoric here does the work of mimesis in other accounts that emphasize the virtuality of games. Bogost's approach is clearly superior to those approaches because it

includes a fuller account of the incorporation and interpretation processes engaged in by players. His analysis also pushes
towards a proper concentration on the aesthetic dimension
– humans are drawn to pattern as a source of beauty – but its
development in this direction is inhibited by reliance on a linguistic paradigm of meaning-communication.

Understood in this way, the enthymeme is a kind of missing
term in an argument that has to be supplied by the player of
the game. Bogost makes such a step the defining moment of
procedural rhetoric and he explicitly identifies it with the idea
of a simulation gap (Bogost 2007: 214). Similarly, simulation
fever now gets re-modelled as the management of conflicting
game logics, as these are present in different procedural arguments (2007: 274). However, while the notion of an affinity, or
analogy between the enthymeme and player action is interesting, it seems that Bogost here presses the dynamic oscillations
and pulsations of gameplay into a much narrower idea that is
a variant of linguistic meaning interpretation. For him, three
things count strongly in favour of the specifically rhetorical
character of video games. First, as procedural arguments, they
are always open to interrogation and involve their audiences
as critical dissemblers as well as participants. Second, they are
concerned with subjective expression, especially on the part of
their creators, and not merely with being technically 'correct'.
Finally, video games persuade people, rather than being discursive in the Foucauldian sense of forming part of an apparatus
that supports ideas which have to be internalized by individuals as a condition of their inclusion in society (2007: 259).
However, while Bogost's thesis conveys much that is important
and distinctive about the video game as a cultural form, his
argument for the specifically rhetorical nature of games is not
itself persuasive. In particular, Bogost fails to specify what it is
about a procedure that makes it representative (of another procedure). In the absence of such a specification, his observations
on how meaning gets into games and on what happens to it
when people play the games are question-begging. It is unclear
how to develop the kinds of evaluation he proposes, which
would aim to establish why and how some games manage to be

more persuasive than others, especially since he has declared meaning irreducibly subjective. Finally, in attempting to articulate the power of games to persuade to a single paradigm of representation (albeit one that is much more innovative and interesting than post-structuralist attempts simply to 'decode' them as ideology) he arbitrarily narrows the scope of aesthetic appreciation of video games. Each of these points will be developed in the remainder of this section.

The power of procedural representation is that it combines action structures (that must be performed by players) with symbols. The latter can be tightly incorporated into the structure of a procedure. A combination of 'high process intensity' and 'tighter symbolic coupling' results in the intense kind of engagement that leads others to write of immersion in games (Bogost 2007: 42). Playing a video game on this description involves exploring the possibilities held out by a set of procedures in a way that is meaningful, not because the processes represented are 'the same as' those the player carries out in other contexts but because of the intensity of the combination of action and symbolism. Bogost evaluates procedural, and other arguments according to how 'vivid' they are. This idea combines the intensity with which the player responds to the game (2007: 35) and its symbolism, which Bogost acknowledges is metaphorical (2007: 52).[3] Procedural representations can be more 'vivid' (2007: 35) than those in films and books and this is because of what Bogost calls their 'sophisticated interactivity' (2007: 42). However, the nature of this fit runs counter to numerous observations, including some in this book, that suggest there is actually a discrepancy that opens up between processes and metaphors that is not detrimental to the pleasures of play. At the very least, the idea of a 'fit' is in doubt and in its absence the notion that physical processes can 'resemble' one another remains unclarified and open to question. This is particularly the case when we consider the importance of those moments of gameplay that have form and 'feel' to the overall experience (Swink 2009). Abstract games can have this property in abundance so there is also a question concerning how, in the absence of any metaphorical level, still less a fit,

these games work to produce intense engagement. What differentiates ludic unit operations from others seems not to be
the role of enthymemes but rather their aesthetic orientation,
as discussed in the current work.

As an example of a persuasive game, Bogost discusses the
'McDonald's video game' (Molleindustria 2006), which he
says 'makes a procedural argument about the inherent problems in the fast food industry' (2007: 31). This web-based
game presents the player essentially with four screens, which
we move between by clicking on items in a menu that is always
present at bottom left. In this way we switch between looking
at a cartoon image of some green countryside containing what
seems to be an indigenous people's dwelling and framed by a
mansion on one side, which represents the political authorities in a South American country, and some blue sea on the
other, which (it turns out) represents coastal erosion and environmental consequences of intensive agriculture. When we
click on this screen we find that we can harvest cattle feed from
the land, or grow cows on it. To do this beyond a certain point
requires that we raze the village and blackmail the authorities
to let us use more of their land. We have other pleasant options
too, like choosing to grow genetically modified crops which are
mysteriously more effective when the game is up and running.
A second screen represents an abattoir. Here we watch over our
cows, which are comically extracted from the fields by a metal
claw and deposited here in a paddock to be fed up on soy before
being butchered. There is a cyclical dimension to the game and
success requires that we ensure a measured flow of cows and soy
from the field to this place. Cows exit here in the form of pink
burgers on a conveyor belt and we find them again on the third
screen, which depicts a McDonald's restaurant. Here our role
is to employ people to grill the burgers and serve at the tills.
The employees have to be watched as they have a nasty tendency to spit in the food. The restaurant has to be kept stocked
with burgers and the staff have to look happy or the sales rate
– represented by queues of cartoon characters – will decline.
You can reward your staff by clicking on a 'badge' icon, repri-
mand them or even fire them. Another screen represents the

management headquarters of the firm and it contains a range of icons to click on that enable you to toggle on or off strategic options for the business. These include bribing a politician, buying a climatologist, various ways of advertising, and so on. Gameplay is ostensibly quite simple in that you click to move between screens and to make decisions on each one and these choices affect the flow of events. As the player you have to set up routines, as when you choose the number of cows to put in the field and time their introduction to the abattoir. You also have to respond to new events. As you commit more fields to agricultural use, for example, messages appear on the screen telling you that environmentalist protests are targeting the business and affecting sales. This is your cue to hire an environmental scientist to represent your interests to the media. The rhythm of the game is set initially by its cyclical routines, but it is soon punctuated by other developments, like misbehaving staff or the inevitable shortages of cows, burger patties or soy. As you rush to respond to one emergency, so another arises. Eventually, inevitably, the bottom line – represented as a figure for profits on the screen – plummets and you are sacked. This is how you die in this game.

According to Bogost, the game is a procedural argument that communicates the dilemmas of an executive managing a fast food corporation. It highlights key political questions. For example, when a given area of farmland has been used too much it goes all swampy and cows will not grow there any more, or when you get low on soy and feed the cows on industrial waste they turn green and have to be torched. These features of the game highlight questions of sustainability in agriculture and public health related to the business. Bogost believes that the procedural element adds something to the presentation of these issues that cannot be achieved using other media. The fact that, as players, we have to involve ourselves in procedures, which means reflecting on our options, acting in and on the game program, responding to changes that occur in the symbolic environment, all adds up to a kind of involvement that enhances our understanding of that part of the real world that is being simulated. In contrast, Bogost rejects the adapted version of *Pacman,* made to accompany the Morgan Spurlock (2004) movie 'Supersize Me'. It is *not* an example of a rhetorically persuasive game because it is essentially just a re-skin of an older game engine. In the movie Spurlock embarks on an insane diet, living entirely off McDonald's fast food, and measures the impact of this on his body. The message of the film is that McDonald's food is essentially toxic to human beings and that through the sales strategy of 'super-sizing', which involves charging less for larger portions, fast food is compromising public health. The video game tries to communicate the same idea by having players steer a re-skinned pac-man, which looks like a cartoon version of Spurlock, through a maze in which the ghosts have been modified to look like Ronald McDonald, the evil clown from McDonald's advertising. In order to progress through the gameplayers must steer their Spurlock to consume various fruits, although paradoxically he also eats burgers along the way and occasionally grabs a McDonald's drink from just below the central cell in the maze.

As argued in Chapter 3, however, it is quite reasonable to interpret *Pac-man* as an *allegory* of greed in contemporary societies. Bogost clearly intends that the procedures in the McDonald's game are something more than allegory. Rather, they 'stand for' recognisable structures of decision faced by executives in real corporations. At the same time, their fit with that experience is not identity, which we might expect if the representation was a simulation. Bogost emphasizes that, 'Procedural representation is representation, and thus certainly not identical with natural experience' (2007: 35). Moreover, he is careful to detach his thesis from the idea of 'visual rhetoric'. It might seem that Pac-man, for example, does not represent greed in society because the game is too abstract, offering just a two-dimensional maze on the screen, while the McDonald's game has charming visual components like moving cartoon cows that look (a bit) like cows, but this is not Bogost's point. He argues that visual elements in games cannot account for their rhetorical character because they do not admit of the same distanciated interpretation that is necessary for an argument to be a piece of rhetoric aimed at persuading us.[4] Images are not propositional, but procedural rhetorics are:

> procedural rhetorics do mount propositions: each unit operation
> in a procedural representation is a claim about how part of the
> system it represents does, or should function. (Bogost 2007: 36)

What makes a game representation more vivid, then, seems to
be the intensity of its interaction fused with the presence in
its sequences of symbols that maintain a connection with the
subject matter at hand. However, as already pointed out and as
Bogost also says in the citation presented above, in the course
of particularly intense gameplay the symbolic, or metaphoric
scenario projected by games largely ceases to be a factor in
players' concerns. The best games are nearly always those that
mean the least when we are playing them. To be sure, interpretation and reflection may follow but these processes are always
partly influenced by this fact of a distance from the meaning
that opened up during play, as discussed in Chapter 5. *Pac-man*
is a good example: in terms of its rhythms and the engagement
that it requires of its players, *Pac-man* is a much more intense
game than the McDonald's game, although (perhaps because)
its symbolic content always remains fundamentally obscure.
Intensity and vividness seem to be two quite disparate features
of a game, highly resistant to being merged in the idea of a 'fit',
whereas this space that opens up from meaning in the course
of gameplay is essential to the form and present in all the most
intense versions of the experience.

Bogost's decision to align video games with a spoken art
form is a regrettable narrowing of the potential for his concept
of unit operation and it actually limits the sense of his claim
that video games can be vehicles for self-expression of designers. Unit operation is a suggestive concept that grasps the way
in which programmed objects interface with their human
users, producing new modalities of human-machine interaction and new patterns in social and cultural practice. If the
concept is restricted to the merely textual then it is actually
a regression behind earlier ideas of cybertext (Aarseth 1997).
However, broken free from its rhetorical straitjacket, it helps
focus our awareness of the wider reconfigurations of experience

associated with digital technical objects and especially their
interface with human beings. The notion of unit operation
comports well with Thrift's (2008) observations, discussed in
Chapter 4, concerning the balletic character of contemporary
social experience. Moreover, this approach can find similar historical resources, in the dance-as-archive, but also in historical
sciences of gesture which, like rhetoric, have been relegated
to the status of near-forgotten knowledge. At the same time
that modern discourse broke with the traditional relation of
language and reality as parts of a seamless whole, which included rhetoric as one of its levels, it also submerged a parallel
tradition in which gesture and embodied action had been understood as part of that same system of meaningful resonances
between the human and the real. Bogost attempts to articulate
video games to an ancient body of knowledge and practice on
the basis of one point of connection (the enthymeme), but there
are many more connections to dance and gesture. As argued in
Chapter 4, this constitutes an integral part of the 'historical
a priori' of our present, just as networks founded on resemblance make the modern regime of discursive representation
possible. Overall, the problem is that Bogost has inverted his
own, correct insistence on the priority of unit operations over
other features of the game object, especially the metaphoric
level. This approach cannot explain why so many games are
not trying to persuade anyone of anything but seem to be concerned with elves and dungeons.

Badiou's inaesthetics

Bogost cites the French philosopher Alain Badiou as the main
philosophical influence behind the concept of unit operation.
As stated above, this concept is an advance on previous scholarship, but it runs into the problem that video games are not a
linguistic medium while the model of representation assumed
in procedural rhetorics is grounded in a particular use of language. It is in Badiou's work that we can locate the source of
the difficulty and some useful ideas relevant to its solution.
Badiou's philosophy offers a definition of truth that involves

a rupture or break with prevailing discursive conditions and would call into question the significance of Bogost's attempt to interpret games as *persuasive*. Drawing on what Badiou (2005a) calls his 'inaesthetics', it is more consistent with his overall framework to situate games as a variant of dance. For Badiou, dance is not and cannot be an artform. At the same time, dance exists and it happens because there is art. Forms that involve movement and the channelling of bodily energies down lines that exist essentially, yet without purpose, are fundamentally tied to the aesthetic regime but they may not be able to take on the meanings, or discursively formulated truths that can be expressed in artistic media. In light of this, there is scope for a Badiou-inspired correction of Bogost and also to suggest that the video game raises a particular problem for Badiou's system, on the broad terms of his own project.

Badiou's argument is in some ways a mathematical version of Heidegger's (1986 [1927]) thesis that different historical situations may differ not just in terms of the comparisons drawn by historians – more or less technology, greater or lesser importance attached to gender in determining social roles, etc. – but that underlying such differences is a more profound one concerning the way that the world as it really is (being) gets disclosed to the members of a given society. For Heidegger, most of our reflection on Greek philosophy, for example, is superficial in that it fails to understand that the Greeks moved within a different revelation of the world so that their discourse and ours are radically incommensurate (Feenberg 2003). The only way, for the later Heidegger at least, to establish any kind of translation between them is through a 'depth hermeneutic' that takes poetry to be a kind of bridge between the two worlds (Dreyfus 2002). Only poetry can do this for us because in the resonances of its use of language we are able to establish a starting point for dialogue with people in a different world and this is primarily because poetry is unaffected by the demands of scientific and technical formalisation. The latter narrows the semantic resources of language and separates us off from the possibility of other ways of being. For Badiou (2007), philosophy is able to speak of such possibilities not because of poetry and its resources but, in sharp contrast to Heidegger, because mathematics discloses the real structure of being. It gains resources in its task from what we might think of as mathematically comprehensible eruptions (Badiou conceives of them as 'subtractions' in a sense to be elaborated below) in each of four domains, which he says are the 'conditions' of philosophy. These domains are art, politics, science and love. In each of them we find periodic disruptions characterized by the appearance of individuals (Badiou's subjects) who are convinced they are in possession of an as yet unrecognized truth and who as a result of their fidelity to that truth, drive through changes that redefine entire situations (Badiou says they inaugurate a new count). It seems strange to suggest that we should understand the proclamation of a new love, or a new direction in politics in mathematical terms, but one of the things Badiou has in mind here, which makes strong intuitive sense (although, like Alex Callinicos (2006) I am not sure that it is anything more than a strong analogy) is that such assertions are a kind of subtraction. When we realize we love someone, much of what has previously been included in our assessment of them simply seems unimportant and the realization prompts us to re-assess the entirety of our relationship to them. Likewise, militants in politics will affirm truths in that sphere, especially equality, and their activity will 'subtract[s] itself from the normative consensus that surrounds the state' (Badiou 2006: 85). If equality is a revealed truth the effect is that structures which support inequality come to seem merely contingent and the associated political practices of liberal democracy, including persuasion are hollow and uninteresting (Pluth 2010: 172). Here we find an essentially subtractive procedure that Badiou will say reflects, or perhaps more accurately initiates a change in the experience of being. Using mathematical terms poetically, he understands such changes as outcomes of 'permutations of the void' (Hallward 2003), because what we see in them is human beings viewing the world not with something added, but free of various kinds of illusion. Responding to a new truth, they illuminate the contingency in what seemed to be solid features of reality. In this activity such people become 'subjects'[5] of a 'truth-event'. The event itself is always out of view – it is uncountable – but when it strikes it leaves behind an 'evental site', from which subjects faithful to the event's truth will work. The illumination shed by the truth includes an idea of the eternal, or infinite. Cantor's discoveries in set theory are the most obvious example of this, since transfinite mathematics opens up a way of thinking about infinity that then makes subsequent work in mathematics thinkable (Badiou 2007; Fenves 2001).

What Bogost takes from Badiou's philosophy is the principle that fundamental or ontological processes can be described in formal mathematical terms. This means that there is a level of description that encompasses the material, linguistic and other constitutive layers of experience. The point of ontology is to establish a common ground for these latter in a theory of being, which for Badiou is set theory. Badiou's ontology reveals a world that is ordered into discrete mathematical operations and Bogost conceives unit operations as an extension of this principle:

> Perhaps the closest philosophical precedent for unit operations is contemporary philosopher Alain Badiou's application of set theory to ontology ...
> Badiou makes several gestures that resonate with my goals, starting with his general support of the extensional over the intensional. More important, however, is Badiou's insistence on 'unit' as the fundamental building block for ontology ...
> ... his transformation of set theory into a philosophical discourse unifies mathematical representation with cultural representation, a core requirement of comparative procedural criticism. (Bogost 2006: 10, 12, 13)

Bogost clarifies the meaning of unit operation with reference to Badiou in order to address the difficulty raised above: How can a process 'represent' another process? Bogost's answer invokes a structural homology that echoes Badiou's strategy of claiming that set theory *is* ontology; that the power-set *is* an account of social power, and that the mathematical specification for generating a state of a situation applies directly to our understanding of the workings of the political state.

The strength of this idea is clear: there is a formally specifiable homology between a process and its representation in a unit operation wherein the mathematics of the situation are grasped and reproduced.

Here it is probably significant that Badiou's innovation in philosophy finds a, perhaps unintended, resonance in computer science – it is normal for programmers to think about computer ontologies in set theoretic terms. The problem, however, with this strategy is that it aligns video games with meaning and representation and, for Badiou, these are implicated in the state of the situation. For Badiou, representation is an effect of a specific operation of power, namely, the power of the state to order and count a presented situation. Established knowledge in and of a situation will be derived from this primary count and, as such, will be essentially conservative. His philosophy charts the intertwined nature of knowledge in this sense with the unacknowledged, uncounted part of being, which features only as a kind of trace in experience, an absence that is nonetheless integral. Throughout, Badiou distinguishes between the kind of meaning that equates to representation, and truth. Mundane meaning is the ticking over of situations structured by power. The truth event is an eruption that originates in the void – the being that is not because it never gets counted – and which makes possible a different kind of world disclosure. It might be compared to Benjamin's idea of sudden illumination from a primal, ur-historical source, which makes alternative futures visible, discussed in Chapter 3. Badiou, however, understands such events in terms of the logical possibilities they open up, that is, the way they make possible an alternative count carried out by people who have been touched by it through contact with its 'evental site'. Such individuals are 'subjects of truth' and their activity in politics, art, science and love constitutes the basis for a more authentic way of life, opening onto new worlds. On this basis Badiou aligns himself politically with those for whom adherence to generic truths has priority over discussion, rhetoric and the pursuit of consensus. He opposes militant fidelity in politics, which involves adherence to such a new world, precisely to those processes that are prioritized by

Bogost in his account of political games.[6] In terms of Badiou's attitude to representation, Bogost's positive assessment of video games as persuasive media would condemn them to the role of extending technical communications media to reinforce the power of the state. Badiou rejects the idea of rational persuasion within the parameters set by liberal norms, therefore the politics of persuasion are alien to him. In its place he puts fidelity to truth and his theory of subjectivity. Being open to persuasion and the conformity to consensus it implies occupy an entirely negative place in his system.

Badiou's notion of inaesthetics and especially his views on dance can be useful to video game studies. Moreover, the next section will suggest that the idea of the truth-event itself also enables us to understand better much of the turbulence that has surrounded the new discipline. At the same time, thinking about video games raises interesting problems for Badiou's philosophy. In particular, it is unclear why Badiou affords the kind of priority he does to art in his system, while games should in principle be denied the status of what he calls 'conditions'. Conditions are privileged locations for the occurrence of 'truth-procedures', in which subjects pursue the implications of their fidelity to a truth-event, and it is these practices that make philosophy possible. The remainder of this chapter will try to clarify the political implications of the video game as an aesthetic object in light of these ideas.

The ludological truth event

As seen in the previous section, for Badiou truth events can occur in any of his four conditioning domains, one of which is art. Badiou writes that in an artwork that effects the kind of eruption he associates with the truth-event, we gain insight into eternal properties of that medium or artform, even as its core elements are being reconfigured in line with the new truth. Badiou writes that, 'a truth is, first of all, something new'. This contrasts with knowledge, which is only of the familiar and is essentially just repetition. For Badiou, 'Distinguishing truth from knowledge is essential' and what he has in mind here is precisely the distinction between formal permutations that cannot yet be comprehended in meaningful terms, that is, do not take the form of judgements and knowledge, which is mere rehearsal of what has already been represented, but actually issue a kind of appeal to the future where the new real will have been fully elaborated. The truth he has in mind, 'must be submitted to thought, not as a judgement, but as a process in the real' (Badiou 2005b: 45). The truth event, therefore, is always something indeterminate, undecidable in principle. The importance of becoming a subject to truth lies in being prepared to take a particular kind of risk, to stake one's self on the importance of the event without actually knowing what it means. The heart of the truth event resides in this, its undecidability, and to maintain fidelity involves taking this risk:

> For the process of truth to begin, something must happen. What there already is – the situation of knowledge as such – generates nothing other than repetition. For a truth to affirm its newness, there must be a supplement. This supplement is committed to chance. It is unpredictable, incalculable. I call it an event. A truth thus appears in its newness, because an evental supplement interrupts repetition.
>
> Examples: the appearance with Aeschylus, of theatrical tragedy; the irruption, with Galileo, of mathematical physics; an amorous encounter which changes a whole life, the French Revolution of 1792. (Badiou 2005b: 46)

What marks such events is their formal undecidability but also the fact that within them we find a glimpse of the eternal, or the infinite which is a property of human thought itself. Consequently, for Badiou, there are privileged dimensions of human cultural life that serve as conditions for philosophy, which is the discourse that subtracts meaning to discern formal truth within these procedures. In identifying philosophy with this truth, Badiou confirms its association with the unchanging, eternal aspects of the human. One of the conditions of philosophy in this sense is the existence of a literary genre like tragedy, because 'Tragedy itself, as an artistic truth, continues to infinity. The work of Sophocles is a finite subject of this infinite truth' (2005b: 47).

Perhaps the most appealing aspect of Badiou's system for video game studies, then, resides precisely in his separation of the dimension of formal truth from that of ordinary sense meaning. Mathematics discloses the movements, or permutations of being in a way that exceeds conventional signification. In *Being and Event* (Badiou 2007) Badiou deals with the question of new movements in art from this perspective. Any such movement in its experimental phase is, he suggests, confusing from the standpoint of established knowledge. There is a struggle to work out what 'operators of faithful connection' (2007: 291) will finally apply and enable people to make the works intelligible. Badiou describes responses to this situation that try to assimilate, or reject the new work by imposing current 'doctrines of the multiple', or the perspective of established art. Neo-classicists, for instance, are not reactionaries so much as they are 'partisans of sense' (2007: 292) because they want to extract coherence according to familiar rules. Similarly, constructionist approaches in Badiou's terms attempt to 'subsume the relation to being' in the new works 'within the dimension of knowledge' (2007: 293) and thereby to 'dominate any excess, that is, any unreasonable hole within the tissue of language' (2007: 294). Fidelity to the truth in the new work, in contrast, works from this 'hole in sense', which is left behind by the truth event, and performs a new count, starting a new world. Badiou's approach allows us to conceive the possibility of forms that enter experience without necessarily becoming subordinate to the demands of discursive meaning. For him, fidelity to this operation is the true meaning of thought and he contrasts it with what passes for thinking within ordinary knowledge: Thought defines the subject who is faithful to a truth.

As discussed in Chapter 4, Badiou views dance as a metaphor for this kind of thought. He writes that dance is, 'first and foremost the image of a thought subtracted from every spirit of heaviness'. He has in mind here not thought in the standard sense, but the special kind of thought that is opened up or made possible in connection with a truth event. Every genuine thought depends upon an event (2005a: 61). Such thought makes new perspectives possible, while at the same time it is conditioned by what was always there, what is eternal. Dance enables us to see the physical world differently; it is a kind of liberation that gives 'a new name ... to the earth' (2005a: 57). He continues,

> Dance is innocence because it is a body before the body. It is forgetting, because it is a body that forgets its fetters, its weight. It is a new beginning, because the dancing gesture must always be something like the invention of its own beginning. And it is also play, of course, because dance frees the body from all social mimicry, from all gravity and conformity. A wheel that turns itself: this could provide a very elegant definition for dance. (2005a: 57–8)

Dance, for Badiou, is a metaphor for the unfixed, which makes it a metaphor for thought itself. As we have seen, comparison of video gameplay and dance eliminates confusion over the nature of the 'virtual embodiment' produced by video games, manifest in symptomatic errors like the conflation of action in a game with looking at it, or too easy assertions of mimetic correspondence between manual operations and simulated actions. The processes that correspond to 'virtual embodiment' when playing a game concern the articulation of hand and body movements to sensations produced, usually through the eye by the operation of moving graphic images. These sensations can be disconcerting and they can be reminiscent of embodied experiences like flying. It is important, however, to remember that they are sensations, integral to the sensorium of a person who is not flying a plane, or a spaceship, but is playing a game and for whom they have a particular import that is not primarily related to anything else. The paradigm for such sensation is, as I suggested in Chapter 4, dance.

Viewed in these terms, the emergence of the video game could be seen as a kind of 'truth event'. As we saw in Chapter 2, the video game is something profoundly new and yet, as ludologists tell us, it is also a continuation of something as old as humanity, namely, games. The video game is a permutation of gaming's void. In it we find a clear example of a new form erupting and introducing drastic change into a long-established field of endeavour. As it reconfigures gaming and the meaning of games in our culture, the video game also prompts new re-flection on the trans-historical, universal character of gaming as an element in human affairs. The video game has its adher-ents, those subjects whose fidelity to the new truth leads them to clarify the nature of play and, perhaps most importantly, the shape of its future. The ludologist is a subject to the truth event of the video game and this explains the conviction and force that animates many of their pronouncements – they are militants faithful to a truth. The vehemence with which many pursue this often seems disproportionate to the significance of the activity or the resistance it encounters. Richard Bartle, in an article in the *Guardian* newspaper illustrates the zeal that is common among video game militants:

> I'm talking to you, you self-righteous politicians and newspaper columnists, you relics who beat on video games: you've already lost. Enjoy your carping while you can, because tomorrow you're gone.
>
> According to the UK Statistics Authority, the median age of the UK population is 39. Half the people who live here were born in 1969 or later. The BBC microcomputer was released in 1981, when those 1969ers were 12. It was ubiquitous in schools; it introduced a generation to computers. It introduced a genera-tion to video games.
>
> Half the UK population has grown up playing video games. They aren't addicted, they aren't psychopathic killers, and they resent those boneheads – that's you – who imply that they are addicted and are psychopathic killers.
>
> Next year, that 1969 will be 1970; the year after, it'll be 1971.
>
> Dwell on this, you smug, out-of-touch, proud-to-be-innumer-ate fossils: half the UK population thinks games are fun and cool, and you don't. Those born in 1990 get the vote this year. (Bartle 2008)

Bartle's polemic continues for another eight paragraphs, in which he points out that demography is on the side of the video game, since each new generation only increases its involve-ment and familiarity with the medium. His article concludes with the words, 'Games are mainstream. Drown, or learn to swim.'

The confidence expressed here in the future also demonstrates that fidelity to the video game is, as with all the truth events that Badiou discusses, a matter of faith – pragmatically, we could not say that current trends in entertainment will continue. The anticipation of a time when everyone will see the truth is not subject to that kind of counter-argument, but an assertion of the universality of the video game as the truth about gaming in our changed situation. When Bartle makes games, just as when he writes about them, he does so in the conviction that he is participating in something important. That other people do not recognize this is not simply a matter of their analyzing the same evidence as him but reaching different conclusions, it is a consequence of them living in a different world, one that is not illuminated by the truth. A superficial reading might be that the force of such a polemic reflects an underlying defensiveness, even insecurity on the part of a grown man who likes to play children's games. However, Bartle can be seen as acting in fidelity to a truth, gambling on the notion that the video game will be as important to culture as aesthetic art was in the eighteenth and nineteenth centuries. In making this wager his conviction is surely grounded in the perception that the form in which he participates is eternal as well as new; it connects with something constant and profound in human beings, even if his argument does not make this connection explicit. This clarifies the point made in Chapter 2, that ludologists guard the truth of video games, although they do not always know that that is what they are doing.

Viewed in this way, the real enemy of the ludological truth-event is not narratology but cultural studies. As Žižek points out:

> In theory, perhaps the main indication of ... [the] suspension of Event is the notion and practice of cultural studies as the predominant name for the all-encompassing approach to socio-symbolic products: the basic feature of cultural studies is that they are no longer able or ready to confront religious, scientific or philosophical works in terms of their inherent truth, but reduce them to a product of historical circumstances, to an object of anthropologico-psychoanalytic interpretation. (Žižek 1999: 155)

More specifically, cultural and media studies are concerned to submerge the account of any event, including the emergence of a new experience of form and play, in the story of its social and historical coordinates. From such a perspective video games are not free-standing structures instantiating timeless principles but polysemic texts woven into the daily lives and cultural practices of millions. To understand video games is to grasp their role in the contemporary meaning economy and their ideological implications as texts.

The clearest illustration of this tendency in cultural criticism has come from those who are concerned with the gender politics of video game narratives and imagery. As we saw in earlier chapters, it is easy and ultimately quite fruitless to analyse video games in this way because the ostensible content of video games tends towards extreme imagery for reasons discussed in Chapter 5, and this makes them easy targets for the manipulative popular press. As Nina Power (2009) has observed, there is a danger of contemporary feminism, including feminist scholarship, getting caught up in an unthinking convergence of concerns with various kinds of authoritarian moralism and the response to video games provides a case in point. The simplistic 'decoding' of graphic violence as representing, well, violence, followed by its swift implication in various discourses in which violence, allegedly, plays an important role propping up male power is a quick route to such convergence. However, such analyses overlook the key properties of video games, failing to position them as aesthetic objects whose formal characteristics condition their points of insertion and articulation to social and cultural contexts. This in no way exonerates video games as wonderful things, but it does require us to think about their pivotal role in the contemporary structure of feeling. Repetitive, largely joyless routines punctuated by moments of frustration, excitement and laughter; tensions in the body, their escalation and release; the revival of play and games within modern culture, and the social diffusion of objects that are the loci of such processes ought to be at the centre of our concerns as critical theorists.

From Badiou's perspective video games, like dance, would differ from conditions in that they do not name a truth. At the same time, however, we have seen that they differ from dance in *not not* naming one. Unlike dance, which flies above the ground, video games crash into objectuality and the result is ugly obtrusion. Dance for Badiou is a metaphor for the unfixed in thought and therefore is undecided – we cannot attach a meaning to it because we cannot recognize any specific truth in it to which anyone might commit. Read in this way, video games are undecided as this differs from the unfixed. Their 'truth' is a kind of joke and, unlike dance, they are fixed there, as the comic reflection of Badiou-ian seriousness. But the only decision this would accommodate would be a cynical challenge to the earnestness of truth.[7] It is at this point, however, that it seems video games raise serious questions for adherents of Badiou's system. In particular, we have to ask why 'gameness' does not feature as one of the four conditions that make philosophy, the study of truth, possible. Games, after all are about as eternal a feature of human cultural practice as it is possible to find. Badiou's attachment to the four conditions (art, science, love, politics) means that his system cannot accommodate the video game as a cynical truth event. It seems to be only an innate conservatism regarding fundamental cultural distinctions and hierarchies that leads Badiou to seize on these conditions rather than other, equally timeless dimensions of human cultural experience.

Dancing our way to where?

It is quite likely that what is political about videogames is not to be found at the level of the kind of message they communicate, but rather in the fact that even the political ones actually eschew politics in favour of form. Alexander Galloway (2006) grasps the notion of the game as a source of patterned movement before it is anything else when he describes the rule structure of games in terms of their algorithmic basis. For him, the route to better, more progressive games lies in producing games that have newer and more complex algorithms – effectively a call for more form in games. This is an important part of the political aesthetic of video games. In so far as they merely consist of established game engines with new skins they fail to offer anything new to their players. However, even if they do sometimes offer new forms in this way, do they really add anything worthwhile to the lives of the individuals who play them? Can they be viewed as a positive contribution to the culture?

Videogames inherently refuse politics as content because they are fundamentally concerned with attacking and negating content in general. This paradox, of a meaninglessness produced through obsessive focus on a meaning, ensures that video games cannot be used as effective tools of political or ideological communication. It makes them frustrating for people who want media to be available for carrying critical ideas to new strata of society. And when they address this by producing 'worthy' or educational games, the results are not inspiring. When played successfully, late into the night, the McDonald's game becomes accomplished supervision of the routines described earlier. It is possible to make the firm sustain healthy profits for many decades, perhaps even centuries, into the future. This generates a feeling of accomplishment that is only possible because the meaning, or symbolic level, has been banished. Moreover, the feeling is itself undermined when we reflect on what we have actually done and gives way to a mild sense of shame both because of the time it took and the symbolic meaning which now creeps back in, only to be cancelled out again as we reassure ourselves that we do not really eat at McDonald's. The meaning of the game is not the one its programmer intended. Rather, it stands as an allegory of the labour process itself in contemporary capitalism. This commonly involves repetitious unit operational processes whose meaning varies according to the context. If we are lucky, it may be that our work produces something positive but it is just as likely to consist in something we do not care about or even approve of (Sennett 2006). As allegory, the game shares its message with countless others and on my interpretation is actually less pointed politically than *Pac-man* whose target has a more visible, if still rather muted, value as its central concern (greed). Similarly, *Sims*

games purport to model human societies, covering every dimension of human existence – labour, love, domesticity, even
pet ownership – but they are actually allegories for the functional segmentation of modern life into various compartments.
They do not criticize it, but they expose its functional, routine
character and the tendency towards segmentation of life itself
into unrelated temporal units. According to research reported
by Richard Sennett (2006), a major difference between contemporary youth and those of the 1960s or 1970s concerns the
tendency for the former to bracket their current activities off
from any over-arching conception of what their life is about; its
overall purpose or meaning. People of Sennett's 'baby boomer'
generation allowed themselves to envision their lives as coherent totalities, but today's young people confront a capitalism
that offers few footholds on which to base such a sense of self.
Instead, they apply themselves to the task at hand in disconnection from any such ordering narrative.

Bogost's view that video games might enhance political discourse by serving as vehicles for the communication of ideas
must confront this ambivalence of games: do they just affirm
the meaninglessness of much of modern life or can they in
some way challenge it? There is a cynicism in video games
that is difficult to shake off and which aligns them with other
aspects of contemporary, digital culture. As Geert Lovink
(2008) points out, after the initial rush of excitement of associated with 'new media' developments like 'web 2.0', or the
'blogosphere', has come a realization that cyberspace and digit-
ally mediated communications are, after all, just an extension
of ordinary society. As such, they are prone to the same logic of
nihilism and apathy (summed up neatly in the title of Lovink's
book, *Zero Comments*) as the rest of political culture. For him,
the outpourings of bloggers, vloggers and YouTube users are
a case of people talking mainly to themselves, with nothing
much serious being said and even less of it constituting effective communication, measured in terms of its ability to actually
change anything. In this context, video games, which Lovink
barely mentions, are perhaps exemplary. Through them we
gain a clear vision of the structure that underlies much of our

activity, stripped of its ostensible meaning. This is a critique in so far as it detaches us from various kinds of rationalisation and pseudo-justification, but it is a blunt one in that it does not point towards anything we might actually do about it.

Most often the games that try, such as overtly political or educational games, just miss their mark. A clear illustration of this is the game *Global Conflict: Palestine* (Serious Games Interactive 2007), which purports to educate its players by offering a simulation of life in the Palestinian territories currently occupied and/or under siege by Israel. Your character in the game is a journalist who goes back and forth between people on either side, having conversations in which they describe their concerns and difficulties. On occasion you can take on missions like carrying packages or information for people who cannot move as freely as a Western journalist, but mainly you progress by successfully submitting 'reports' to your editor, based on what you have been able to find out. The goal of the game designers is the worthy one of deepening players' understanding of the situation in occupied Palestine. Unfortunately, however, the game is dull because it shades into mere simulation. The boredom of standing in line, part of the dull reality of oppression, comes through loud and clear but this is probably not the message intended by *Global Conflict: Palestine*'s designers. The game illustrates a general point which is that games can only really teach people how to play games. In his work on the educational benefits of video games, James Paul Gee (2003) disagrees, arguing that in mastering a game we learn its processes and therefore deepen our understanding of whatever the game is about, but this just assumes the obviousness of the latter. The problem, illustrated by *Global Conflict: Palestine* is that the more obvious the meaning content is, the less likely it is that the game will work as a game: its content is inimical to its form. There are exceptions to this, where the meaning is allegorical. Frasca's game, *September 12th* which involves shooting characters marked as 'terrorists' in an increasingly crowded marketplace is an example. Each time you hit a character who is not a terrorist the number of terrorists increases. I believe it is impossible to win this game, or establish long periods of equilibrium as in the *McDonald's* game, so the only outcome is a world full of terrorists and this is an allegory of the futility of countering terrorism with military force. It surely helps this game make its point, however, that futility is its theme. Its message could just as well apply to resistance to oppression through armed struggle, or indeed any model of passive resistance that involved repetitive movement of any kind. What the game is really 'about' is the pointlessness of action and beyond that its signs are secondary and ambiguous. As such, it has the character of a cynical gesture (Sloterdijk 1987) at power rather than being a searching critique articulated to any kind of political practice. At the same time, video games' refusal of meaning is itself a gesture with political significance when viewed in context. It is a fundamentally childish move that comports with both the notion of a prevailing cynicism, which Lovink calls 'creative nihilism', and with more positive investments that might be placed in the resurgence of play. Video games are ambivalent between these two possibilities.

Badiou's politics are interesting and relevant to this discussion because underpinning his view is the idea of an ontological difference. This powerfully reworks an idea that has been important to critical theory and seemingly becomes more important in the current period. Work in critical theory normally associates the notion of ontological politics with the transition to a more meaningful world. This approach associates the aesthetic with the meaningful. Consequently, for some the fact that video games project worlds of colour and fantasy, that they resurrect the simplistic moral worldview of childhood (albeit to throw in a few twists and turns here and there), point towards a medium that may be suggestive for a better way of life in the future (Dunscombe 2007). More commonly, of course, video games have been derided by critical theorists as part of a culture of commodification and distraction (Stallabrass 1995). Focusing on the formal element of video games enables us to view this ambivalence differently. Herbert Marcuse (1964) argued that technocratic societies could only be changed by cadres within the technocratic elite who would have the ability to redesign technology in the direction of an alternative civilization. He linked this to the goal of a more aesthetic technology that would resonate with the technical basis of crafts and be compatible with a more integrated life-labour process in which humans appear as more than just impersonal cogs in a monolithic machine. Marcuse understood this 'aestheticisation' of technology, which he extended to his vision of an entirely reformed culture, in terms of play and form. From this perspective changes to design culture, in the direction of aestheticisation, play a key role in the politics of transition to a better society. Describing the role of play and form in these processes Marcuse (1979) acknowledged his debt to Adorno, who rejected the foundational role of ontology in some twentieth-century philosophies. It is clear, though, that Marcuse also envisaged the transition as one that involved an altered relation to being itself – in other words, radical politics as ontological politics. Understood in this way, the element of form, described above as an aspect of gaming that constantly resurfaces and undermines the meaning, is a kind of recurring obtrusion of functionality and a reminder that the game is a technical system.

This idea has been developed by Andrew Feenberg in his theory of 'technical politics'. The transition to what he calls an alternative civilizational model will require interventions within technology design. The diffusion of technologies throughout society and changes in the human-machine interface associated with digitization make it increasingly feasible that social groups can make such interventions. There are numerous examples of this. For example, in the UK in recent years property owners have experimented with a device called a 'mosquito', which emits a sound at very high frequencies that can only be heard by people under 21. The sound is uncomfortable to the ear and the mosquito is used to discourage groups of youths from loitering on street corners. Some young people have recorded the sound on their mobile phones and use it as a ring tone. This enables them to receive calls while they are at school because teachers cannot hear the sound. Hacking technology that was designed to be used against them, they have created a tool for conviviality and resistance. Another example of technical politics concerns the use of traffic lights to control cars in urban spaces. Campaigns in the south of England and Scandinavia have led to the removal of traffic lights and cars now negotiate a slower, more even course through towns where pedestrians feel confident enough to move among them and cross in front of them safely. If video games are allegories perhaps the best ones point not to futility but to an enhanced sense of our abilities to work with the obtruding technical element, to play with it and to successfully fold it back into the production of new routines and practices.

Such processes necessarily have an aesthetic dimension: technology needs to feel different and to be an integral part of the texture of life in the new civilization. Viewed in aesthetic terms, play with a video game involves the reconciliation and synthesis of a variety of kinds of rule systems. In play are the technical rules of the programmed object; the rules of a (normally) competitive game; the rules of social practice (when other people are playing too), and the rules of one's own ethical conduct in connection with the game (Sicart 2009). In earlier work I have argued that the dynamics of this process are akin to those of a robust modernism. The cynical player plays by corroding the meaningful shell on the game, working her way down to the harder levels of the game object in order to master procedures that are thereby rendered meaningless in the terms of the game's fiction (Kirkpatrick 2004). However, we should also notice that aspects of a different modernist aesthetic are also present. The rhythms of dance with a video game object are pleasurable because they comport with those of natural form and this appeals to something innate within the human creature. The salience of natural and supernatural imagery in games and the enormous energies devoted to presenting us with compelling illusions are essential to the appeal of this work we have to do with them to bring them to life. Viewed in terms of this more naturally-oriented modernism (Feenberg 2002; Ranciere 2007), the game is a challenge to synthesize a pleasing unity from its elements through active, physical play. The attachment to empty procedure that works against this goal and yet is essential to its realization is the central dynamic of gameplay and of videogame aesthetics. It is not in any sense progressive in itself, but it can be considered a kind of opening; an allegory for the work of thinking about and making alternative worlds.

Notes

1 Ted Friedman (1995) argues that players see through interfaces to underlying simulations in the course of playing the game. His analysis is similar in certain respects to the one advanced here but he retains an emphasis on the idea of the simulation as *of* some other situation, namely the deisgner's theory about the situation portrayed on the interface even where the two are discrepant, whereas I am arguing it is the tensions between the player's embodied experience of responding to the game program and the messages on its interface that is all-important.

2 It's important to notice that there *is* a blunting of meaning here if we assume, with the Enlightenment, that rhetoric, while affecting is actually an inferior mode of communication because of its aesthetic standard of truth.

3 Bogost discusses *Taxman* as a good example of what he has in mind. However, he considers it regrettable that the game uses locomotion – manipulating an on-screen character to 'avoid' objects that stand for tax responsibilities – as its central metaphor because as it exploits a one-sided understanding of movement as a 'graphical property' of games. This argument is similar to the one made above (see Chapters 2 and 3) but Bogost's solution is to substitute his own bias towards discursive or linguistic meaning rather than to widen the scope of our analysis of movement in games (Bogost 2007: 51–2). This failure is implicit in his attachment to the idea of 'interactivity'.

4 This observation may be related to Benjamin's comments on the power of the image to overwhelm us; see Chapter 3 above, although Bogost denies that images can be dialectical (Bogost 2007: 36).

5 It's important to note that Badiou, in contrast to most philosophers and sociologists, withholds this term from most individuals most of the time. To be a subject is to be the subject of an event, it is to be faithful to the insight associated with that event and to work towards a reconfiguration of the world in light of that

truth. People not subject to truth in this way are not subjects in Badiou's sense. Sicart's (2009) use of this idea, in which he suggests people become subject to specific game characters seems anomalous.

6 As Christopher Norris puts it in his commentary on Badiou: 'On his account politics – in any valid or meaningful sense of that word – takes rise from a disruption to the normal functioning of all those discourses, representations, "democratic" procedures, systems of knowledge or modes of ideological containment that typically masquerade as "politics" under presently existing conditions' (Norris 2009: 245–6).

7 We should not forget that far from being dishonest or opposed to truth, cynicism is one of its faces (Sloterdijk 1987).

Bibliography

Printed sources

Aarseth, E. (1997) *Cybertext: Perspectives on Ergodic Literature*. Baltimore, MD: Johns Hopkins University Press.

Aarseth, E. (2001) 'Video game studies year one' editorial, *Game Studies* 1(1).

Aarseth, E. (2004) 'Genre trouble: Narrativism and the art of simulation', in N. Wardrip and P. Harrigan (eds), *First Person: New Media as Story, Performance and Game*. London: MIT Press.

Adkins, L. and B. Skeggs (2004) *Feminism after Bourdieu*. Oxford: Blackwell.

Adorno, T.W. (1991) *The Culture Industry: Selected Essays on Mass Culture*. London: Routledge.

Adorno, T.W. (1994) *Minima Moralia: Reflections from Damaged Life*. London: Verso.

Adorno, T.W. (2002 [1970]). *Aesthetic Theory*. London: Continuum.

Adorno, T.W. and M. Horkheimer (1997 [1946]) *Dialectic of Enlightenment*. London: Verso.

Adshead, J. (1988) *Dance Analysis: Theory and Practice*. London: Dance Books.

Allen, W. (1971) *Getting Even*. London: Star Books.

Althusser, L. (1984 [1970]) *Essays on Ideology*. London: Verso.

Apollinaire, G. (2004) *Calligrammes: Poems of Peace and War 1913–1916*. Berkeley, CA: University of California Press.

Arsenault, D. (2008) 'Guitar Hero: Not like playing guitar at all?', *Loading...* 2(2).

Atkins, B. (2003) *More Than a Game: The Computer Game as a Fictional Form*. Manchester: Manchester University Press.

Bachelard, G. (1984) *The New Scientific Spirit*. Boston, MA: Beacon Press.

Bachelard, G. (1994) *The Poetics of Space*. Boston, MA: Beacon Press.

Badiou, A. (2005a) *Handbook of Inaesthetics*. Stanford, CA: Stanford University Press.

Badiou, A. (2005b) *Infinite Thought*. London : Continuum.

Badiou, A. (2006) *MetaPolitics*. London: Verso.

Badiou, A. (2007) *Being and Event*. London: Continuum.

Bartle, S. (2008) 'We've won: Get over it', *Guardian*, 28 April.

Baudrillard, J. (1994) *Simulacra and Simulation*. Ann Arbor, MI: University of Michigan Press.

Benjamin, W. (1968) *Illuminations*. New York: Schocken.

Benjamin, W. (1979) *One Way Street*. London: Verso.

Benjamin, W. (1985) *The Origins of German Tragic Drama*. London: Verso.

Berger, J. (1974) *Ways of Seeing*. London: BBC and Penguin.

Bergson, H. (2007 [1940]) *Le Rire*. Paris: Quadrige/PUF.

Bergson, H. (2008) *Laughter : An Essay on the Meaning of the Comic*. Rockville, MD: Arc Manor.

Bogost, I. (2006) *Unit Operations: An Approach to Videogame Criticism*. London: MIT Press.

Bogost, I. (2007) *Persuasive Games: The Rhetorical Power of Video Games*. London: MIT Press.

Bojin, N. (2008) 'Play and the private', *Loading …* 1(3).

Bolter, J.D. and R. Grusin (2000) *Remediation*. London: MIT Press.

Bourdieu, P. (1990) *The Logic of Practice*. Cambridge: Polity Press.

Bourdieu, P. (1993) *The Field of Cultural Production*. Cambridge: Polity Press.

Bourdieu, P. (2001) *Masculine Domination*. Cambridge: Polity Press.

Bourdieu, P. (2010) *Distinction*. London: Routledge.

Bramwell, T. (2004) *'Katamari Damacy* Import review', Eurogamer e-zine, www.eurogamer.net/articles/r_katamaridamacy_ps2.

Brandstetter, G. (2005) 'The code of Terpsichore the dance theory of Carlo Blasis: Mechanics as the matrix of grace', *Topoi* 24.

Buck-Morss, S. (1991). *The Dialectics of Seeing*. London: MIT Press.

Burnett, R. (1995) *How Images Think*. London: MIT Press.

Butler, C. (1993) *Early Modernism*. Oxford: Oxford University Press.

Caillois, R. (2001). *Man, Play and Games*. Urbana, IL: University of Illinois Press.

Callinicos, A. (1989) *Against Postmodernism*. Cambridge: Polity.

Callinicos, A. (2006) *Resources of Critique*. Cambridge: Polity.

Carnagey, N.L. and C. Anderson (2004) 'Violent video game exposure and aggression: A literature review', *Minerva Psychiatrica* 45.

Carter, A. (1998) *The Routledge Dance Studies Reader*. London: Routledge.

Castronova, E. (2005) *Synthetic Worlds: The Business and Culture of Online Games*. Chicago: Chicago University Press.

Chabot, P. (2002) *La Philosophie de Simondon*. Paris: Vrin.

Chabot, P. and S. Laloux (2009) *Territoires Intimes Michele Noiret la danse-cinema*. Bruxelles: Editions Alternatives Theatrales.

Chee, F. (2005) 'Understanding Korean experiences of online game hype, identity and the menace of the "Wang-tta"', paper presented at Digital Games Research Association conference, Vancouver, 16–20 June.

Chipp, H.B. (1968) *Theories of Modern Art: A Source Book by Artists and Critics*. Berkeley, CA: University of California Press.

Classen (1993) *Worlds of Sense: Exploring the Senses in History and Across Cultures*. London: Routledge.

Collins, K. (ed.) (2008) *From Pac-Man to Pop Music: Interactive Audio in Games and New Media*. Aldershot: Ashgate.

Comment, B. (2002) *The Panorama*. London: Reaktion Books.

Consalvo, M. (2007) *Cheating: Gaining Advantage in Video Games*. London: MIT Press.

Copier, M. and J. Raessens (2003) *Level Up: Digital Games Research Conference Proceedings*. Utrecht, the Netherlands: Utrecht University Press.

Crary, J. (1992) *Techniques of the Observer: On Vision and Modernity in the Nineteenth Century*. London: MIT Press.

Crogan, P. (2010) 'The Nintendo *Wii*, virtualisation and gestural ana-logics', *Culture Machine* 11.

Danto, A.C. (1995) *Art After the End of Art*. Princeton, NJ: Princeton University Press.

Darley, A. (2000) *Visual Digital Culture: Surface Play and Spectacle in New Media Genres*. London: Routledge.

Davidson, D. (1980) *Inquiries into Truth and Interpretation*. Oxford: Clarendon.

Dewey, J. (2005 [1934]) *Art as Experience*. New York: Perigee.

Diderot, D. (1994) *Selected Writings on Art and Literature*, edited by G. Bremner. Harmondsworth: Penguin.

Dill, K. and J. Dill (1998) 'Video game violence: A review of the empirical literature', *Aggression and Violent Behaviour* 3(4).

Dovey, J. and H. Kennedy (2006) *Game Cultures: Computer Games as New Media*. Maidenhead: McGraw-Hill.

Dreyfus, H. (2002) *Heidegger Re-examined: Art, Poetry and Technology*. London: Routledge.

Dunagan, C. (2005) 'Dance, knowledge and power', *Topoi* special issue on dance 24(3–4).

Dunscombe, S. (2007) *Dream: Re-imagining Progressive Politics in an Age of Fantasy*. New York and London: The New Press.

Dyer-Witheford, N. and G. de Peuter (2009) *Games of Empire: Global Capitalism and Video Games*. Minneapolis and London: University of Minnesota Press.

Edge (2008) 'Independent Minds' May.

Egenfeldt-Nielsen, S., J. Smith and S. Tosca (2008) *Understanding Video Games*. London: Routledge.

ESA (2009) 'Essential facts about the computer and video game industry', Entertainment Software Association, www.theesa.com/facts/pdfs/ESA_EF_2009.pdf, accessed 25 May 2010.

Eskelinen, M. (2004) 'Towards computer game studies', in N. Wardrip, P. Harrigan (eds), *First Person: New Media as Story, Performance and Game*. London: MIT Press.

Feenberg, A. (1991) *Critical Theory of Technology*. Oxford: Oxford University Press.

Feenberg, A. (2002) *Transforming Technology*. Oxford: Oxford University Press.

Feenberg, A. (2003) *Heidegger and Marcuse: The Catastrophe and Redemption of History*. London: Routledge.

Feenberg, A. (2009) 'The ten paradoxes of technology', unpublished paper, cited with author's permission.

Fenves, P. (2001) *Arresting Language: From Leibniz to Benjamin*. Stanford, CA: Stanford University Press.

Focillon, H. ([1934] 1992). *The Life of Forms in Art*. London: Zone Books

Fortunati, L. (2002) 'Italy: Stereotypes true and false', in J. Katz and M. Aakhus (eds), *Perpetual Contact: Mobile Communication: Private Talk, Public Performance*. Cambridge: Cambridge University Press.

Foster, S.L. (2005) 'Choreographing Empathy', *Topoi* 24.

Foster, S.L., P. Rothfield and C. Dunagan (2005) 'Introduction', *Topoi* 2(3–4).

Foucault, M. (1983) *This is Not a Pipe*. Minneapolis, MN: University of Minnesota Press.

Foucault, M. (1994) *The Order of Things*. London: Routledge.

Franko, M. (1995) *Dancing Modernism/Performing Politics*. Bloomington, IN: Indiana University Press.

Frasca, G. (2003a) 'Simulation versus narrative: Introduction to ludology', in M. Wolf and B. Perron (eds), *The Video Game Theory Reader*. London: Routledge.

Frasca, G. (2003b) 'Ludologists love stories too: Notes from a debate that never took place', DiGRA conference proceedings, University of Utrecht, the Netherlands.

Friedman, T. (1995) 'Making sense of software: Computer games and interactive textuality', in S.G. Jones (ed.), *Cyber-society: Computer Mediated Communication and Community*. London: Sage.

Fullerton, T. (2008) *Game Design Workshop: A Playcentric Approach to Creating Games*. Amsterdam: Elsevier.

Funk, J., G. Flores, D. Buchman and J. Germann (1999) 'Rating electronic games: Violence is in the eye of the beholder', *Youth & Society* 30(3) March.

Galloway, A. (2006) *Gaming: Essays in Algorithmic Culture*. Minneapolis: University of Minnesota Press.

Galloway, A. (2009) 'The Unworkable Interface', *New Literary History* 39.

Game On (2002) Exhibition on the history of the computer game at the Barbican Centre, London.

Gee, J. P. (2003) *What Video Games Have to Teach Us about Learning and Literacy*. London: Palgrave.

Geertz, C. (1991) 'Deep Play: Notes on the Balinese cockfight', in C. Mukerji and M. Schudson (eds), *Rethinking Popular Culture: Contemporary Perspectives in Cultural Studies*. Berkeley, CA: University of California Press.

Genette, G. (1980) *Narrative Discourse*. Oxford: Blackwell.

Grau, O. (2000) *Virtual Art: From Illusion to Immersion*. London: MIT Press.

Grodal, T. (2003) 'Stories for eye, ear, and muscles: Video games, media and embodied experiences', in J.P. Wolf and B. Perron (eds), *The Video Game Theory Reader*. London: Routledge.

Habermas, J. (1984) *The Theory of Communicative Action Volume 1: Reason and the Rationalization of Society*. Cambridge: Polity.

Hallward, P. (2003) *Badiou: A Subject to Truth*. London: University of Minnesota Press.

Hardt, M. and A. Negri (2000) *Empire*. Cambridge, MA and London: Harvard University Press.

Hardt, M. and A. Negri (2005) *Multitude*. London: Penguin.

Hayles, N.K. (1999) *How we Became Post-human: Virtual bodies in Cybernetics, Literature and Informatics*. London: University of Chicago Press.

Heidegger, M. (1986) *Being and Time*. Oxford: Blackwell.

Herber, N. (2008) 'The composition-instrument: Emergence,

improvisation and interaction in games and new media', in K. Collins (ed.), *From Pac-Man to Pop Music: Interactive Audio in Games and New Media*. Aldershot: Ashgate.

Hetherington, K. (2008) *Capitalism's Eye: Cultural Spaces of the Commodity*. London: Routledge.

Himanen, P. (2001) *The Hacker Ethic and the Spirit of the Information Age*. London: Secker & Warburg.

Honneth, A. (2008) *Reification: A New Look at an Old Idea*. Oxford: Oxford University Press.

Huizinga, J. (1950) *Homo Ludens: A Study of the Play Element in Culture*. Boston, MA: Beacon Press.

Husserl, E. (1970) *The Crisis of European Sciences and Transcendental Phenomenology*. Evanston, IL: North Western University Press.

Husserl, E. (1993) *Cartesian Meditations: An Introduction to Phenomenology*. Dordrecht, the Netherlands: Kluwer Academic Publishers.

Ihde, D. (1990) *Technology and the Lifeworld*. Bloomington, IN: Indiana University Press.

Jameson, F. (1975) *Marxism and Form*. Princeton, NJ: Princeton University Press.

Jenkins, H. (1992) *Textual Poachers: Television Fans and Participatory Culture*. London: Routledge.

Jenkins, H. (2006) *Convergence Culture: Where Old and New Media Collide*. New York: New York University Press.

Johns, J. (2006) 'Video game production networks: Value capture, power relations and embeddedness', *Journal of Economic Geography* 6.

Jones, S. (2008) *The Meaning of Video Games: Gaming and Textual Strategies*. London: Routledge.

Juul, J. (2001) 'Games telling stories: A brief note on games and narratives', *Game Studies* 1(1).

Juul, J. (2003a) 'The game, the player, the world: Looking for a heart of gameness', in M. Copier and J. Raessen (eds), *Level Up: Digital Games Research Conference Proceedings*. University of Utrecht, the Netherlands.

Juul (2003b) 'Just what is it that makes computer games so different, so appealing?', International Digital Games Research Association, Ivory Tower Column, April, www.jesper.net/text/justwhatisit. html, accessed 19 November 2010.

Juul, J. (2006). *Half-Real: Video Games Between Real Rules and Fictional Worlds*. London: MIT Press.

Kant, I. (1960 [1795]). *Critique of Judgement*. Oxford: Clarendon Press.

Kant, I. (1992) *Immanuel Kant's Critique of Pure Reason*, trans. N.K. Smith. Basingstoke: Macmillan.

Katz, J. Aakhus, M. (eds) (2004) *Perpetual Contact: Mobile Communication: Private Talk, Public Performance*. Cambridge: Cambridge University Press.

Kerr, A. (2006) *The Business and Culture of Digital Games*. London: Sage.

Kiaer, C. (2005) *Imagine No Possessions: The socialist objects of Russian constructivism*. London: MIT Press.

King, G. and T. Krzywinska (2006) *Tomb Raiders and Space Invaders*. London: I.B. Tauris.

King, J. R. (1999) *Magic: The Gathering. The Thran*. Berchen, Belgium: Wizards of the Coast.

Kirby, L. (1997) *Parallel Tracks: The Railroad and Silent Cinema*. Durham, NC: Duke University Press.

Kirkpatrick, G. (2003) 'Modernism and the aesthetics of personal computing', *Journal of Cultural Research* 7(2).

Kirkpatrick, G. (2004). *Critical Technology: A Social Theory of the Personal Computer*. Aldershot: Ashgate.

Kirkpatrick, G. (2008) *Technology & Social Power*. Houndmills: Palgrave-Macmillan.

Kirkpatrick, G. (2010) 'Gender, technical capital and aesthetic politics in video game design', *Information Communication & Society* 13(6).

Klevjer, R. (2007) 'What is the avatar? Fiction and embodiment in avatar-based singleplayer computer games', dissertation for degree of doctor rerum politicarum, University of Bergen, Norway.

Kline, S., N. Dyer-Witheford and G. De Peuter (2003). *Digital Play: The Interaction of Technology, Culture and Marketing*. Montreal and Kingston: McGill-Queens University Press.

Kluitenberg, E. (2008) *Delusive Spaces: Essays on Culture, Media and Technology*. Amsterdam: NA Publishers, Institute of Network Cultures.

Kolko, B.E. and T.L. Taylor (2003) 'Boundary spaces: Majestic and the uncertain status of knowledge, community and self in a digital age', *Information Communication and Society* 6(4).

Kucklich, J. (2003a) 'The playability of text versus the readability of games: Towards a holistic theory of fictionality', *Proceedings of*

DiGRA Conference, Utrecht, the Netherlands.

Kucklich, J. (2003b) 'Perspectives of computer game philology', *Game Studies* 3(1).

Laclau, E. and C. Mouffe (1985) *Hegemony and Socialist Strategy*. London: Verso.

Langer, S. (1953) *Feeling and Form*. London: Routledge Kegan & Paul.

Lash, S. and C. Lury (2007) *Global Cultural Industry*. Cambridge: Polity Press.

Latour, B. (1987) *We Have Never Been Modern*. Cambridge, MA: Harvard University Press.

Latour, B. (2005) *Re-assembling the Social*. Oxford: Oxford University Press.

Laurel, B. (1995) *Computers as Theatre*. Reading, MA: Addison-Wesley.

Lefebvre, H. (1991) *The Production of Space*. Oxford: Blackwell.

Lefebvre, H. (2004) *Rhythmanalysis*. London: Continuum.

Leslie, E. (2007) *Walter Benjamin*. London: Reaktion Books.

Levy, S. (1984) *Hackers: Heroes of the Computer Revolution*. Harmondsworth: Penguin.

Lovink, G. (2008) *Zero Comments: Blogging and Critical Internet Culture*. London: Routledge.

Lunn, E. (1984) *Marxism and Modernism: Lukacs, Brecht, Benjamin, Adorno*. London: Verso.

Mallarmé, S. (2006) *Collected Poems and Other Verse*. Oxford: Oxford University Press.

Maravall, J. (1986) *Culture of the Baroque: Analysis of a Historical Structure*. Manchester: Manchester University Press.

Marcuse, H. (1964) *One Dimensional Man*. London: Ark Books.

Marcuse, H. (1979) *The Aesthetic Dimension*. Harmondsworth: Macmillan Papermac.

Marx, K. (1977) *Economic and Philosophic Manuscripts of 1844*. London: Progress Publishers.

Missac, P. (1995). *Walter Benjamin's Passages*. London: MIT Press.

Montalvo, J. and D. Hervieu (2007) *On Danse*. Edinburgh: Edinburgh International Festival.

Morris, R. (1995) *Continuous Project Altered Daily: The Writings of Robert Morris*. London: MIT Press.

Morris, R. (2005) *Blind Time Drawings, 1973–2000*. Gottingen: Steidl.

Mukerji, C. and M. Schudson (eds) (1991) *Rethinking Popular Culture:*

Contemporary Perspectives in Cultural Studies. Berkeley, CA: University of California Press.

Murray, J. (2001) *Hamlet on the Holodeck: The Future of Narrative in Cyberspace.* Cambridge, MA: MIT Press.

Nadeau, M. (1978) *The History of Surrealism.* Harmondsworth: Penguin.

Nakamura, R. and H. Wirman (2005) 'Counter-playing tactics of female players', *Game Studies* 5(1).

Ndalianis, A. (2004) *Neo-Baroque Aesthetics and Contemporary Entertainment.* London: MIT Press.

Nordmann, C. (2006) *Bourdieu/Ranciere: La politique entre sociologie et philosophie.* Paris: Editions Amsterdam.

Norris, C. (2009) *Badiou's 'Being and Event'.* London: Continuum.

Palmer, F. (2008) 'The critical ambivalence of play in media art', *Proceedings of the International Symposium on Electronic Art.* Singapore.

Piaget, J. (1972) *Play, Dreams and Imitation in Childhood.* London: Routledge Kegan Paul.

Pluth, E. (2010) *Badiou: A Philosophy of the New.* Cambridge: Polity.

Poole, S. (2000) *Trigger Happy: The Inner Life of Video Games.* London: Fourth Estate.

Poster, M. (1995) *The Second Media Age.* Cambridge: Polity.

Poster, M. (2006) *Information Please.* London: Duke University Press.

Power, N. (2009) *One Dimensional Woman.* London: Zero Books.

Ranciere, J. (2006) *The Politics of Aesthetics.* London: Continuum.

Ranciere, J. (2007) *The Future of the Image.* London: Verso.

Ranciere, J. (2009) *Aesthetics and its Discontents.* Cambridge: Polity.

Roberts, D. (1991) *Art and Enlightenment: Aesthetic Theory after Adorno.* Lincoln, NE: University of Nebraska Press.

Rosewater, M. (2006) 'Timmy, Johnny, and Spike Revisited', http://wizards.com/default.asp?x=mtgcom/daily/mr220b, accessed 22 April 2006.

Ryan, M-L. (2001) *Narrative as Virtual Reality: Immersion and Interactivity in Literature and Electronic Media.* Baltimore: Johns Hopkins University Press.

Saisselin, R.G. (1992) *Enlightenment against baroque: Economics and Aesthetics in the Eighteenth Century.* University of California Press.

Schiller, F. von (2008 [1795]) *Letters on the Aesthetic Education of Mankind.* Whitefish, MT: Kessinger Reprints.

Scholes, P. (1970) *The Oxford Companion to Music.* Oxford: Oxford University Press.

Sennett, R. (2006) *The Culture of the New Capitalism*. New Haven, CT: Yale University Press.

Shields, R. (2003) *The Virtual*. London: Routledge.

Sicart, M. (2009) *The Ethics of Computer Games*. Cambridge, MA: MIT Press.

Skinner, Q. (1994) *Reason and Rhetoric in the Philosophy of Hobbes*. Cambridge: Cambridge University Press.

Sloterdijk, P. (1987) *Critique of Cynical Reason*. Minneapolis: University of Minnesota Press.

Stafford, B. (1994) *Artful Science: Enlightenment Entertainment and the Eclipse of Visual Education*. London: MIT Press.

Stallabrass, J. (1995) *Gargantua: Manufactured Mass Culture*. London: Verso.

Suits, B. (1978) *The Grasshopper: Games, Life and Utopia*. Edinburgh: Scottish University Press.

Sutton-Smith, B. (2001) *The Ambiguity of Play*. Cambridge, MA: Harvard University Press.

Swink, S. (2009) *Game Feel: A Game Designer's Guide to Virtual Sensation*. Amsterdam: Morgan Kaufmann.

Tanke, J. (2009) *Foucault's Philosophy of Art*. London: Continuum.

Taylor, T.L. (2006) *Play Between Worlds*. London: MIT Press.

Thrift, N. (2008) *Non-Representational Theory*. London: Routledge.

Todoroff, T. (2009) 'Les instruments virtuels interactifs pour la musique electroacoustique', www.arts-numeriques.culture.be/fileadmin/sites/art_num/upload/art_num_super_editor/art_num_editor/documents/Articles/Culture_en_action2WEB.pdf, accessed 19 November 2010.

Trotsky, L. (2005) *Literature and Revolution*. Chicago: Haymarket Books.

Troup, G. (2006) *Bad Twin*. London: Transworld/Channel 4 Books.

Tsivian, Y. (2004) *Lines of Resistance: Dziga Vertov and the Twenties*. Sacile/Pordenone, Italy: Le Giornate del Cinema Muto.

Tufnell, M. and C. Crickmay (2008) *Body Dance Image*. London: Dance Books.

Turkle, S. (1984) *The Second Self: Computers and the Human Spirit*. London: Granada.

Wajcman, J. (2004) *Technofeminism*. Cambridge: Polity.

Wajcman, J. (2006) 'The feminization of work in the information age', in M. Fox, D. Johnson and S. Rosser (eds), *Women, Gender and Technology*. Champaign, IL: University of Illinois Press.

Waldberg, P. (1997) *Surrealism*. London: Thames and Hudson.

Walton, K. (1990) *Mimesis as Make-believe*. Cambridge, MA: Harvard University Press.

Wardrip-Fruin, N. and P. Harrigan (eds) (2004) *First Person: New Media as Story, Performance and Game*. London: MIT Press.

Weber, S. (1991) 'Genealogy of modernity: History, myth, allegory in Benjamin's "Origins of the German Mourning Play"', *MLN* 106.

Williams, R. (1961) *The Long Revolution*. London: Chatto & Windus.

Williams, R. (1991) 'The dream world of mass consumption', in C. Mukerji and M. Schudson (eds), *Rethinking Popular Culture: Contemporary Perspectives in Cultural Studies*. Berkeley, CA: University of California Press.

Winnicott, D. (1971) *Playing and Reality*. London: Tavistock Press.

Wittgenstein, L. (1992) *Philosophical Investigations*. Oxford: Blackwell.

Wolf, M. and B. Perron (eds) *The Video Game Theory Reader*. London: Routledge.

Žižek, S. (1999) *The Ticklish Subject: The Absent Centre of Political Ontology*. London: Verso.

Games and other sources

Artoon (2002) *Blinx: The Timesweeper*. XBox.

Atari (1972) *Pong*. Arcade machine.

Bandai/Atari (2003a) *dot.hack: Infection*. PS2.

Bandai/Atari (2003b) *dot.hack: Mutation*. PS2.

Bandai/Atari (2003c) *dot.hack: Outbreak*. PS2.

Bandai/Atari (2004) *dot.hack: Quarantine*. PS2.

Bungie (2004) *Halo 2*. XBox.

Capcom (2005) *Resident Evil 4*. GameCube, Wii.

Electronic Arts (2008) *Mirror's Edge*. XBox 360.

Frasca (2008) *September 12th*, www.newsgaming.com/games/index12.htm, accessed 17 September 2008.

Hasbro (2004) *The Lost Experience*.

Hasbro (2008) *Cluedo Reinvention*.

Id Software (1994) *Doom*. PC.

Jodi (2008) *Doom*, experienced at *Deep Screen: Art in Digital Culture Exhibition*, Stedelijk Museum, Amsterdam.

Metanet/Atari (2006) *N*. PC.

Metanet/Atari (2008) *N+*. PC.

Midway (2004) *Mortal Kombat: Deception*. XBox/PS2.

Molleindustria (2006) *McDonald's Videogame*, www.mcvideogame. com/, accessed 2 July 2010.

Namco (1980) *Pacman*. Arcade.

Namco (2004) *Katamari Damacy*. PS2.

Next Level Games (2007) *Mario Smash Football*. Wii.

Nintendo (1981) *Donkey Kong*. NES.

Nintendo (1989) *Tetris*. GameBoy.

Nintendo (1998) *The Legend of Zelda: Ocarina of Time*. N64.

Nintendo (2002) *Dr Kawashima's Brain Train*. DS.

Nintendo (2006a) *Sound Voyager*. GameBoy/DS.

Nintendo (2006b) *Wii Sports*. Wii.

Nintendo (2006c) *Electroplankton*. DS.

Red Octane/Activision (2005) *Guitar Hero*. PS2 XBox.

Rockstar (2001) *Max Payne*. PS2/XBox.

Rockstar (2002) *Grand Theft Auto: Vice City*. PS2.

Serious Games Interactive (2007) *Global Conflict: Palestine*. PC.

Super Size Me (2004) dir. M. Spurlock. Wisconsin: Kathbur Pictures.

Team17 (1994) *Worms*. Commodore/PC.

Treasure (2002) *Ikaruga*. Dreamcast/XBox.

Twilight Creations (2005) *Mid Evil*.

UbiSoft (2008) *Lost: Via Domus*. XBox, PS3, PC.

Valve (1998) *Half Life*. PS2.

Wizards of the Coast Inc/Hasbro (1993) *Magic: The Gathering*.

XBox (2010) www.xbox.com/en-GB/Kinect/Home, accessed 20 November 2010.

Index